The Jossey-Bass
Business & Management Series

The Third Shift

It all goes back, of course, to Adam and Eve—
a story which shows, among other things,
that if you make a woman out of a man,
you are bound to get into trouble.

Carol Gilligan, In a Different Voice

Contents

Acknowledgments   ix

About the Author   xi

Introduction: Managing the Third Shift:
Choices and Challenges for Women   1

Part One: The Identity Challenge: Who Are We?   25

1   The Myth of Androgyny:
    Who Are We Supposed to Be?   29
2   Gender at Work: When Does It Matter?   62
3   A Business of One's Own: Who Are We
    When We're on Our Own?   99
4   From High-Rise to Hearth and Home:
    How Do We Thrive?   135

Part Two: The Task Challenge: What Are We to Do?   169

5   Management 101 for Women:
    Doing What Matters   175
6   Women Entrepreneurs: Balancing
    Logic and Emotion   207
7   Women at Home: Understanding
    the Job Description   243

Part Three: The Balance Challenge: Who Comes First?   279

8   The Crux of the Matter: Defining
    Personal Achievement   283

Afterword 315

Appendix: The Women of the Study 323

Index 329

Acknowledgments

This book is about women, but I cannot even think about acknowledging the many people who believed in me and made this book possible without first thanking and acknowledging my family members, male and female. My thanks go first to my husband, Roy, who appears to suffer from no third shift whatsoever. Without appearing arrogant or being a know-it-all, he is blessedly free of the doubts, reservations, and uncertainties that plague so many women. His confidence helped me overcome my doubts. His strong sense of himself has always allowed me to take all of the space that I need.

I am also grateful for the understanding of my two children, Evan and Clare. Evan allowed me to watch his soccer games from the sidelines, ignoring the fact that I had a book chapter on my lap, my red pen poised in midair as he neared the goal posts. I thank Clare for allowing me the space to write this book, although she said several times that it was "taking too long." (I quite agreed.) But she loved the idea that I was writing about "grown-up women," even though it necessitated that I often lock myself into my office and type away all afternoon.

I have never met a woman I didn't learn from, and in compiling data and ideas for this book I have been influenced by far too many women to acknowledge them all. At the very grave risk of omitting some who undoubtedly deserve my thanks, I would like to mention those women who will surely earn a place in "entrepreneur's heaven" for helping so many other women live their dream: Sue Layman, Pam Rasmussen, Kelli Richards, Joanne Springer, and all the other women who helped to launch and run the Center to Develop Women Entrepreneurs at San Jose State University. I am particularly in awe of the support and personal efforts of Cheryl Domnitch, Christine Flores, Carla Griffin,

Swati Jalnapurkar, Robin Jessup, Sudha Mani, Jackie Pickett, and Rolland Pollard. But there were many, many more who served. And dozens more who set aside the time to be interviewed for this book. Thank you all.

I also wish to thank my business partner and longtime friend, John Baird, for supporting my need to express myself through this book, although there were many days when it took me from other work in our partnership.

I am deeply grateful to the careful and tactful suggestions of my editor at Jossey-Bass, Susan Williams, who reads between the lines every bit as well as the lines themselves! My thanks go as well to Julianna Gustafson, who answered all my questions with accuracy and friendliness. I would also like to acknowledge the careful scrutiny and professional typing of Pauline Watson on parts of this manuscript.

Finally, it is to my agent and new friend, Sheryl Fullerton, that I give my most profound thanks and respect. She believed in me and this project from the outset. She gave of herself, her advice, and her little purple pen unstintingly. She is a smart professional and a very wise woman, and I have enjoyed working with her immensely.

Los Gatos, California   MICHELE KREMEN BOLTON
April 2000

About the Author

Michele Kremen Bolton, Ph.D., is a founding partner of ExecutivEdge of Silicon Valley, an executive development and management consulting firm located in Los Gatos, California. She is a "recovering academic" and former professor of management, having recently retired from nearly twenty years on the faculty of the College of Business at San Jose State University. She taught M.B.A. courses in visionary leadership, strategic management, entrepreneurship, and team building. While at the university, she received several awards for outstanding teaching and leadership, including a Presidential Special Recognition Award. She is the author of numerous articles in such journals as *Organizational Science, Organizational Dynamics,* the *Journal of Management Education, California Management Review,* and the *Journal of Management Studies.* She is active in a number of scholarly and professional associations and has reviewed for the IEEE, the National Science Foundation, and several other journals.

She has served as an advisory board member on a venture capital firm, a business incubator, and a range of nonprofit organizations, from Big Brother/Big Sisters to Hope Rehabilitation. In 1993, she cofounded a community mentoring organization to guide women entrepreneurs, the Center to Develop Women Entrepreneurs, at San Jose State University, which won the Community Organization of the Year Award from the Silicon Valley chapter of the National Association of Women Business Owners. As its first executive director, she led the organization in helping more than twelve hundred women entrepreneurs find the courage and direction to move toward their dreams.

Bolton has been an executive development consultant for fifteen years. She works both with individual clients as an executive coach and with larger teams. She conducts seminars and training and gives keynote presentations. She has appeared in *Business Week* and *Inc.* and on National Public Radio. Her clients include start-ups and Fortune 500 companies as well as educational, government, and community organizations. She has consulted to individuals at all levels, including CEOs and their executive staffs, boards of directors, senior managers, and technical or scientific employees in nonsupervisory positions. She specializes in executive development in strategic leadership, leadership style, and gender issues. Her recent clients include Apple Computer, Applied Materials, Cadence Design Systems, the California State University, Compaq/Tandem, The Gap, Genelabs, Hewlett-Packard, Intuit, Microsoft, National Semiconductor, Nike, Silicon Graphics, Sun Microsystems, and the University of California.

She lives in the Santa Cruz Mountains with her husband, two children, and three dogs.

The Third Shift

In memory of Evelyn Berman Kremen

Managing the Third Shift

Choices and Challenges for Women

*Oh dear, how hard it does seem to take up
our packs and go on.*
LOUISA MAY ALCOTT, *Little Women*

The idea for *The Third Shift* began the night our six-year-old daughter, Clare, was to spend her first overnight with her best friend, Yael. She was extremely excited and feeling *so* grown up. My husband of twenty-three years was also thrilled, especially after we arranged a last-minute overnight for Clare's nine-year-old brother, Evan; it looked like we'd have the house to ourselves for a cozy evening.

The bubble burst at ten o'clock that night when the phone rang. Yael's harried father was calling to explain that Clare had been sobbing for an hour and wanted to come home. She wanted to sleep in her own bed. *And she wanted her Daddy.*

I was devastated.

With that single, innocuous phone call, I was reminded that as a woman a continuous inner dialogue second-guesses whatever decisions and acts fill my days. A first shift at work and a "second shift"[1] at home can be physically tiring, but the third shift is psychologically relentless; it ranges over professional anxiety about workplace assignments and self-perceived derelictions on the home front. In essence, every day is lived at least twice, like a videotaped instant replay that won't shut off.

Some women are far more vulnerable than others to this self-destructive and exhausting ritual. But most suffer at least a mild case of third-shift angst because it stems from the universal difficulty of choosing wisely and remaining satisfied with our personal life choices as contemporary women. A few women apparently live the third shift throughout the day, whenever they face hard decisions and trade-offs. For them, the third shift may feel more like an *endless* shift! But most of the women I interviewed for this book seemed to use their private, quiet time—in the car, in the shower, before falling asleep at night—as a psychological third shift after finishing the actual first and second shifts that made their days too busy to fully think through their actions and choices.

Adapting the particulars to your own situation, have you ever spent unpaid time toiling over questions such as these in the privacy of your own third shift?

- *Am I doing it "right"?*
- *Am I sacrificing time with friends and family for the false gods of ambition and material success?*
- *Is the high of luring a new client as lasting as the joy of watching my son smash a double way into the outfield?*
- *Am I turning my back on career success by settling for the "mommy track"?*
- *Am I a "good person" if I prefer to spend my precious allocation of personal free time with my nose in a book rather than selling scrip for our kids' school, like the other moms?*
- *Am I lacking commitment as a businesswoman because I want to spend more time expressing myself outside of work?*
- *If I quit my job to stay home with my family, will I feel bored and restless? Or guilty?*
- *Can I really be a good mother even though I have no idea what my kids most like to find in their school lunchbags?*
- *Am I spending enough time with my aging parents when they visit, or do they feel bad because I don't take more time off from work when they come?*

Despite the uncertainties revealed by these questions, our inner third-shift dialogue can help us find our most profound and enduring strength as women. This is because our third shifts are composed of twin voices: one a negative whisper of self-doubt, the other a more positive utterance of self-awareness. By listening to both of these inner voices, we can honestly appraise ourselves, our actions, and our choices, thereby improving how we make the important decisions in our lives.

Unlike the first and second shifts, the third shift is a psychological rather than a literal phenomenon. It can become a virtual "inner oasis" of self-awareness that we can summon in our minds when we feel frazzled and frustrated by everyday demands. For example, on our good days, our third shift can provide true harmony: the inner guidance, self-confidence, and acceptance that allows women to feel at peace with their choices. Yet for many of us, this journey inward can be even more daunting than the dizzying climb through the glass ceilings of the outer workplace. Rather than providing the serenity of an oasis, our third shift offers negative, self-critical voices, shouting at us what we are doing wrong, not what we are doing right. This occurs when we succumb to feelings of guilt or attacks of the "shoulds" because our choices as women rarely allow us to do everything we want as well as we think we should.

The third shift is a widespread feminine phenomenon today precisely because we live in an era of social transition, when gender roles for women are in enormous flux. As the poet W. H. Auden said, we live in an Age of Anxiety. Women are expected to fulfill significant responsibilities and leadership roles at work; prove themselves; master new industries and occupations (and in the process overcome biases and stereotypes); and *also* retain a nurturing, other-oriented role in the family and broader community.

Overlaid onto women's dual responsibilities is the question of how to behave, with stereotypes of "male" and "female" behavior changing rapidly. For example, new studies conducted at the nonprofit Families and Work Institute in New York indicate that "daddy stress" is on the rise, and today's fathers want increased ability to both provide for and spend time with their children.[2] Journalists who specialize in work and family issues, such as Sue Shellenbarger of the *Wall Street Journal,* report on a new unity in values between men and women.[3]

These studies, however, find no evidence that men are sharing the deeper, *inner* dilemma—beyond work-family balance—faced by women today. In her book *The Mismeasure of Woman,* social psychologist Carol Tavris describes the relentless mental yo-yo of a woman's third shift:

> A woman who leaves her child in day care worries that she is failing as a mother; but if she leaves her job temporarily to stay home with her child, she worries that she will fail in her career. A woman who cries at work worries whether crying is good, since she is a woman, or wrong, since she is a professional. A woman who spends endless hours taking care of her husband and ailing parents feels that she is doing the right thing as a woman, but the wrong thing as an independent person. A woman who cannot penetrate her husband's emotional coolness alternates between trying to turn him into one of her expressive girlfriends and trying to cure her "dependency" on him.[4]

My own research reinforced what Tavris is describing. Between 1994 and 1998, I conducted an intensive longitudinal study with a research team of graduate students from San Jose State University, where I was a faculty member, interviewing 117 women aged twenty-three to sixty-six.[5] The sample was restricted to the Silicon Valley geographical area, which may bias the outcome, but the underlying diversity of the study population reduces that possibility.[6] We conducted structured interviews with each woman at least once and repeated the interviews annually for approximately one-third of the sample. We talked to aspiring entrepreneurs and entrenched corporate women, senior professionals and reentry women, young stay-at-home moms and community activists. They represented multiple ethnic and racial groups; crossed socioeconomic classes; and differed by marital status, occupational group, and education attained.

Despite all of these differences, from every woman I heard variations on the third-shift theme: living in harmony with choices. The common theme was clear. Rather than deriving joy from their choices as women—to work, to stay at home, to help out in the community—many women are half-crazed by the constant demands, options, and trade-offs. Even if their outer life looks reasonable and nicely balanced, on the inside many women remain prisoners of their own third shift. On a positive note, as the examples in this book illustrate, many women also effectively harnessed their third shifts, resulting in greater self-acceptance, more effective decision making, and smoother transitions in their lives when they sought new choices. Either way, the inner, third-shift dialogue played a powerful role in how women viewed their lives, their personal achievements, and their deepest satisfactions or disappointments.

Thirty-some years from the beginning of the modern women's movement, it is time to refocus our inquiry and efforts for gender equality—and equally important, for genuine understanding between the sexes. Instead of worrying quite so much about the first shift at work and the second shift at home, we must concentrate further on the third shift *in our minds*. On the outside, millions of women look like heroic mountain climbers, successfully staggering up the steepest slopes. But on the inside, they're struggling even more, in ways that are often invisible to outsiders.

The Dilemmas of the Third Shift

What's behind this struggle, and what can we do about it? As a card-carrying member of the baby-boomer, Woodstock generation, I was raised to believe that anything is possible—if you try hard enough, if you go to school long enough, if you protest loudly enough, or if you apply the wonders of modern science and technology cleverly enough. Nothing can hold women back anymore. But I'm not so convinced as I once was that brute force and easy belief in continuous improvement result in genuine advances in our lives as women.

Thus, I began to sift through the interview transcripts for answers as well as the common thread that would make sense out of the thousands of pages. Initially, I launched my study to understand why some women move ahead in their lives, while others hold themselves back. I was inspired by four talented and energetic female graduate students who had written persuasive and comprehensive business plans for start-ups as the thesis requirement for their M.B.A. But none of these four women seriously considered launching a start-up. One felt "the time wasn't right." Another said it would cost too much to get going (she was right). A third insisted her idea was "strictly a learning experience" and she couldn't see herself "as a real entrepreneur." The fourth had a hot idea, but icy cold feet; "just guts" is what she said she needed. Hers was an inner deficit, an "internal glass ceiling" more powerful than any external block to opportunity.[7]

I so much wanted these bright young women to succeed. I was frustrated that none of them seemed ready to pursue her dreams, no matter how she rationalized her disinclination. Instead of launching their own businesses, the four graduate students joined me to found a nonprofit mentoring organization, its mission "to provide courage and direction" to aspiring women entrepreneurs. As women from the community formed waiting lists for our programs and personal mentors, my initial research questions kept circulating through my head:

- *What kind of internal dialogue were the women having who took chances with their lives?*
- *What kind of inner voices were women listening to that made them afraid to move forward?*
- *What made these two groups of women so different?*
- *What did they hold in common?*

If I were ever to substantively help women (including myself) improve how they make choices in their lives, I knew that I needed to generate a conceptual framework that would allow me to generalize my learnings from a hundred-plus Silicon Valley women to a larger female population. I also knew that as an academic I had been trained to discern patterns; hence I was pleasantly surprised when the oral work histories of the 117 women who ultimately participated in this study coalesced into a consistent picture of three unrelenting dynamic tensions these women faced.[8] These three dilemmas stimulated internal questioning, which in turn colored the external decisions they made about their lives. The dilemmas emerged again and again as pivotal points around which these women's third shifts swirled:

1. *The identity challenge:* expressing yourself as you really are versus trying to be who others will accept
2. *The task challenge:* getting the job done versus worrying about how everyone feels

3. *The balance challenge:* spending time on achievements for yourself versus service to others

The Third Shift begins with the identity challenge because it deals with the most basic issue of all, our core sense of ourselves as authentic women in a largely patriarchal society where male needs and definitions of success prevail and color the thoughts and behaviors of both sexes. A female airline pilot who is shunned by her male peers yet doesn't want to hang around with women coworkers because she might be taken for a flight attendant is an example of a woman facing a true identity challenge. A woman supervisor who leaves a crucial, late-afternoon meeting early to pick up her children at day care serves as a second example of the identity dilemma. In both cases, the women struggle with compet-ing selves, not just conflicting demands.

Next, *The Third Shift* tackles the task challenge, the tension of focusing on getting the job done versus attending to how people are feeling. A woman who suppresses conflict because she "just wants to be one of the guys" feels internal conflict when she observes others at work making decisions that ignore the human component at the expense of a delivery schedule. Or a rookie en-trepreneur may sell her services far too cheaply because she is overly worried about her relationship with her new client. In both cases, the women struggle to attain dual objectives: satisfaction that the work gets done, plus peace of mind that they've stepped on no toes in the process.

The third distinctively female issue addressed by *The Third Shift* differs somewhat from the other two dilemmas, each of which pos-sesses issues that stem from a woman's choice of a corporate career, entrepreneurial effort, or stay-at-home life. The balance challenge is a meta-issue, rather than a parallel challenge like the others, involving the trade-off between attention to self versus others. A woman who raises four children before attending college for the first time highlights the tendency of women to place others first. A senior female executive with a resume-to-die-for and a fat pen-sion, but without the children or husband that she once hoped for, represents the darker side of shattered glass ceilings, and a persis-tent reminder of hard trade-offs.

The data from the study clearly illuminated how these three dilemmas are fluid, *dynamic* tensions that never disappear altogether but must be managed daily.[9] No once-and-for-all solutions seem to exist. My goal with this book, therefore, is to help you effectively manage the three dilemmas of the third shift—identity, task, and balance—so you can live harmoniously with the choices you make.

Living with Your Choices

The examples in this book demonstrate that women can focus and discipline their third shifts to attain personal satisfaction no matter the path they take—corporate life, entrepreneurial endeavor, or stay-at-home lives and community work. But *inner harmony stems from self-acceptance, rather than simply the choices themselves.* Every woman must learn this valuable lesson, as have I.

Like many of you, I suffer from my own third shift and unrelenting internal and external demands. I'm the mother of two young children and a wife of more than two decades, but also a founding partner in a management consulting firm. I'm a "recovering academic" who left the ivory tower after twenty years, looking for new challenges and new freedom. I needed a change because my life wasn't working anymore. At forty-something and with the big five-oh hovering just around the corner, I felt I'd arrived professionally.

But on the home front, I rate myself a C+ at best, even though my domestic arrangement is probably the envy of most women I know. Locally, my husband, Roy, is known as "the paragon." He elected a few years ago to step back from his career and take over the kids and house. Roy is a veritable icon at their school, accepted by the other moms as "one of them" (unless the talk drifts too closely to the most intimate, clinical details of cervical dilation and breast pumps).

I, on the other hand, bring home the bacon and rarely have a chance to eat it with my family. I treasure my many wonderful moments with our children. Now at eight and eleven, they're smack in the middle of the golden years of childhood and a real delight to be with. But typically I'm the "fun" parent rather than the custodial one: the Old Maid partner, the Monopoly guru, the one who teaches them how to play jacks.

On the outside, I probably look like the perfect nineties career woman, right? I'm "doing it all." *But am I doing it right?* Why do I often feel like I'm not a real mother, but just some cardboard Glinda in a pink taffeta dress with a magic wand who wanders in occasionally, sprinkling cheer and good times on the kids? Why is it still so hard to live with my choices as a working woman? Why can't I manage my own third shift effectively?

Self-Awareness and Self-Doubt

As I mentioned previously, the third shift's power comes from its twin voices, one of self-doubt and the other of self-awareness. It is worth examining these voices in greater detail because we manage our individual third shifts according to how we balance them. Beginning with a personal example may be helpful.

In my own case, the voice of self-doubt seemed to be winning because I just couldn't put the evening of Clare's sleepover behind me. Unsettled by persistent uncertainty, I shared my third-shift doubts with my husband. Despite his most heroic attempts at empathy, and dutiful active listening, he simply couldn't get it. "Clare's fine," he said, his voice carefully neutral as he tried to ferret out what was bothering me. "She's over it. Don't make it into a big deal. It isn't one."

But it was for me. Roy isn't afflicted with a third shift of his own. In his mind, the problem with Clare was solved. She stopped crying that evening and fell asleep, and we learned that she was still too young for sleepovers. I, however, was clearly stuck, my third shift spinning out of control. Breaking down my inner dialogue to analyze it productively, I realized I was having an acute attack of the shoulds, first blaming myself and then pointing the finger at others.

I should be around more so my daughter turns to me when she's upset.

I should worry about my daughter, and not make this incident about *me*.

I shouldn't stereotype men, but I can't help wondering if Yael's father is doing a good job of handling an emotionally laden situation like this.

A full blown case of the shoulds exemplifies the negative voices in our third shift, the self-doubting litany that can escalate from a small event to broader self-attack about one's choices. My research showed that it is precisely these self-doubts that can keep women stuck on the inside, no matter the tangible, economic progress on the outside. I am convinced that this need to attain both inner and outer satisfaction makes contentment for women more elusive than not. On the night my daughter called home, looking to my husband for comfort, I was forced to come to exceedingly painful terms with the price of my own need for workplace achievement: fear that I wasn't sufficiently involved with my own family; fear that I wasn't needed for the nurturing and succoring traditionally performed by women; and a genuine sense of loss (tinged with pride and gratitude for my husband's role in the family) that I was being pushed aside. In short, in some ineluctable way I felt that I had let my own daughter down—an especially shameful downfall, given that I prided myself on building my career, at least in part, around mentoring and coaching women.

Of course, the self-aware part of me knows that succumbing to the shoulds with the fervor of a tragedy queen is a self-indulgence no working woman can afford. Happily, my third shift also includes the calm voice of reason and self-awareness that listens to, but then drowns out, the negative voices. This frees me to step back and remember that my family is happy, healthy, and well-adjusted. I am actually a pretty decent role model for my daughter (and for my son). Most important, I do the best I can, and I'm forever learning more about my own needs and those of others I care for, adjusting my day-to-day decisions as a consequence. My life is busy, but it's also exceedingly rich and satisfying.

I wrote this book to help other women undertake the psychological sorting process that the twin voices of the third shift amount to. I have learned, as Susan Chira has expressed it in *A Mother's Place,* to no longer "search for absolutes that don't exist."[10] I also recognize that on some days, my choices—like many of yours—may not be particularly easy to live with. But other choices may entail even worse trade-offs.

To understand fully the rich dialectic of self-doubt and self-awareness, read the chart below and contrast the dual voices, keeping in mind that they come from the mind of the same woman. For some women, the differences between the two columns are blurred and subtle. For others, the lines of demarcation are sharply drawn:

Self-Awareness	*Self-Doubt*
It's wonderful that my daughter has such a close relationship to her father. The research states over-whelmingly that adult female self-confidence stems from a close father-daughter tie.	I'm spending far too much time worrying about my business when I should be spending more time with my daughter. She needs a mother.
I've taken for granted all my life the ability to have a choice about whether I work, or how much I work. The important thing is to try my best, not to be perfect with my decisions.	Why am I never satisfied? It's selfish and adolescent to focus on myself so much. I should just hunker down and stop obsessing.
If my kids can go to a private school, they may have a more enriched curriculum, more exposure to new experiences, and ultimately more choices in their lives.	I could spend more time at home if I didn't keep adding expenses into the budget. The exposure our kids need is to their own family, not to some fancy school.

In each successive chapter, *The Third Shift* helps you actively examine and manage your personal mix of self-awareness and self-doubt, particularly as the two pertain to the specific challenges inherent in the identity, task, and balance dilemmas. Undergoing this reflection process is essential if you are to use your third shift to truly enrich your life. The alternative is daunting. An expert on anxiety, Dr. Edward M. Hallowell, calls "toxic worry"—a third shift gone awry—"a disease of the imagination. It is insidious and invisible, like a virus. It sets upon you unwanted and unbidden, subtly stealing its way into your consciousness until it dominates your life. As worry infiltrates your mind, it diminishes your ability to enjoy your family, your friends, your physical being, and your achievements because you live in fear of what might go wrong. It undermines your ability to work, to love, and to play. It interferes with your starting a new task or even enjoying the completion of an old one."[11] Fortunately, few healthy women suffer from so painful an inner threat. But in today's climate of personal choice for women, none of us is immune from some degree of unease, self-questioning, and occasional anxiety when we closely scrutinize our lives. It's my goal to explore the positive use of the third shift in the hope of helping women make key decisions about their lives.

The Hope Diamond for Women

If the oasis of the third shift seems like an elusive mirage, it is worth noting here that women's successful development as adults requires meaningful connections to others, in addition to personal achievement.[12] After analyzing the interview data, I quickly saw that the feminine need to adequately develop and preserve relationships with others—whether at work or on the home front—is the *sine qua non* of the three dilemmas:

1. Identity: Should you reveal yourself as you truly are, or go along to meet *others'* expectations?
2. Task: Should you take time to worry about *others,* or just concentrate on the job at hand?
3. Balance: Should you focus on attaining achievements for yourself, or remain available to serve *others* who are important in your life?

At home, or at work, I could easily recognize "the girlish compulsion to solicit approval"[13] at the root of these three dilemmas—a developmental footnote for most men, but the Hope Diamond for women in terms of a successful adult identity. For most men, fame, fortune, and achievement can allow them to feel successful. For women, these attainments—however glorious and necessary to self-worth—are rarely enough unless accompanied by moderately satisfactory connections to others. These differences may be innate, or they may be culturally programmed; most current researchers cite the interactive influence of both factors.[14] But without doubt, the unique pathway to adult development for women, as compared to men, means that a collision between inner and outer needs was inevitable once women en masse entered increasingly responsible and demanding careers. For as women scale the higher echelons of their chosen vocations, they increasingly come into contact with a workplace culture visibly defined by the narrower, more linear developmental needs of men. Some women adapt, but others leave because they are unable or unwilling to reinvent themselves.

Nina Gordon (a pseudonym, as are the names of all the women in my study) was a corporate exile whose core identity was poorly validated in her current job. She wanted more from her career than achievement and tangible accomplishments. She wanted a connection to others. One day she simply got tired of the good fight and quit. Rejecting the idea of starting her own business, as have millions of other women who left corporate America, Nina realized she wanted to work in the community. She recognized that she had never truly felt at home in the world of business despite a modestly successful career: "I have a hard time believing that the energy it would take to distinguish me from the crowd is worth the energy I want to put into starting a company. It isn't like I have a unique product concept or a niche that isn't being filled out in the marketplace. The people who know my work say that I undersell myself, that I'm really very good. Part of the problem is that when things come easily to you, you tend not to think it's a major deal."

Nina turned to volunteer community work, a category of endeavor often marginalized as "women's work." But she looked at it differently, viewing her career change as a return to herself. A realist, she also acknowledged her freedom of choice since her husband earned a sufficiently sizable salary to keep the household running without her financial contribution. Although most of us may not share Nina's financial flexibility, we can learn from her perspective on work and its role in her life. Her view about what is important is rooted in genuine self-awareness and months of thoughtful reflection in her third shift about the years she spent unhappily toiling for others in corporate America: "When you get paid in money, then the currency comes with a price. People can criticize you, they can ignore you, they can change what you have done, they can use what you have done, without giving you credit. When you work as a volunteer and you do professional level work for them, you get paid in the currency of respect, appreciation, friendship, and a sense of community. At my stage in life, this is what I want. Being a kept woman doesn't hurt. If I were a single parent, I would probably have to be hustling out there."

Nina serves as a stellar example of a woman whose inner third-shift reflections allowed her to identify what she needed to bring her outer life into better harmony with her inner needs. In a world where men's and women's "currencies" can be markedly different, the conditions are set for an increasingly vocal, inner third shift to dominate the decision making of many successful women, even those who are deeply satisfied with their workplace experience.

The Quest for Inner Harmony

To a large degree, the problem is that no single choice in today's society gives a woman everything she wants. In this context, effectively managing the identity dilemma sometimes requires women to make excruciating choices. Indeed, healthy adult development involves the ability to make and then live with the consequences of one's important life choices. With respect to the third shift, the problem comes when women make a decision and act on it but then continue to second-guess themselves, eroding their happiness and self-confidence.

Carole Hawthorne, a thirty-seven-year-old from my study, still wonders whether she was right to leave graduate school two years after her second child was born. She was on a promising research track, with sufficient grants rolling in to keep her from toiling at part-time work and diffusing her focus from either her family or her studies. Returning home each day after hours in the lab or in front of the computer, she was always excited to be greeted by her six-year-old, an impish first-grader, with his younger sister toddling alongside. In a flash, her world as a scholar vanished, replaced with the softer, deeper pleasures of family life. Carole knows that she suffered from an "abundance of blessings." When she was at school, she loved the intellectual challenges posed by her courses and research projects. The possibility of a far-reaching research career excited her. But when she was at home, she recognized that absolutely nothing in the world felt better than the moments she spent with her children, both of whom fortunately were easygoing, healthy, and happy from the moment of birth.

Reflecting on the months before she left graduate school, Carole commented:

> They're such a kick to be with. They're loving and endlessly
> fascinated by the new things they are learning about their worlds
> everyday. It's embarrassing, really, how smoothly everything was
> going. I used to wonder if something was wrong with me that I
> wanted to change anything. Amy was in a great day care program
> at our church she seemed to like very much. My neighbor picked
> up Tommy three afternoons a week from school, and he actually
> preferred to be over at their house because they have a pool and
> two bigger kids. He was at that age when he loved to shadow an
> older boy. I never had one single hint from Tommy that he wished
> I were around all day instead of at school.
>
> Plus, I knew that Amy, my little one, would probably be my
> last. In theory I'd like to have three kids, but the thought of going
> through the whole pregnancy thing again is just too hard. I'd be
> over forty by the time I had everyone out of diapers. So this is it for
> me. My husband is one of those guys who goes with the flow. I put
> him through graduate school, and now it's his turn to foot the bills.
>
> One day I just began wondering if this half-life of school and
> being a mom was the right way to go. I remember not feeling as
> connected to my courses as I used to be. I would sit in my cube
> staring at Amy's picture, practically able to smell that little girl
> smell she has—you know, grape jelly and baby lotion.
>
> I began to miss them so much, even though I knew I was going
> to be home in a few hours. First I thought I was going nuts. If I
> gave up my fellowship I was afraid I would never get another one
> like it again. Besides, I knew that I could probably finish this degree
> in two or three more years if I just kept going full-time and didn't
> pick an outrageous thesis topic.

Several months later, Carole approached her advisor for a leave from the program. After a semester off, she decided not to return because she realized she wanted to remain home. But Carole's third shift is rarely silent about her choice. A residual piece of her uncertainty never disappears altogether, and she continues to question whether she should have given up in the middle of her program rather than forcing herself to complete her degree. The third shift doesn't evaporate because we make a particular choice on a given day. It lurks always in the background, the uncertainties of the identity, task, and balance dilemmas creating a richly textured backdrop for the decisions in our lives as women. Carole is no better off staying home than she was attending graduate school if she still feels that her decision is a "bad" one. (Fortunately, she doesn't.) But this is exactly why the real key to inner harmony today is effectively managing our third shifts, not just attaining salary equity between men and women, or shattering glass ceilings.

Psychological Walls

To the extent that men do not direct their lives via an active third shift of their own (and may even consciously or subtly denigrate others who appear to "suffer" from one), the inner voices of women can become an additional psychological burden, rather than a source of renewal and creativity. Particularly in the workplace, the third shift can become a kind of psychological divide between the sexes. It is easy to feel distant from your male counterparts, especially high-ranking ones, because they don't necessarily ruminate about the same inner or outer struggles that you face. Many men don't care to be viscerally reminded of what they've given up to get to the top. Moreover, they are culturally conditioned to appear macho and decisive rather than vulnerable and reflective, and therefore reticent to take the time to ruminate about their choices, at least in public. A residual image of the "male workhorse, connected to family, but disconnected from self" is a tragic caricature, as slow to change as are culturally conditioned expectations for women.[15]

The third shift remains a largely female phenomenon precisely because there persist widespread differences in perception of gender equality in our society that continue to separate the frame of reference from which members of each sex view workplace interactions with the other. It is crucial to call out these gender-dependent experiences of the workplace so women can understand why they still may feel alone or confused, even though nearly one in two workers in the United States today are women. This sense of "otherness"—even if it is felt only occasionally—can catalyze the inner third-shift dialogue.

In one study, only 2 percent of male supervisors believed that their female subordinates faced any difficulties because of their gender, although two-thirds of women reported such experiences. In another survey, two-thirds of the men and three-quarters of the male business leaders polled didn't believe that women face significant discrimination for top positions. Yet 95 percent of senior posts in Fortune 500 companies are held by white males, as are 80 percent of Congressional legislators, 90 percent of newspaper editors, and so forth.[16] In this climate of denial, it can feel especially lonely at the top. Women start to question themselves, wondering if they aren't mistakenly obsessed with a problem that others—their male counterparts—don't see and can't solve.

A successful controller in a fast-growing high-tech company where few other women had attained her rank, Yvonne Daly confided her loneliness during an interview: "I just woke up one morning and I was sitting in my company office. I looked outside and there were all these people walking past. I'm in a two-story building with a beautiful courtyard. I looked down on the people walking, wondering what they do. How do they get to be outside and I'm here on the inside? The more I observed those people walking, the more I was drawn to run, to run away."

Like many women in my study, Yvonne attained significant and visible achievements in the workplace. Yet her third shift continued to plague her with doubts about the true meaning of her choices. She confided that other women seemed to understand her ambivalence about her career attainments, but she was uncomfortable exploring the topic with the men with whom she worked. It was as though an invisible psychological wall—not just a glass ceiling—stood between them.

What's Next

It is worth repeating that not all women feel the depth of dissatisfaction with their choices and workplace experiences that Yvonne Daly and Nina Gordon do. Indeed, *The Third Shift* is replete with the energized tales of successful, satisfied women—those with careers as well as stay-at-home moms—who have discovered effective techniques and strategies to manage the dilemmas that undermine other women. To share these valuable practices and techniques, *The Third Shift* is structured into three sections and solidly based on the actual stories of women interviewed for this study. I have also drawn from two decades of my professional experience as a professor and management consultant in the field of executive development.

Beginning with a brief overview, Part One successively examines how the identity challenge—expressing yourself as you really are versus trying to be who others accept—affects women in corporate, entrepreneurial, and stay-at-home settings. Each chapter begins with a short case study, a composite woman drawn from the interview data in my study. To the largest extent possible, I use the actual words expressed by the interviewees (lightly edited for brevity), not only because they bring light and life into the book but because it is the women's actual voices that convey the myriad ways in which these women experience and overcome their challenges. Oral histories, like journals, are a crucial link to our understanding of ourselves and our times, affording depth of understanding not available from pure statistics or quantitative surveys. The themes extracted here are consistent with a large body of scholarly research on gender, which is cited where appropriate in endnotes throughout the text. Each chapter examines the specific areas of self-awareness and self-doubt that create the most inner tension in a woman's third shift; each chapter also recommends practical techniques and behavioral strategies to effectively manage the dilemma and "make your third shift work for you."

Specifically, Chapter One helps women understand how to initiate a process of realistic personal reflection, "looking in the mirror" to face their demons and manage them. The chapter discusses specific strategies to help corporate women acknowledge their true identity by breaking away, taking risks, jettisoning nonessentials, and enlisting adequate support from others.

Chapter Two continues its investigation of the identity challenge in the workplace, showing women how to effectively assimilate without losing authenticity. The chapter focuses specifically on how women can play the gender card at work, rather than denying or mismanaging it. Topics discussed include developing one's voice and persona as a woman, soliciting feedback, and leaving behind a personal legacy.

Chapter Three shifts the focus of the identity challenge from the corporate realm to entrepreneurial life. The discussion begins with ways to help women assess their true readiness for entrepreneurship, a rewarding but risky and lonely path that involves an inward journey first, acknowledging one's personal strengths and limitations. The chapter provides examples of how women can turn personal visions into business concepts, designing products or services in ways that reflect their unique identities. The chapter concludes by admonishing women to enjoy their success and take only those risks they can live with.

In Chapter Four, the identity challenge is examined from the perspective of women at home and in the community. The discussion focuses on how women can express confidence in their choice to stay at home, being clear about their expectations and relaxing sufficiently to actually enjoy nurturing their family members. Awareness of one's true needs is crucial, as is the ability to rein in the negative voices of one's third shift. The chapter specifically addresses a common problem faced by active career women who have sojourned homeward: proving themselves again and again by overscheduling themselves and their families. The chapter also offers insights into how stay-at-home parents can increase their psychological involvement with their children—a deeply rewarding accomplishment, if not *the* goal for stay-at-home women. The chapter concludes with concrete suggestions for how family responsibilities can be shared equitably.

After a brief overview, Part Two explores the second dilemma of *The Third Shift* in great detail: getting the job done versus worrying about how everyone feels. Here, as in Part One, I examine how women in corporate, entrepreneurial, and stay-at-home roles are confronted with this challenge.

Chapter Five discusses how to compete as a woman at work, controlling their thoughts, building respect from men in power, and "acting as if." The chapter is direct and practical, helping women devote attention to both task and people's feelings, explaining the importance of properly decoding one's boss and lining up critical players before taking on any important action. The chapter ends with a reminder that it's OK to fail and make mistakes. Women have to recover and move on if they are to learn and grow. From the standpoint of the third shift, this means harnessing the inner voice of self-awareness, rather than the demon of self-doubt.

Chapter Six examines the task challenge from the perspective of women entrepreneurs. The discussion jumps right into how to show others (and yourself) that you're in charge. Entrepreneurs must show their conviction and effectively manage their time and energy, concentrating only on the essentials, rather than getting bogged down by details and detractors, worrying about the customers—but all without being overly accommodating. It's a delicate balancing act—on the outside, as well as in the third shift—and the tricks revealed in this chapter end with the observation that it's lonely at the top, so experts and associates can make all the difference.

The final chapter on the task challenge, Chapter Seven, reveals the joys as well as the fears of women who elect the stay-at-home life. Beginning with the need to define their personal relationship to work, the chapter guides them through a process to solicit personal, concrete approval from others for their choices. The chapter builds upon recent parenting research to highlight practical and rewarding techniques of focusing stay-at-home time developmentally upon the children, without involving needless self-sacrifice. Finally, the chapter discusses how women can effectively structure their days and set limits. This allows them to enjoy themselves and develop an intellectual life. Like any tough job, staying at home can leave women vulnerable to burnout. The chapter concludes with ways to trim the shoulds in the lives of stay-at-home women.

Part Three builds upon the initial focus of the book, the task and identity challenges. In Chapter Eight, I offer a detailed discussion of the meta-issue of balance: spending time on achievements for yourself versus providing service to others. This concluding chapter tackles the biggest dilemma of all for women, understanding "who comes first." Seeking a unifying focus, this chapter blends together the wisdom of women from multiple life paths—corporate, entrepreneurial, and stay-at-home. Balance is an issue not only of work-family conflict but of a broader internal conflict for women: focus on self versus others, whether those others are family members, employees, friends, or prospective customers. In Chapter Eight, you learn how to reach out to others, sharing your third shifts rather than bottling them up. The chapter also addresses ways to broaden your perspective on your life's true work, while reminding you that such work must involve a "double win": affording true meaning to yourself as well service for others.

Finally, a brief Afterword comments on how women today are literally reinventing female adulthood; it also notes the guiding principles and assumptions used in this research. An Appendix follows to extend insights into the demographic makeup of the women whose voices proclaim the lessons of this book.

Throughout, concrete strategies and practical suggestions are highlighted or offset in boxes to help readers not only reflect on their situations in their inner third shifts but to act on them in the real world every day.

Notes

1. Arlie Russell Hochschild, *The Second Shift* (New York: Avon, 1989). The much-cited "second shift" refers to the extra month of housework and child care the average working woman spends, relative to her working husband, over the duration of a year.

2. James A. Levine and Todd L. Pittinsky, *Working Fathers: New Strategies for Balancing Work and Family* (Orlando: Harcourt Brace, 1997). For example, they quote a 1997 poll finding that 84 percent of men in their thirties and forties say that *success* means being a good father. A 1993 Roper Organization study reported that 76 percent of adults said that mothers and fathers should be "equally responsible" for children and infant care. Those authors conclude that we should rethink our perceptions of the second shift. Although men on average spend less time on housework and child care than do mothers, their participation has increased. By 1997, employed fathers were spending at least one hour per nonworking day with their children more than in 1977, while mothers' nonworking day time with their children held constant. On workdays, employed fathers have increased their time for children by a half-hour, from 1.8 to 2.3 hours, while employed mothers have held steady at about three hours per workday. Clearly, continued progress is necessary, but the point of *The Third Shift* is that we may be focusing on a narrow slice of indicators of progress, with respect to gender equality.

3. For example, a poll of 1,015 Americans by the National Partnership for Women and Families found that 56 percent of men and 53 percent of women expect to care for elderly relatives in the future. A Catalyst study showed that men want the freedom of "sequencing" their careers—slowing job progress during family-focused stages of

life, then speeding up again without prejudice from employers—citing data that 65 percent of men and 72 percent of women would be interested in such a career-family strategy (Sue Shellenbarger, *Work and Family: Essays from the "Work and Family" Column of The Wall Street Journal* (New York: Ballantine, 1999). I am cautiously optimistic but not convinced that surveys about men's *intentions* translate into concrete actions. In our social climate of politically correct behavior, it is easy to check the box on the survey with the socially desirable behavior. For many women, it is exceedingly uncommon to experience institutional support from the workplace for their desires to balance work and family life. Thanks to cultural stereotypes and division of labor between the sexes since the Industrial Revolution, men may find it even more difficult than women to obtain workplace support for their goal of balancing work and family.

4. Carol Tavris, *The Mismeasure of Woman: Why Women Are Not the Better Sex, the Inferior Sex, or the Opposite Sex* (New York: Touchstone, 1992), p. 23.

5. I initiated the study in 1994 with individual structured interviews of eighty-three entrepreneurial women from Silicon Valley. Each was a participant in the Center to Develop Women Entrepreneurs, a community mentoring agency I cofounded with four recently graduated MBA students, Susan Layman, Pamela Rasmussen, Kelli Richardson, and Joanne Springer. Because the study was designed as a longitudinal research project, a full third of the subjects were interviewed three times, at one-year intervals, to determine their tangible progress or changing attitudes over time. Initially, the study was designed to address four basic but powerful questions: Who are these women? What are they looking for? What moves them forward? What holds them back? As the study proceeded, I broadened the focus to include corporate, community, and stay-at-home women, adding thirty-four new participants to the study. After performing systematic content analysis on the interview data, we shifted the study from a niche project about Silicon Valley women entrepreneurs to a far broader inquiry into dilemmas faced by contemporary women.

6. The sample is geographically diverse. Only 21 percent of the sample actually grew up in the local area. Subjects come from a remarkable range of locales, from Los Angeles to Seattle, Texarkana to Rhode Island, Johannesburg to Delhi. The Appendix provides a brief summary of the study's demographics, which show that the three challenges women face—identity, task, and *balance*—are deeply rooted, and they exist regardless of the workplace choices the women selected: corporate life, entrepreneurial life, staying at

home, or working in the community. On the basis of the study population, the challenges can be said to exist for economically disadvantaged "ghetto escape artists" trying to become entrepreneurs; for high-octane corporate executives; and for late-blooming, reentry women from gen-Xers in their twenties to baby boomers and women a decade past menopause. The challenges appeared for women working in every industry, from custom dollmaking to high-tech, from health care to frozen foods. The sample involved women of color and middle-class white suburban women, childless women, moms, and grandmothers. Most of them had a first shift, and many experienced a second shift. All of the women voiced the internal tug-of-war that I call the third shift.

7. I discuss the concept of an *internal glass ceiling* fully in the final chapter. The term refers to self-imposed limits on actions and genuine lack of self-knowledge about one's true needs and desires.

8. In fact, I used a grounded-theory approach to data collection and interpretation. Consistent with the work of Barney G. Glaser and Anselm L. Strauss (*The Discovery of Grounded Theory: Strategies for Qualitative Research;* Chicago: Aldine, 1967), I used an inductive approach to research, mapping the trends and patterns after data collection, rather than inductively developing hypotheses to test before initiating the study. Using this technique, the ultimate conceptual framework is "grounded" in the data. The research team was trained in using specific interview protocols and techniques consistent with the approach in Catherine Cassell and Gillian Symon, *Qualitative Methods in Organizational Research: A Practical Guide* (Thousand Oaks, Calif.: Sage, 1994). After an initial analysis of the interview text, a template or "codebook" was developed around themes relevant to the research questions. As appropriate, revisions were made as new data unfolded, with the pattern of themes interpreted qualitatively rather than statistically.

9. Using dynamic tensions as a conceptual framework for the reality of women's challenges is a useful and proven methodology. In teaching, for example, there exists an immutable, dynamic tension around teaching and learning. Every teacher must determine, for each student, in each situation, how much to let a student struggle and learn, versus how much direction, advice, and answers must be given to teach that student the material.

10. Susan Chira, *A Mother's Place: Taking the Debate About Working Mothers Beyond Guilt and Blame* (New York: HarperCollins, 1998).

11. Edward M. Hallowell, M.D., *Worry, Hope and Help for a Common Condition* (New York: Ballantine, 1998), p. xiii.

12. The topic of female adult development is explained in detail in Chapter One, including references to specific research that has noted differences between male and female adult development.

13. Phyllis Rose, *The Year of Reading Proust: A Memoir in Real Time* (New York: Scribner, 1997), p. 11. In both her well-received study of Victorian women, *Parallel Lives: Five Victorian Marriages* (New York: Random House, 1984), and her prestigious anthology of women's autobiography, *The Norton Book of Women's Lives* (New York: Norton, 1993), Rose observes a common theme in women's lives and memoirs: the life-affirming importance of pleasing others, without which, she observes, women can fall into "an existential sinkhole."

14. See, for example, Eleanor E. Maccoby, *The Two Sexes: Growing up Apart, Coming Together* (Cambridge, Mass.: Belknap Press, 1998). A professor emerita of child development psychology at Stanford University, Maccoby writes of an *explanatory web,* including "biological," "socialization," and "cognitive" components of gender differences that appear in early childhood and are sustained through adulthood.

15. In William Pollack, *Real Boys: Rescuing Our Sons from the Myths of Boyhood* (New York: Random House, 1998), persistent evidence showed that adolescent boys feel profound anxiety about their futures as men, particularly that work pressures will rob them of connections to the more emotional, intimate world of family life. Pollack concludes that "adolescent boys are deeply ambivalent about becoming men and dealing with the responsibilities, limitations, and loneliness that appear to go with adulthood" (p. 168). Like today's baby boomer women who came of age as part of a crossover generation with respect to gender roles and stereotypes, this generation of adolescent boys will be different from their predecessors when they attain power in the executive suite of corporate America. But how different remains to be seen, and their own needs and fear of being perceived as "wimps" may take precedence over lending a helping hand to women. For the foreseeable future, therefore, the third shift can become a kind of workplace psychological divide between the sexes.

16. These studies are cited in Deborah L. Rhode, *Speaking of Sex: The Denial of Gender Inequality* (Cambridge, Mass.: Harvard University Press, 1997).

PART ONE

The Identity Challenge: Who Are We?

Expressing Yourself as You Really Are Versus Trying to Be Whom Others Accept

There are some moments in life that are like pivots around which your existence turns, small intuitive flashes, when you know you have done something correct for a change, when you think you are on the right track. . . . [These are] moments of pure, uncomplicated confidence— and last about ten seconds.
ROBYN DAVIDSON, *Tracks* (a woman's solo trek across seventeen hundred miles of Australian outback)

No matter how hard we try, or how long it's been since the beginning of the modern women's movement, we are sometimes alone as working women in a sea of men. Whenever I undertake soul-deep reflection on women's identity challenge—expressing yourself as you really are versus trying to be whom others accept—an evening from many years ago flashes before my eyes. It took place in a different culture, but it is food for thought nonetheless in a book devoted to the challenges faced by women in the United States.

I was accompanying my husband, Roy, on a business trip to Hong Kong. He was finalizing a deal with his Chinese partners overseas, zealous investors in the Silicon Valley land rush of the early 1980s. One evening, we snuck away from his business acquaintances (all men) for an evening on our own. We picked a dinner house recommended to us by the concierge of our hotel in Kowloon, who neglected to mention that the restaurant was a local businessman's haunt. The food was fragrant and exquisite, but the service more problematic. The waiter never once glanced at me. Even when I was speaking, the tall young Asian man looked only at Roy. He scribbled nothing on his order pad until my husband spoke.

So engrossed had we become in our conversation about the day's accomplishments that we failed to notice that I was the sole woman in the restaurant, a large and gaudy banquet room filled to bursting with dozens of round tables, *around which sat only men.* My husband did everything he could to help me through the evening and lessen my discomfort. Still, I felt completely alone. More to the point, I deeply resented feeling that way. After all, I had struggled to earn an M.B.A. and a Ph.D.; I had become a successful businesswoman with a clear professional identity. How could a roomful of men bother *me?* For the first ten years of my professional life, more often than not, I had been the lone woman in many rooms. But to experience this in a restaurant? I was caught completely off guard. By the time our waiter rolled the trolley of Peking duck up our table, I was too unnerved to enjoy the succulent, steaming meat. But it was too late to leave, and I simply sat silently, pretending that I was no different from anyone else in the room.

But I *was* different, though I chose not to draw attention to myself that evening. Although, like those men, I had a professional identity—after all, I was in business, I had credentials, I was successful—I found myself questioning my own identity in this situation. It had become invisible—and so had I. As women in a professional world defined more often than not by men, the evening in Kowloon always reminds me that we are ever at risk of losing ourselves, in others' eyes if not in our own. In a Chinese restaurant, or in an important executive presentation at the office, working women continue to struggle with building a clear identity. The women I've talked with for this book remain deeply troubled that their expectations at work are still so difficult to fulfill, their questions about their own identity ever evolving.

The word *identity* comes from a Latin root meaning "the same"; the dictionary explicitly defines it as unity and persistence in personality. That night in Kowloon, there was neither unity nor identity. Instead, there was a feeling of disintegration, loss of the ability to manifest the identity I had so carefully developed and cultivated through years of education, training, and successful work experience. What was left? What was essential? What was visible and apparent to others? Simply the fact that I was female.

Whenever I reflect on women and their identity, it's clear to me that the challenge for us is to express ourselves as we really are versus trying (or appearing) to be whatever others will accept. An endless internal litany plays back our doubts to us as we seek to assimilate ourselves into the corporate work world; our third shift toys with balancing whether we are defined internally through our own beliefs and needs or externally through the expectations and needs of others. My evening in Kowloon always serves as a visceral reminder that our unique identities as women must guide any of our career and life choices—whether we work in a Fortune 500 conglomerate, whether we design and launch our own business, or even whether we stay home. In each of these arenas, women continue to feel their way, uncertain where to look or whom to trust to develop a clear and stable sense of identity.

The reality is that the working life for women continues to be marred by choices that we have grown weary of making, choices we would have liked to put behind us long since. But without a clear identity to center our lives, our choices imprison rather than liberate us because we still yearn for what we don't have, rather than finding harmony in what we've chosen. Many of our choices entail more transient satisfaction than we hope for, because our lives as women are ever unfolding and changing in a way that most men's lives do not.

I had lunch recently with a woman who first blazed an entrepreneurial trail in Silicon Valley more than twenty-five years ago, building her company into one of the largest woman-owned businesses in the state. She delegated the day-to-day running of the firm to her daughter several years ago and turned her considerable energies to nonprofit leadership. Three years later, here she was picking at her sushi across the table from me, bored and dissatisfied, looking for something else beyond her grandchildren to help her feel truly alive. In her adult life, she had experienced multiple strong and powerful identities. She had read *Passages* and could cite the trials and tribulations of her midlife transition chapter and verse. She was astonished after all this to find herself in her early sixties, once again unable to experience true harmony from her accomplishments and within multiple selves. Why did she have multiple selves?

How easy it would be to explain away this woman's unease as the symptom of a restless soul, the search for her so-called identity a quixotic pursuit. But I think otherwise, not only because I have so much respect for her but because I have learned how women relentlessly question themselves, their actions, their directions, their decisions. This questioning is the third shift that is the focus of this book. It can be a great strength if it leads to more awareness of our true selves and our hopes and dreams; it can drain and demoralize us if it takes the pure form of second-guessing and self-doubt. The trick is to use the third shift productively to develop our true identities, rather than let it mire us in the quicksand of confusion and guilt.

The four chapters in Part One illuminate the inner journey to discover and rediscover our identities, a journey we embark upon every day as contemporary women. The chapters also offer practical guidance specific to the three realms—corporate, entrepreneurial, and stay-at-home—we can in general choose as women today. Chapters One and Two concentrate on the identity challenge in corporate America, Chapter Three examines the challenge in the entrepreneurial arena, and Chapter Four explores how women fare with the identity challenge when they elect to stay at home. Each chapter also reveals the distinctive voice of the third shift as it plays out in each path. From the women portrayed in Part One, we can gradually piece together a picture of how to successfully use our third shifts to manage the identity challenge. We also see that the women experiencing the greatest internal harmony and external success have learned to integrate their moments of self-awareness with their internal chorus of self-doubts. Only then can a woman truly accept herself for who she is, rather than plaguing herself with fears about being someone or somewhere else.

CHAPTER ONE

The Myth of Androgyny
Who Are We Supposed to Be?

*Why could one never do a natural thing without
having to screen it behind a structure of artifice?*
EDITH WHARTON, *The House of Mirth*

She's just turned forty, and she feels every day of it. Gwen Allen[1] has made it big time. She is the highest-ranked executive woman in her company, a major Silicon Valley computer manufacturer. As an "early badge" employee and one of a handful of females with an elite technical degree in manufacturing engineering, she worked at a furious pace for sixteen years, finally earning promotion to vice president and general manager of a crucial and rapidly growing product division. Known and respected as a strong people manager with great manufacturing instincts, she is now trusted to build the company's future. Beyond her elite title, the company has rewarded Gwen's efforts with an enviable amount of stock. Even on the days that the NASDAQ goes into free-fall, Gwen is a millionaire three times over.

As for real life, Gwen has struck gold there, too. She is the mother of three great kids, all in elementary or nursery school, and all doing well. Her husband-turned-consultant is proud of Gwen's career but admits that he doesn't see enough of her. Although no slouch himself, he's not as driven as his superstar wife. As a veteran of the high-tech wars in a software start-up, he understands the mind-numbing hours executives spend on the job, and the seductiveness of the raw intellectual challenges of high-tech business.

Beyond his consulting practice, his job is to work with the nanny and make certain all the pieces fit together for the family. Gwen, however, constantly battles an inner voice that tells her she's not spending enough time at home. The family tightrope sways quite a bit from time to time, but no one has fallen off. Yet.

Lately, however, something has changed. The higher Gwen climbs in the company, the worse she feels. After the glow dimmed from her promotion, she was left only with the cold reality of the vice presidency. It's not exactly a Louisiana chain gang, but the hours are long, the competitive problems complex and worsening, the personnel issues relentless. She cries regularly, as much as once a week. Her tears help release the pressure for a few moments, but afterward nothing really changes. Inside, she's deeply ashamed. What's wrong with her? Can't she cut it?

Gwen has never been a great sleeper, but now her insomnia feels out of control. She regularly wakes up in the middle of the night, exhausted but unable to keep her mind from performing countless instant replays of the day's highlights. Worst of all, she lives with an icy trickle of fear that never goes away completely: with all her success, why does she still feel like a failure?

The Dream Is Dead

Gwen Allen is suffering from the *identity challenge,* the most basic of the three dilemmas (identity, task, and balance) that create angst and uncertainty in contemporary women. Played out in the corporate workplace, the identity challenge involves the choices a woman makes about who she is at work. It surfaces most often in a male-dominated environment, although even women working in a "pink ghetto" environment such as nursing or elementary school teaching can face the identity challenge, particularly if they are interested in moving up the ranks.[2] In Gwen's case, how much of herself can she reveal? How much of herself should she ignore? Should she try to become like the men since they can't, or won't, become more like her? Should she follow the nostrums for entry into the club, strategically arranging her days and relationships to charm her way into the comfort zone of men in power? Or will hard work and excellent performance pave her way to acceptance?

One of the reasons the identity challenge is so difficult to manage at work is because it colors *every* choice a woman makes as she develops her leadership style. It affects the little issues. (Gwen, for example, still wonders whether she should sit next to other women in a staff meeting, or try to become more gender-blind.) It also impacts the grander questions (should she forge new ground for women as she rises up the corporate pyramid, or lie low, awaiting the day when she is truly an insider?). It's exhausting to cope with these continuous anxieties day after day, a third shift that has expanded to an endless shift.

For many women I've seen over the years, this distress appears unavoidable, the inevitable result when two disparate workplace cultures, one male and dominant, one female and subordinate, grind and writhe below the surface like the genderized equivalent of California's San Andreas Fault. Thirty years into the feminist movement, we have not yet reached either a general cultural equilibrium or specific rules of engagement to determine how men and women are to partner effectively in the workplace. Instead, taking only the female viewpoint in this book, we have the women, as the subordinate culture in most workplaces, seeking to learn more about the dominant culture—often finding out more about how the men operate than they know about themselves—pleasing them, accommodating them, and disguising their real selves when necessary. This deprivation hurts both sides, because the subordinate and dominant groups lose valid knowledge about each other during the charade. Moreover, the subordinate never really feels truly comfortable, because she assumes the role of the outsider, a trespasser rather than a resident, until the persona becomes more real than one's inner self.

In her groundbreaking work on the psychology of women, Jean Baker Miller points out that "a subordinate group has to concentrate on basic survival. Accordingly, direct, honest reaction to destructive treatment is avoided. Open, self-initiated action in its own self-interest must also be avoided."[3] Is authenticity at work truly incompatible with subordination? If so, the women's movement has further wonders yet to perform.

The next step to being one's self at work is to move women from imitating men and the dominant culture to developing a feminine professional identity of their own. This is a difficult transformation that—as we shall see in this and other chapters—evolves over time with experience and conscious reflection. The important point to highlight here is the universality of the identity challenge. No matter how senior, how wise, or how outwardly successful the women executives that come into my office for executive coaching, they all have had to come to terms with this issue. Those who don't acknowledge the problem—a condition I term "gender denial"[4]— are not only less successful in achieving their goals at work; they can also be walking time bombs, likely to wake up one day and repudiate all that they have gained in search of something, or someone, they cannot yet envision.

Highly driven professional women with significant parental pressures can suffer the most. Their expectations of themselves and the workplace are often the highest. No wonder Gwen Allen has indisputably arrived at her breaking point, a deeply painful meltdown ensuing from years of trying to fulfill contradictory demands of her work, her family, and her self-imposed internal needs for increasing achievement as well as personal satisfaction. The elaborate and disciplined systems she has always relied upon to keep her balance while on the working woman's tightrope so long keep her personal high wire from swaying dizzily beneath her feet. She's afraid to look down, to turn back, or even to take another step forward to safety. All the major symptoms are there: exhaustion, sadness, lack of trust in her own instincts, decreasing self-esteem and sense of inadequacy, inability to act or make decisions, and "a peculiar, unassailable, overwhelming bewilderment."[5]

That Gwen is a demanding, self-critical perfectionist makes her situation more extreme than the norm. But the underlying dilemma paralyzes and torments thousands of contemporary working women, hitting overachievers the hardest. Sociologist Martha Beck, author of *Breaking Point: Why Women Fall Apart and How They Can Re-Create Their Lives,* attributes this phenomenon to a deeply rooted double bind our society imposes upon women. American women are caught in the cultural schizophrenia of mutually exclusive expectations, facing increasing pressure (and opportunities) to assume increasingly active responsibility in the workplace, while at the same time encouraged to remain in traditional roles in a society hammered daily by haunting media exposés of neglected children. The unstated subtext is that street-corner violence, adolescent drug and alcohol addiction, and even teenage pregnancy would be lessened if mothers stayed at home and tended their flocks. On the other hand, the second income of working women makes our consumer society hum. *True androgyny—acting out both gender roles simultaneously—is a myth, rather than a reality for most women.* The dream is dead. Instead, it's all a question of trade-offs.

A Developmental Catch-22

It would all be laughable if it weren't so counterproductive—the basic human tendency to analyze an unsatisfying situation and then look around for someone to blame. Men as a group constitute a convenient scapegoat for the women's identity dilemma, but effective strategies to proactively manage it may be more fruitfully sought by turning to the field of human development. Borrowing from the work of Mary Catherine Bateson, women "compose a life" from different themes and roles, forming a richer but much more varied mosaic than men's linear progress through life and career.[6] Only recently has the broader field of human development acknowledged that "life structures"—the underlying patterns, designs, needs, and choices in a person's life—operate somewhat differently for women than men. Freed from Adam's rib, women must establish their own distinctively feminine standard of success, prizing improvisation as genuine achievement, rather than slap-dash accommodation to a masculine developmental clock.[7]

Nor do the yearnings and private satisfactions of women perfectly mirror men's inner needs. A woman's identity is based upon relationships, not just deeds, at work as at home. Gwen Allen, for example, never feels a true sense of accomplishment with completing a project at work unless the work is done well *and* the participants have felt good about their involvement. The pure getting-it-done-right isn't enough for her. She is far from unique in this regard. Joan Kofodimos, a researcher at the Center for Creative Leadership in Greensboro, North Carolina, and an experienced organizational consultant, observes that men seek "mastery" throughout their organizational lives, "the experience of developing and exercising one's abilities and powers," while women are more likely to seek "intimacy," or connectedness with others and with their inner self.[8]

In a decade of work as an executive coach, I have observed this phenomenon more often than not. Because the corporate workplace demands attention primarily to tangible results, women often place *additional* expectations and burdens upon themselves by trying to achieve excellence in two spheres: an outcome, and a distinctive legacy that can be traced back to their different developmental paths as they grow to adulthood. On their good days, the need for a stricter standard of success enhances their satisfaction and productivity. On their darker days, self-doubts remove the pleasures of heightened self-awareness and sensitivity to others.

Consider the following example of mental gymnastics I tracked in one of my female clients, a project manager who had released a software upgrade on time and with minimal bugs but had experienced great discomfort pushing her team to meet the deadline. Her inner third shift involves the dialogue she maintains with herself, vacillating back and forth between self-awareness and self-doubt:

Self-Awareness	*Self-Doubt*
We are the only team this quarter that met the deadline. I was very anxious about pushing everyone so hard. It was uncomfortable for me to overrule all their excuses for delaying the release.	I wonder if anyone will ever want to work on my team again. My lead developer said he didn't want to work so hard anymore.
I need to talk with the team about how we should handle our next project. I want their ideas about how to meet the deadline, without ending up with too many bugs, but I want them to own more of the responsibility.	I'm afraid of what they'll say to me if I announce a postmortem. I don't think they like working with me.
I want to appear as a strong manager with this group, but I really do care about how they feel. It is hard to reconcile both of these things. I think we should celebrate our victory and move on. This is a learning experience for everyone. I may lose one or two key people who need to be doing something else.	I suppose they don't think I'm a whuss after this last quarter. But maybe they think I'm something worse. I know that Tim is thinking about leaving. I wonder what I did wrong.

In presenting this portrayal of an actual third shift, I did not exaggerate the language in the right-hand column of self-doubt. I have seen the most competent women at the vice-presidential level demur at decisions because of personal doubts about how to manage their need to relate well to others while at the same time drilling down and nailing the project goal. I have worked with numerous high-level men who are also quite indecisive, but their reluctance to make the call stems more often from the need to properly play the politics and not offend any critical players. Women—not all, but so many that I have seen—are more likely to worry about hurting others' feelings; there are clear data from the workplace in support of visibly different developmental needs of men and women. This can be hard for men to understand, let alone to value.

Real Men Don't Bond

Thus the first difficulty stemming from the identity challenge for women in a corporate setting is that the dominant workplace culture—usually developed and designed by men—values first and foremost mastery and tangible accomplishment. The intimacy-oriented approach is quite rare among male managers, despite all the joking about male bonding. In Kofodimos's study, the men experienced tremendous discomfort with intimacy, often avoiding it actively. I've often noticed how human nature tends to devalue what can't be easily understood or practiced. It's no surprise that even though women crack open glass ceilings daily and experience statistical success in entry-level and midlevel hirings, the core identity of corporations remains firmly masculine.

Paradoxically, the more that women seek intimacy in the work setting, the more they become outsiders, and the more their relational needs at work are seen as threatening, uncomfortable, or inappropriate to men. If women mask their feelings and intimacy needs, they become less authentic and the workplace inserts a powerful wedge between their behavior and their true needs as women. To be sure, the strength and persistence of the wedge varies according to the individual woman, but it is a true case of denial to insist that men and women possess the same needs in their adult working lives. The developmental catch-22 of the workplace creates a no-win situation for the identity of working women. This is why Gwen Allen looks successful on the outside yet is slowly disintegrating from within.

As if the mastery-versus-intimacy problem isn't tough enough to manage, thousands of women groan under an even more daunting load on the corporate tightrope. These women actually want to *integrate* their mastery and intimacy needs, rather than settling for only one. That is, they want to meet both needs, *at the same time*— a truly audacious goal that even highly ambitious and interpersonally skilled men would never try to pull off. Yet most women executives I've met try to stagger beneath this double load, raising once again the specter of the myth of androgyny.

On the one hand, integration may reflect a superior level of ability and morality on the part of women, as feminists such as Carol Gilligan would have us believe. Women, Gilligan implies, are superior to men because they can acquire adult power without losing their innate feminine sensitivity and compassion.[9] Her book, *In a Different Voice,* struck a deep chord within the field of adult development because it contrasted significantly with the view of the day, first articulated by Erik Erikson, that adult development requires separation from others, rather than intimacy, and that it is an adolescent, unrealistic yearning to attain integration of both needs.[10] Gilligan was among the earliest to conclude that this party line of adult development fails to consider women. In biting language, she likens the male adult development cycle to Virgil's journey, an "arduous struggle toward a glorious destiny."[11] Relationships constitute a clearly subordinate role in this journey and may even inhibit "individuation"—updated terminology for the separation that Erikson articulated as central to healthy male development.

Women in the corporate world can become frozen between two standards of adult development. Masculine separation looms as an "empowering condition of free and full self-expression, while [feminine] attachment appears a paralyzing entrapment and caring an inevitable prelude to compromise."[12] The real irony is that relational abilities, or "emotional intelligence" as it is currently termed, increase in importance as one moves upward in the corporate world.[13] The soft relational skills—self-awareness, empathic, and social skills—are more critical than pure intellect for success in the upper echelons. Women have no monopoly on these soft skills, but in my experience of the past decade they are more likely than men to value them.

Take the case of Maria Rodriguez, an energetic regional sales director for a multinational pharmaceutical house. She extracted her last promotion over four equally talented peers (three men and one woman) because she had a reputation for bringing people together. Her new job involved integrating two formerly separate geographic territories that had historically been at odds with each other—the legacy of her predecessor, an overtly competitive manager whose motto was "take no prisoners."

Maria came into her new job with solid experience and plenty of raw brainpower to back up her time in the trenches. But the key success factors were her willingness and ability to personally work with each peer—no matter how defensive and irritating, or how large their egos—and emerge from her discussions with commitments and win-win decisions. In her own way, she also took no prisoners. Her peers would be the first to say that it was no use fighting her; as one confided to me, "In the end you'll lose, and you'll even like losing to her!"

The downside of Maria's approach, of course, is that it takes time, hours of it, because this relational approach is so labor-intensive. All the key players have to be approached individually as well as in group settings. They have to be checked back with and stroked. There's no let up. For the first ten or twelve years of her management career, Maria was willing to put in the extra time. The rewards of accomplishing the goal and keeping the troops happy were enough. Her third shift was healthful rather than demonic. But somewhere along the line, Maria began to feel that she was "losing her edge," as she put it. The old thrill was gone. Her children had all successfully finished college, and her husband was happily launching his third start-up. The harder she tried to feel connected to people at work, the emptier she felt. In our sessions together, we traced the root of her problem. For years, she had been fighting an uphill battle in her company to make people count ahead of products and technology. For many years, she felt that she was making progress, but recently a new division president had been hired who set her work back by a decade. This new boss was interested purely in results, and he managed through intimidation. Whether he was threatened by relational needs or simply unable to relate to them, the new president made it clear to everyone that Maria's style was ineffective and too time-consuming. "She just isn't tough enough," he insisted.

Of course, "it wasn't personal," but after a particularly terse and unsatisfactory meeting between the two of them, Maria allowed herself to feel—for the first time in years—that her need to attain both happy campers and successful accomplishment was adolescent and unnecessary. Her third shift was like an internal dial of her own mental health, the needle creeping from self-awareness over to self-doubt. She began to lose both her confidence and her eagerness to come to the office. She worked for the new president for another six months, her needs sidelined again and again until she learned to ignore them, to recast them, and even to turn against herself, thinking there was something the matter with her. One day she simply resigned, giving up much she loved in the company, but knowing she no longer fit. After a brief search period, she found a new job with a competitor with exciting responsibilities, a compatible boss, and a work culture that seemed more attuned to her values. Who is the real loser here?

This is how a woman's hold on her true identity begins to slip, one day at a time. It took Maria Rodriguez six months, Gwen Allen sixteen years, for the process to percolate through the haze of promotions, stock options, and successful strategic initiatives these women launched at their respective companies. The internal tug-of-war left both women exhausted, defeated, indecisive, and self-questioning. Gwen certainly doesn't feel the way a vice president should. Most days she doesn't feel like anybody at all, just a bundle of nerves. Since she is the only female vice president, who can she ask what she is supposed to be feeling? Surely not the other women on the ladder below her. She's supposed to be their shining star, the woman who has made it and can do it all. The myth of androgyny has duped Gwen, just as it has duped others into the belief that women don't have to pay a price for their position on the corporate front lines. If true androgyny is a dead hope for today's exhausted and puzzled women, what should they do next?

The Keys to the Kingdom

In 1994, Mary Pipher published *Reviving Ophelia, Saving the Selves of Adolescent Girls.* Thousands of panicked mothers across the nation yanked their preteen daughters from middle schools and junior highs, thrusting them into all-girl academies. Even the public school systems have tentatively begun to research the legality and efficacy of same-sex classrooms. Pipher depicts American adolescence as physically and emotionally dangerous for girls. "Something dramatic happens," she writes; "just as planes and ships disappear mysteriously into the Bermuda Triangle, so do the selves of girls go down in droves. They crash and burn in a social and developmental Bermuda Triangle. In early adolescence, studies show that girls' IQ scores drop and their math and science scores plummet. They lose their resiliency and optimism and become less curious and inclined to take risks. They lose their assertive, energetic and 'tomboyish' personalities and become more deferential, self-critical and depressed. They report great unhappiness with their own bodies."[14]

For the Gwen Allens of corporate America, who escaped Ophelia's fate as preteens, it appears that the danger is far from over just because they've reached adulthood. Of course, it doesn't happen to everyone. A recent study of one thousand women, published in *Working Mother,* reported that multiple roles agree with *ambitious* women, who report happier marriages than their less ambitious counterparts, even when combining stressful professional lives with family responsibilities.[15] The ambitious women were also more likely to perceive themselves as good mothers than were those who characterized themselves as less ambitious.

Why these results? The study's authors offer up a no-brainer: successful women are more positive and have more energy to begin with. Everything in their life works better for these exciting, powerful women with well-rounded lives. *These women feel good about themselves because they are clear about who they are.* The multiple roles in their lives contribute to their strong sense of self, rather than fragmenting their identity. Their third shifts support rather than tear down their belief and confidence in themselves as working women.

But there can be a thin line between the profile described by the *Working Mother* survey and the Gwen Allens of corporate America. When the high wire starts to unravel, the woman doesn't merely stumble; she tends to plunge downward through the thin safety net our society provides for working parents. Hence, Gwen's unhappiness despite all her success. It's more than overload; it's her very identity at stake after years of the androgynous life. Not every woman need end up like her. Indeed, many may feel quite content with their corporate careers. But for every such fortunate woman are many others who are struggling to fit into a workplace that is slow to recognize, value, and act on their crucial needs as women—from the freedom to use a "softer" feminine style, to the flexibility to better balance family life with job requirements. The identity dilemma occurs when workplace practices and values collide with a woman's true personal beliefs and inner needs. The symptoms, first and foremost, include a third shift that brings pain rather than pleasure to its owner.

Making Your Third Shift Work for You: Managing the Identity Challenge

With closer examination, we can identify a number of practices to help women better navigate their professional lives and use their third shifts to their advantage. These practices stem from twenty years of work with adult learners in graduate courses, private clients in my consulting practice, and structured sessions with women in my research interviews. Each can serve as an important starting point to help women develop a positive working identity without sacrificing the inner territory of their souls, or without requiring everyone else to make all of the changes.

- Look in the mirror regularly. Face yourself. Face your demons.
- Develop an effective breakaway strategy, either virtual or the real thing.
- Go against the grain. You can't help others without starting with yourself.
- Take a risk. "Jump at the sun."
- Jettison part of the load. If you keep carrying it, no one else will.

- Enlist support. Change efforts require encouragement and understanding from others.
- Invest in yourself. Is your credit more important than your sanity?
- Be realistic. True, lasting harmony in our society is elusive.

Look in the Mirror Regularly

Of all the steps, the hardest is this first one. For most of us, facing our true selves can be a difficult chore, one we shun without provocation. It is never easy to detach and spend the hard time necessary to look in the glass and accept the image that stares back. In Gwen Allen's case, her natural achievement drive, her excitement at the new intellectual challenges unfolding at work, and her complete preoccupation with the everyday demands of leadership kept her from dawdling in front of the mirror to review her own progress and personal growth. Early in her career, she deliberately submerged too much reflection about where she fit into the system. As a woman in manufacturing engineering, she was already an oddball. Why spend even more time fretting over something that couldn't change? Better to learn how to operate successfully with the men around her. Besides, she wasn't looking for a fight. She was looking for a chance.

Approaching her thirtieth birthday, Gwen and her husband decided it was time to start a family. Having succeeded in everything she had tried to date, she was certain she could combine motherhood with a career. After her oldest was born, she strode confidently back into the workplace, certain she could handle the new pleasures and challenges of a child. Oddly enough, the entrance of a baby into her life was the very first time that gender raised its head. Naturally, she worked with many male parents, but none of them had abdomens jutting out like the prow of a ship after nine months. For the first time, she noticed that others were treating her differently—nicely, but differently all the same. She just ignored the special treatment.

After her second child was born, Gwen again promptly returned to work, focused on how to keep her new family from inconveniencing either herself or others at work. She downplayed any maternal image that might leak out at work. She groomed herself meticulously each morning to eliminate lurking Cheerios from her hair, and she purged her office of all but two small pictures of each child. She concentrated on the practical, assuming the whole trick was straightforward scheduling. With her third and final child, she allowed herself the luxury of four months of maternity leave before returning to the office, having learned from her first two. With her middle daughter, Gwen's comfort with the situation became somewhat more precarious as she endured a year of nursing into a breast pump behind the closed doors of her office, since her daughter couldn't tolerate formula or cow's milk.

Gwen stayed upbeat through the entire experience, knowing it was a transient dilemma. *It will get better,* she told herself, though she was torn every day as she left work with reports undone, or left home with a baby in tears in someone else's arms. Struggling to control the disparate parts of her life, she simply picked up the pace, literally running from home to work, meeting to meeting. I can well imagine that there was little time to look into the mirror. A day at a time, Gwen continued to lose herself, until the authentic woman underneath the juggled balls was buried as deeply as last year's headline news.

It all finally came crashing down after her promotion to vice president. Transitions—*even the positive ones*—can yank a woman like Gwen right off the working woman's tightrope. It was clear to me that her promotion was a turning point because the new title involved even more work and responsibility, with the added dimension of a subtle yet crucial change in her leadership style toward a more hands-off approach. Now she was managing a large organization without really understanding everything about the business. She had to delegate decisions, not just work, to senior people she barely knew and didn't necessarily trust. She had to give up control, even as she was perceived as being more powerful with her new rank. And with the exception of the lone human resource professional on her staff, she managed all highly competitive men, several of whom were still fuming that she'd been promoted over them. When Gwen finally took a real look in the mirror, she took the first step of acknowledging the severity of her problem, rather than running away from it. She stopped using her work as an anesthetic, her busyness walling her off during the day, her exhaustion a narcotic at night.

To nourish her first small glimmer of hope and change, I urged her to get away. For the first time in years, she took a few weeks off, without planning an elaborate family vacation. With minimal but typically efficient voice mails to her staff, she arranged to be absent for three weeks—a short period, but in the company where she worked a veritable windfall of time. Another woman, one whose personality was less hard-driving or less extreme, might not require such a complete time out. Another woman might have made many other choices and compromises along the way, taking longer at home with each child, trying part-time work for the first year while breast-feeding, putting up more family pictures at work and not worrying about how others saw her, or even—God forbid— temporarily turning down a promotion, sensing it would be incompatible with three young children. But like many other women who've come into my office with manic third shifts, Gwen didn't do any of these things. So she had to take a different step to help find herself again.

Develop an Effective Breakaway Strategy

"I decided to run away!" Gwen shouted with a giant smile as she burst into my office for our last visit before the sabbatical she had maneuvered for herself. Joking aside, in our masculine, westernized culture, deliberately removing oneself from the firing line is often seen as weakness, rather than a sensible and life-affirming strategy, a kind of workplace hooky and an unjustified absence in many of Silicon Valley's high-tech palaces. Nonetheless, if you seek to understand your own choices and make clearheaded decisions about your life, it can be extremely useful to take yourself out of the game temporarily. Some women are able to extend their vacations for this purpose, or take sabbaticals or unpaid leaves. Naturally, many women must make do with "virtual" breakaways: stolen moments, afternoons, or evenings when they are not distracted by other demands.

Taking a true sabbatical or breakaway from your work can involve career and financial risks. But I remain firmly convinced that it's a strategy well worth fighting for, even if your company is one that frowns on the practice, and even if it seems out of reach financially. An analogy is our love affair with the biblical Moses. Most people's vision of this great prophet is a single powerful image of him striding defiantly out across the desert, the Israelites in tow. They forget about the years he spent in quiet solitude, resting in the hills as a reclusive shepherd, preparing himself for the real work ahead. For women apprehensive about their true reputation in a male-dominated workplace, a breakaway may accurately be feared as career-limiting. But it is senseless for women depleted from mental, emotional, or physical exhaustion to delay their breakaway for too long, or naïvely assume that a vacation with the family or a few moments of quiet meditation substitutes for the real thing.

The real thing is a voyage of self-discovery, a test of one's third-shift voices. Though many will disagree, I firmly believe that most contemporary working women with children at home simply cannot develop the requisite psychological disengagement for genuine, deep reflection without getting away physically. It is equally clear to me that not every woman requires this extreme form of breakaway strategy. Moreover, some women, like Gwen Allen, can afford a true sabbatical extending over several months, while most others may have to manage with a week or so, or even less. The latter women have to live with a virtual, armchair breakaway: say, an afternoon off in a quiet place removed from one's normal surroundings. The results associated with each strategy may vary, however.

A breakaway is not simple rest but a sustained, solo, deeply personal journey, involving mental and spatial distance from the workplace with the objective of reflecting and, if necessary, *healing*. For women like Gwen who have reached a breaking point, healing is not possible without time away from the source of the pain. Time out, however, need not be expensive, because the destination for a breakaway is development of a *new* perspective about one's life and one's choices. One can go to the mountains, the seashore, a dumpy motel outside town, or a solitary walk down the road, so long as one makes a clean exit, leaving cell phones, pagers, and even the most well-meaning friends and loved ones behind. If taken regularly, breakaways can require no more than a day off or an occasional weekend away (which, granted, is a stretch for single mothers without close family in the area). In my experience, by taking some regular time out for yourself you can avoid the depth of trauma that Gwen Allen was experiencing; you can also avoid taking months off work, which might be a luxury you can't afford.

To put it another way, a true breakaway involves *sacred time,* a concept familiar to followers of eastern and Native American religions but suspiciously New Agey to most American executives. In these cultures, sacred time typically involves physical removal from one's routine daily life, whether in a trek to a remote hillside, within a community of peers in a sweat lodge, or in a quiet garden where profound meditation can occur naturally. Of course, pursuing sacred time in our modern culture requires practical adjustments, but in principle they may be as much psychological as physical.

There may be envy mixed with the skepticism, but most executives break out in a rash when they hear a phrase like "sacred time"—no matter how piteously they themselves whine about the need for their employees to take time out to think and "become more strategic," "get out of the weeds," and "look at the big picture." These same executives can become like cardboard caricatures, with limited opportunities to retool or renew. No wonder they have difficulty thinking outside of the box.

Regardless of whether you can take an extended leave or must squeeze your breakaway into a rigid schedule with limited financial resources (I discuss some ideas for this later in the chapter), the crucial essence of the breakaway strategy is dramatic departure from the status quo, which is necessary to catalyze self-reflection, questioning of your values and true identity, as well as creative development of new choices and practices for your return to the world after the breakaway period. To stimulate your own voyage of self-discovery, reflect as follows:

Questions for Reflection During a Breakaway

- *What is the role of work in my life?*
- *What do I expect from my work?*
- *What changes have I experienced over my life in my relationship to work?*
- *Am I happy about these changes?*
- *What brings me joy at work?*
- *When do I feel unhappy at work?*
- *What is the "right" work for me?*
- *What changes in my life will make me happy? So why don't I make those changes? What is blocking me?*

In Gwen's case, her breakaway period didn't solve everything, but it crystallized many feelings she had spent years trying to ignore. Most significant of her learnings was her response to the first question on the list, the role of work in her life. After her breakaway, Gwen knew with startling clarity that she would never again allow work to have such a choke hold on her life. In her case, she was clear that she couldn't have gained this perspective without the time away. But she also couldn't imagine life without an important job where she could constantly test herself and hone new skills. She wanted to come back, and she needed a senior, visible position with considerable challenge; but she had learned that she didn't need any more visibility, any more seniority, or a grander title than the one she currently possessed. Using Gwen's own metaphor, in the tapestry of her life the silver thread of a senior vice presidency was not sufficiently different from the golden thread of executive VP. For her, the rewards for the higher-level position fell woefully short compared to the additional sacrifices she would need to make. She had enough.

From the actual work itself, Gwen expected the opportunity to see tangible results from her efforts as a manufacturer of innovative products. She took particular pleasure in guiding her team to new levels of quality with each successive product generation. This satisfied her intense achievement need and desire for mastery. She realized that though she liked most of her coworkers, upon reflection she knew that she could walk away from nearly all of them in a heartbeat. Her important relationships and her need for intimacy were met elsewhere, with close friends and family. This revelation allowed her to loosen up the demands of her third shift somewhat because she could see that she didn't have to agonize over every personnel and business decision at work, trying to make other people happy.

To skip to the bottom line for Gwen, we found that the right work for her involved lifelong change and continuous learning. If she reached a point where she became bored or felt slighted by her decision not to pursue a further promotion, then she would take a lateral move elsewhere, maybe even to another industry where she could learn something completely fresh. Flashing her dimples at me, she mused, "I might even go out and start my own company. Why not?"

Go Against the Grain

During an emergency in an airplane, the flight attendants always tell parents to put on their own oxygen masks before affixing the yellow plastic cup to their child's face. This clearly goes against the grain for most mothers, but in a grave emergency the wisdom of placing oneself first makes sense. Still, for women like Gwen the need to break away may be compromised further by their fears that they already spend too much time at work and should therefore give any remaining time and energy to their children. Giving up one's needs is laudable at first, even noble on occasion, but it then becomes a bad habit, one that occurs without thought.

Sainthood, however, is only acceptable in saints. It is often not until middle life that serving others at the expense of ourselves catches up with us. But why wait until our forties? In his refreshing best-seller, *The Aroused Heart: Poetry and the Preservation of the Soul in Corporate America,* David Whyte reminds us of the perils of this path: "Finally reaching the height of our powers at midlife, we approach the very temple of our identity. Everything for which we have striven is represented by this place. Work becomes, as we sacrifice everything on the corporate altar, the be-all and end-all of our identity."[16]

In literature and at the movies, we laugh at the caricature of the all-sacrificing Jewish (or Italian) mother. Who actually respects that woman? Gwen must ask herself what she really gets from dedicating her life to pleasing and serving others. You don't need to be Sigmund Freud to guess that Gwen feels fulfilled by helping others accomplish their goals. Maria Rodriguez derived exactly the same sense of inner satisfaction. Indeed, it is this very skill at developing subordinates and building an organization that has gained both women their senior titles. But Gwen took it to extremes, turning her greatest strength into a weakness, in both her personal and professional lives.

Other women have succumbed to this trap. Elyssa Franklin is only thirty-one, but she's already wondering if medicine is the right career for her. After a daunting number of years given over to cramming physiological and scientific facts into her consciousness as an undergraduate, a medical student and intern, and a resident, she is now in her first specialized year of an ob-gyn residency, the field she chose for herself after a wise and compassionate gyne-cologist in college helped her through a difficult abortion.

Elyssa is astounded by the draconian cuts to patient service she observes at the public health facility where she works grueling back-to-back shifts. Everyone around her simply seems to accept them, so she has held her tongue. Nor has she said anything about the surprisingly crude, locker-room humor that blankets every pro-cedure when the patient is unconscious. She had picked her field especially because it involved more contact with women, over-looking the fact that it is a low-prestige, low-paid specialty. Al-though peopled with a larger percentage of female physicians than any other specialty, it is nonetheless ruled by masculine prac-tices and expectations. This is what disturbs her most. She knows that the profession is changing, but will it happen fast enough for her? She wonders if she should change her specialty, or leave med-icine altogether, or put her head down and bear it, or try to become a change agent. "Some days I feel like I just want to run and hide," she admitted to me. "Is this what I really should be doing with my life?"

It was clear to me that Elyssa was one of that special breed of women who take the imperfections they see around them very much to heart. She simply could not stand idly by because to her inaction was a kind of silent collusion. On the other hand, her posi-tion as a young resident gave her few options to influence a system she felt was wrong yet could be improved. We began to search for ways she could influence *something*, first openly and nonjudgmen-tally discussing her lifelong tendency to take too much upon her-self. Throughout her career, I told her, I thought she would always need an *objective* way to gauge whether she was doing fine, or whether she was simply being too hard on herself.

We began with her current situation, seeking to discover if it was really her profession that was a poor fit for her, or her inabil-ity to act on her beliefs that was the true problem. We discussed what was appropriate and realistic for residents to improve, as opposed to senior department heads. This helped to remove some of her worst guilt while constructively identifying concrete work-place conditions and practices that upset her (but that she could indeed act on without undue risk to her career).

We also took steps to identify when Elyssa's third shift of self-doubt became most strident; we quickly concluded that it flared up when her sleep patterns were disturbed by her working hours. As a useful technique, I suggested she actually keep a two-column journal of her third shift, tracking it across time and the hours worked as best as she could, given the little bit of time she could find for herself as a resident. This practice proved highly effective, allowing her a clearer perspective without ignoring or discounting her feelings, the positive ones as well as the negative. As women, we become healthier and more powerful as we integrate, rather than substitute one aspect of our third shift for the other. I have included an excerpt from Elyssa's journal here:

Self-Awareness	*Self-Doubt*
Dr. Thompson is unequivocally the worst role model I'll ever have as a doctor. When I have my own residents, I will be very clear about what not to do. With all due respect, he really is a jerk. He has no idea how to bring out the best in others.	Dr. Thompson always makes me feel like I'm an idiot. Why can't I ever please him? If only there were some way to work with someone else, I wouldn't feel so bad.
I don't think anyone could have done a better job with that delivery. It was very complicated. I definitely need more experience if I'm going to excel. I don't ever want to be in a situation with a patient where I'm over my head.	I felt like I didn't know what I was doing. The stakes are so high! I'm really not cut out for this. I wonder if I should change my specialty to something easier.

In Gwen Allen's case, the need to effectively align her own values with those of her workplace led her to a similar impulse for action. We discussed how she could have the most impact as a leader by her attention to "human asset" issues, deliberately focusing on the people elements and the work culture, delegating to her strongest subordinates some of the process-oriented, strategic-planning components of her job. The idea is to make her mark as a leader by building upon her strengths rather than trying to do everything herself. The question she might want to ask herself is, *"What do I want to be known for as a leader?"* This deliberately narrows the expectations and will probably greatly improve the results and the legacy she leaves behind her in the organization. It also forces her to focus on building and expressing a unique workplace identity.

At home, Gwen might discuss with her children how they really want to spend time with their mother. It is often quite a jolt to find that spending two extra hours to make homemade brownies, as opposed to buying the packaged kind from the bakery, makes absolutely no difference to anybody but oneself! Better to spend the time playing a card game or shooting a few hoops, if those are activities that the kids really enjoy.

It is also worth remembering that many employees and children *always* want more than any single boss or parent can—or should—give them. A significant portion of professional development for employees at work, as well as personal development for children at home, is letting one's dependents learn and grow on their own. Indeed, this is probably what Erikson had in mind when he identified separation as a healthy element of growth. Women who take on too much may sometimes be denying others what they need the most.

Take a Risk

Every day for the first week of her breakaway, Gwen had to physically restrain herself from calling the office. She seemed to be experiencing more, not less, stress by staying away. Away at school all day, her children didn't need her. She filled the time with extra sleep, listless afternoons of reading, and numerous trips to the gym, alarmed to find that she had little more energy in the evenings to play with her rambunctious young children than she normally did. She feared that her strength and enthusiasm might never return. She worried that her peers were plotting behind her back while she was gone (and, of course, they were).

Her husband counseled patience, never Gwen's long suit at any time in her life. She hung on, and very slowly the fog started to lift. One morning, nearly three weeks into her breakaway, Gwen woke early with a noticeably higher level of energy. She decided to take an additional three weeks off and told her boss she'd call when she was ready to come back. Finally, six weeks to the day after Gwen left her elegant office behind, she called up Ron, the brashest and most ambitious but also the strongest of all her direct reports. "The keys to the kingdom are yours, Buddy," she said. "I'm taking six months' leave." Ron tried halfheartedly to hide his glee, and Gwen tried not to shudder, but she felt as though someone had just walked over her grave.

Hanging up the phone, she paced and ruminated. Had he won and she lost? At Gwen's level, a lengthy breakaway was undoubtedly career-limiting. Tom Peters could hang out in a Vermont farmhouse, and John Sculley could probably get away with time on his yacht between engagements, but for Gwen, a self-imposed sabbatical was political suicide. In her company, the corporate culture was like the last few moments at the Alamo. All hands were expected to keep firing until no one was left. The strategy worked because, unlike the Alamo, there were always fresh young recruits on the way to replace the dead or departed.

I tried to help Gwen see that transitions always involve loss as well as gain. She was losing her blind and unquestioning loyalty and the sense of security she always experienced when working long and hard at a problem. She was also losing the adrenaline-charged excitement that accompanies life atop the anthill. It was an unnerving, difficult time for Gwen; she was taking an enormous risk to step back and literally forge a new and broader identity for herself. Her career had always served as the true north of her entire adult life; she squeezed everything else that mattered to her around it.

At forty, was it now time to forge a different path, or change how she traveled on the one she had chosen? Anna Quindlen once remarked about women that "no matter what choice we make, we're going to get nailed for it. So we might as well choose what makes us happy."[17]

During her time away, Gwen recalled an exhortation from her childhood: "Jump at the sun. You might not land on the sun, but at least you'll get off the ground." She realized that she wanted to return to work. Her professional career wasn't more important to her than her children, but it was as compelling. It was who she was. But if she returned, she would need to change her perfectionist ways, remove herself from the details, and simply let a few things in her life go. What seemed like simple common sense to others felt like tremendous personal risk to her.

Jettison Part of the Load

The field of psychotherapy has established that profound individual breakthroughs involve three steps: (1) enlightenment, (2) experimentation with new behaviors, and ultimately (3) internalization of the desired new behavior and attitude. The essence of the breakaway strategy is its power to lift one out of the whirlwind and into the calm eye of the storm. The solitude affords the *opportunity* for enlightenment to occur—if one is willing, and if one dares to see oneself as others do. Breakaway without the next step—experimentation with new behaviors—never achieves a visible, concrete result. I knew that nothing would change in Gwen's life unless she followed enlightenment regarding her demons with actual, sustained changes in the daily conduct of her life.

Tremendous willpower is needed for highly driven managers like Gwen to truly transform how they accomplish their goals, even when their behavior is clearly self-defeating. This is because their visible behaviors—such as the need to perform every detail themselves—is not just a habit, but a representation of themselves as human beings. Leaving out anything represents failure to them, not simple forgetfulness. By taking the time to think through her perfectionism and to initiate discussion of it with others, Gwen enlarged her perspective. She reluctantly realized that her achievement drive had imprisoned her. She placed extraordinary demands on herself as well as others, rarely allowing herself to see how unrealistic the expectations were. Because she was so well liked and respected, her staff tended to rescue her, rarely giving her realistic feedback that she was taking on too much by herself. No one wanted to hurt Gwen's feelings, and she literally became cocooned, with no external pressure to change.

During her breakaway, her activity level ratcheted way down, allowing her defense system to shrink back as well. Some of the external messages from others began to seep into her consciousness. Perhaps for the first time, Gwen actually heard her husband when he said, "You don't need to bake those cookies yourself for the school assembly. Just stop at Safeway on your way to school." Or "The house is clean enough. No one is going to be looking through the closet. Relax and go out for a walk." Or "The kids are fine. You don't have to feel guilty if you want to take a nap." She began to see parallels with her style at work, thinking back through all the Saturdays she had come in to the office just to clear off the clutter on her desk and complete quarterly reports exactly the way she thought they should look. She had always assumed, as do most workaholics, that someone else was in even worse shape than she was (hence she was fine). If she stayed at the office all day Saturday, she'd point to a colleague who stayed until closing time on Sunday.

Similarly to Elyssa's journaling, we began by tracking Gwen's activities rather than her third shift, both at home and after she returned to work. She was going to put her perfectionism and her penchant for detail to new use. She jotted down how she spent her time in half-hour increments. By the end of the month, she was able to see a clear pattern. Her knee-jerk reflex was always to overdo. If her intent one morning was to simply pick up a few toys in her daughter's room, she'd end up going through the closet looking for giveaway items. If she began reading a book for fun, she'd stop a chapter into the volume and pick up the latest issue of *Forbes,* thinking she'd better catch up on the industry. By monitoring how she spent her time, she was able to figure out that a surprising amount of what she took on didn't really need to be done.

Focus on the essentials. You have to jettison part of the load; there's no other way.

Enlist Support

Barbara Killinger, a Toronto psychologist with years of experience treating workaholics, suggests that underneath their superhuman exteriors workaholics are deeply dependent upon approval and admiration from others.[18] She terms workaholics the "respectable addicts," describing how our modern society prizes work above all else, accepting if not encouraging workaholism while vociferously decrying drug, alcohol, and other addictions. Of the many practical suggestions Killinger advances in her book, one rises above all else: allow others to be in charge on occasion. At their roots, perfectionism and workaholism are about control.

But Gwen's workaholism, like that of many other executives, also stems from a broader cultural endorsement of overwork. Going against the tide of our Calvinistic, work-obsessed culture requires tremendous internal stamina and courage, particularly for women who have spent decades trying to batter their way into the corporate citadels. Placing one's work in perspective, then, requires a change in one's role models and associates to include networks beyond the workplace. It also requires an exceptionally strong sense of self.

As Gwen's breakaway allowed her to begin seeing herself through new eyes, she needed new insights and perspective in her life along with clear feedback, but also unconditional support during this transition period. For the first time in her life, she began to need the company of women. Also for the first time, she actually had time to fit them in. She joined a fitness center, not just to pare a few pounds from her thighs but to deepen her relationship with several other career women who seemed plagued by similar workplace ills. She no longer felt so alone, and she didn't take herself quite so seriously any more.

Gwen also carefully enlisted the support of the two individuals in her life whom she most respected: her husband and an old friend from college with whom she maintained close contact. When she first returned to work, Gwen had turned to her boss for support—before quickly realizing that her own breakaway was extremely threatening to him. At best, her boss, a very nice guy, was ambivalent about the "new, improved" Gwen. At worst, he was cynical and clueless. Gwen knew that he would probably never feel quite the same about her again, but she doggedly began to rebuild his confidence, involving him closely in her efforts to prioritize and focus her assignments. She passed a lot of work to her staff that she would have taken home previously.

During this period, I also encouraged Gwen to take advantage of other types of professional support. Many of my other clients benefit tremendously from developing closer working relationships with in-house organizational development specialists who can give them practical, concrete, and inside advice to help shift their management styles, while building on their true inner identities. In fact, a great many of these OD specialists are women who have chosen these staff positions precisely because they enjoy the opportunity to counsel others.

Gwen was able to share her personal goals with such an individual in her company (it turned out to be a he), ultimately distancing herself from her work and leaving more details to others. She focused on getting her division to perform at the same level as before her breakaway so she could regain credibility with the company. From the OD specialist, she also learned to use a magical phrase whenever her employees came to her office with problems to solve: "How do you want to handle this? Give me several recommendations, and tell me which one you like best."

The one stubborn fly in the ointment was Ron, to whom she had passed the reins during her extended breakaway. He just couldn't get over her return to her old position, and he fought her at every opportunity. She would have loved to somehow regain his trust and loyalty, but she realized that this was definitely a battle she would never win. She finally had a meeting with him; the emotional session ended with her committing to find him a new position elsewhere in the company at a significant promotion from his current level. Her breakaway had taught her that there were simply some hills it was better not to climb.

Gwen's return to work was surprisingly stressful for her, even though she was deliberately trying to juggle fewer balls. We were both fearful that her good intentions would dissolve and she would find herself quickly flailing again, retreating to old habits and practices. Without continued support—each in very different ways—from her boss, the OD specialist, her husband, and old and new friends, her resolve to change would have been inadequate to the task. Indeed, willpower alone is rarely sufficient for successful senior executives to change. In *Beyond Ambition*, Robert Kaplan, senior fellow at the Center for Creative Leadership, emphasizes that sustained change requires a set of people who will cooperate with the executive as she tries to be different.[19] From a strictly practical standpoint, this is not always possible, or at least in many of the companies where I consult. Moreover, experimenting with new behaviors is unsettling and destabilizing. For achievement-oriented executives like Gwen, with high need for control, it is a tremendous personal triumph of will over habit to explore and act on a new self. A combination of external pressure and external support is the best prescription for internalizing new behaviors over time and forging a new identity. This is also why a formal breakaway period acts as a profoundly useful antecedent to genuine change for women like Gwen. (Again, many readers do not need, nor can they afford, so extreme a strategy.)

Invest in Yourself

By talking with a new group of women, most of whom were a bit further down the corporate food chain than she was, Gwen realized just how fortunate she was to have the financial strength to take several unpaid months away from work. In most cases, finances preclude a woman's breaking away to press the reset button. For women without Gwen's plush stock options, what can be done?

It is heresy, no doubt, to suggest that taking time out must transcend other, more immediate financial needs. Except for women in families at the very bottom of the socioeconomic scale, where absolutely no financial flexibility is possible, the bulk of middle-class women can rearrange their short-term financial requirements *if they so choose*. The difficulty is putting one's own needs first, not dealing with the creditors. Think about it. The average American family is saddled with significant amounts of unsecured credit, the legacy of years of catalogues and credit cards coming uninvited through the mail. For women at the breaking point without a financial nest egg, an unpaid month away from work can only be paid for by maxing out a credit card. I've talked with women who routinely run up their credit lines to the limit every day for jewelry, clothes, and furniture. Yet they resist putting their credit on the line for something incalculably more important: themselves. Is such a practice risky? Awkward or embarrassing? Most likely. Can it be done? Assuredly. Is it any crazier than doing nothing at all, grinding away at work every day, making no changes, and pretending that things will get better?

Alternatively, I've listened to women in my study talk about hanging on by their fingernails at work for a six-month period, shutting down every optional expenditure until thirty days of breakaway money is carefully sequestered in a bank account. This requires thoughtful discipline as well as a firm eye on the goal. The strategy must be temporary—waiting for years rather than months is a senseless sacrifice. As a permanent strategy, a less severe approach is to regularly question one's minor daily purchases: the extra lunch out here, that third pair of black slacks there, the name-brand running shoe instead of the house brand at Penney's. Over time, with regular small sacrifices, most middle-class families can probably keep thirty days of living money in an account as a security blanket.

Does a thirty-day grace period do the trick for every woman suffering from superwoman's disease? There is no magic break-away pill that suggests what the appropriate time is for a woman to rediscover what is truly important to her. Not every woman even needs a full-fledged breakaway. Rather, she needs the feeling of control over her work life, the sense that she can make a choice and take a different path that fits her true needs and identity, should she so choose. Obviously, the trick is for a woman to avoid letting herself get so overextended that she can dig herself out of her situation only with extreme measures. This means monitoring one's stress level and making time for oneself regularly, in small but frequent doses. Above all, it means investing in oneself.

To end this section, I include in this discussion the plight of the single mother. The idea of a breakaway—of even an afternoon—must feel out of reach for this hardworking woman. However, it is possible for even a harried woman in this group to set limits with the children; ask them to play quietly for a bit longer; put them to bed earlier than usual; ask a friend, neighbor, or family member to take a child for an afternoon or evening; or use the TV-babysit-ter more than she might like on an afternoon when she is desper-ately trying to think through whether she needs to make some changes in her life. Because these elusive, catch as-catch can moments may feel sporadic and random, I strongly advise you, in this situation, to keep a journal to fill in during the solitary moments. This helps you pick up the thread of your earlier reflec-tions much more quickly and accurately between the breakaway moments you manage to steal from your busy life.

Be Realistic

True, lasting harmony in our society is elusive. Highly driven career women talk a good game about searching for harmony, but observers may very well wonder. Why do their choices so often take them away from peace? Why are they forever adding more to their plates, rather than less? Why do they continue to want it all? Psychologists advance the hypothesis that such women (and men) are trying to drown out internal negative emotions—fear of failure, fear of boredom, fear of laziness, and even fear of self. Such individuals build their external lives into palaces of achievement, taking highly visible jobs where others can look up to them. They hear other women talk about balance and wonder what's wrong with them. They are always trying some new scheme to change themselves and slow down, but the changes never seem to take. They can control astounding responsibilities at work, yet they can't seem to get themselves under control. Even when they don't mean to, they raise the bar ever higher for themselves.

This type of frenetic, type A behavior is well known in male executives, but the female version can be much worse, since these women add the universe of domestic obligations to their already bulging portfolio of job demands. In our patriarchal society, where women do not have wives—a nanny or a housekeeper is a limited substitute, at best—overload is inevitable, and the cycle of activity becomes ultimately self-defeating rather than rewarding. What Gwen Allen and her ilk have forgotten is that the central task of successful adult development is self-acceptance, a state dependent upon who one is, rather than what one does. In the algebra of life, this is an equation that is far harder to solve for women whose paid work leaves such an indelible stamp on their lives. Activity and achievement without self-acceptance yield results alone. But the real scorecard for women—the one that includes the third shift—requires harmony for a true win.

My conversations with more than one hundred women made it very clear that women today dislike narrow choices, such as staying at home or going to work. They are shooting for a higher goal, balance across the two spheres and simultaneous satisfaction of one's feminine and masculine needs through life choices. But is this not the myth of androgyny? In the kingdom of science there exist only rare, androgynous mutants in plants and animals with physical characteristics of both sexes. The difficulty in attaining this nirvana-like, androgynous state leaves women feeling incomplete, frustrated, and deeply self-critical, with only mediocre performance in both spheres. In fact, the more one seeks a satisfying professional identity by moderating each choice, the more elusive harmony actually becomes. For women with high standards, balance becomes an unacceptable, and largely unsatisfying, convergence to the Confucian middle because there is no zone of excellence where the inner woman feels complete and successful.

Harmony, therefore, is attainable only for women who truly accept trade-offs; it continues to be elusive for the rest. Harmony, not just balance, is the real prize that women desire, above even choice, equal pay, and equal work. Harmony is a reward reaped in concert with a series of lifetime choices, rather than a single event or job. The greatest requirement for attaining harmony is honesty. Elsa Friedlander, a youthful seventy-two-year-old in my study, concurs. Trying to decide whether to start an entrepreneurial venture at her age, she colorfully voiced her quandary: "At my age, I ain't exactly gonna go out there and become a pitcher for the Yankees, am I? I have to be realistic. I have to set my goals on something that's important to me. But it would be nice to know if there were a ladies' softball league out there somewhere, for old broads like me. We'd just take the bases a little slower, that's all."

The final ingredient for harmony is sufficient self-confidence to listen to oneself. If harmony is a matter of meeting one's own expectations, it is inevitable that one's secret, unvoiced dreams and expectations will clash at times with the hopes of others. Listening to one's inner voice, rather than fulfilling only the demands of friends or parents, children, bosses, or the larger society, is the final key. On the day that Rosa McCauley Parks held onto her seat in that Alabama bus, and in the lonely days that followed in a Montgomery jail, this otherwise quiet and ordinary woman, a poorly paid seamstress, listened to herself, allowing her voice to be heard. For today's working woman in search of harmony, the place to begin is inside oneself.

What's Next

The next chapter examines some further implications for a woman's identity in the corporate workplace. Specifically, it addresses gender denial—wishful thinking that many women retain in believing that gender is largely irrelevant to one's professional identity, needs, and success. The women portrayed in Chapter Two possess multiple *layers* of identity, from their innermost spirit to their attitudes and beliefs, to their behavior and professional style, to the visible and tangible appearance evident to others. To remain true to themselves, women must make workplace choices in harmony with each layer of their identity. They must make peace with their internal third shift while learning how to use their external behavior, style, and appearance to advantage. In short, these corporate women must learn how to best play their own gender card.

Notes

1. Gwen Allen (a fictitious name), like the other case studies in this book, is actually a composite of several women from the interview data, rather than representing a single, real individual.

2. I would argue that even women working in "more female" atmospheres work in a surprisingly patriarchal work culture. Elementary education, for example, always the province primarily of female teachers, is very much colored by the masculine influence of educational leadership. Principals and superintendents, more often than not, are men. Or take publishing, replete with high-level females doing the workaday tasks, thereby an industry superficially on womanly ground. Yet widespread corporate acquisition of independent publishers means that the real players are still men, the real decisions handed down from the males at the helm of the Fortune 500 media giants.

3. Jean Baker Miller, *Toward a New Psychology of Women* (Boston: Beacon Press, 1988, 2nd ed.), pp. 9–10.

4. Gender denial is a main topic of Chapter Two.

5. Martha N. Beck, *Breaking Point: Why Women Fall Apart and How They Can Re-create Their Lives* (New York: Times Books, 1997), p. 7.

6. Mary Catherine Bateson, *Composing a Life* (New York: Atlantic Monthly Press, 1989).

7. For many years, the entire psychology industry—both its practitioners and its scholars—considered development as a formal discipline of study relevant only between birth and adolescence. With the 1978 publication of Daniel Levinson's classic *The Seasons of a Man's Life* (in collaboration with Charlotte Darrow, Edward Klein, Maria Levinson, and Braxton McKee; New York: Knopf), it became clear that predictable stages could describe adult development, in males at least. At the same time, Levinson also noted that a separate study would be necessary to discern whether predictable passages

occurred in the lives of adult women, a research project he completed nearly twenty years later and published as *The Seasons of a Woman's Life* (in collaboration with Judy D. Levinson; New York: Ballantine, 1996). From both studies, he verified what we observe around us every day: distinctive periods of separate adult life, involving a "novice" phase in early adulthood, followed by a period of "midlife transition" and concluding with a "culminating life structure" in later adulthood. Each successive era brings its own challenges. Transitions can be painful, and each stage bears the fruits of developmental progress gleaned during earlier seasons. The pattern is straightforward, characterized by alternating periods of building, maintaining, and transitioning.

8. Joan Kofodimos, *Balancing Act: How Managers Can Integrate Successful Careers and Fulfilling Personal Lives* (San Francisco: Jossey-Bass, 1993).

9. Carol Gilligan, *In a Different Voice* (Cambridge, Mass.: Harvard University Press, 1982).

10. Erik Erikson, *Identity: Youth and Crisis* (New York: Norton, 1964).

11. Gilligan (1982), p. 152.

12. Gilligan (1982), p. 157.

13. Daniel Goleman, *Working with Emotional Intelligence* (New York: Bantam Books, 1998).

14. Mary Pipher, *Reviving Ophelia: Saving the Selves of Adolescent Girls* (New York: Ballantine, 1994).

15. Special Report, "The New Achievers," *Working Women,* Dec.–Jan. 1998, pp. 22–27.

16. David Whyte, *The Heart Aroused: Poetry and the Preservation of the Soul in Corporate America* (New York: Currency Doubleday, 1994), p. 209.

17. Anna Quindlen, *Thinking Out Loud: On the Personal, the Political, the Public and the Private* (New York: Random House, 1993).

18. Barbara Killinger, *Workaholics: The Respectable Addicts* (Buffalo, N.Y.: Firefly Books, 1991).

19. Robert E. Kaplan, with Wilfred H. Drath and Joan R. Kofodimos, *Beyond Ambition: How Driven Managers Can Lead Better and Live Better* (San Francisco: Jossey-Bass, 1991).

CHAPTER TWO

Gender at Work

When Does It Matter?

*. . . she leaves the table like a man, without
putting back the chair or picking up the plate.*
SANDRA CISNEROS, *The House on Mango Street*

From behind, Jennifer Caldwell looks as if she's getting ready to sprint the hundred-meter dash. She darts down the aisles between cubicles as though her hair's on fire, her pager vibrating furiously against her hip. She talks fast, she thinks fast, and she works fast. Her coworkers roll their eyes skyward when they talk about her, admitting her capability but wondering if she ever winds down. For a productive marketing expert at a giant food conglomerate, she hasn't been promoted very quickly. She does all assignments at the 120 percent level, but somehow, instead of receiving real rewards and recognition, her better-than-average work tends to get taken for granted. The more she produces, the more others expect from her. It's just started dawning on her that outdoing everyone else isn't paying off.

In conversations about her career, Jennifer states that she's "never had any issues" about being a woman, and her appearance confirms her disinterest in the topic. She deliberately downplays herself, selecting her business-casual dress (typically navy or beige polo shirts and khakis) to be nearly indistinguishable from the guys' wardrobe. Her shoulder-length hair is shaggy and shapeless.

In fact, she seems genuinely surprised when gender is brought into the discussion. "I make my own opportunities," she asserts staunchly. Having just left her late twenties behind, she is too young to remember the boomer motto not to trust anyone over thirty. Ironically, the generation currently in control of the workplace is largely these same boomers—men brought up to succeed alongside women. But something seems to happen to the guys as they near the top of the corporate pyramid. Women are all just one more competitor, and men like to win. Judy Rosener, an expert on women's leadership, says it straight out: "Girls play until they get bored rather than until they win. Boys, on the other hand, focus on their scores and how well they're doing. . . . Boys play to win, not just to have fun."[1]

Jennifer hasn't even heard of Judy Rosener, and she trusts everyone—until they let her down. She is gender-blind and expects others to be. She has never made a special effort to connect with other women at her office, although a female senior director has more than once tried to mentor her—even offering her one-to-one "face time," that most precious of all commodities in today's time-starved corporation. But somehow the weeks have gone by and Jennifer has never even gotten around to scheduling the first meeting. Now she's embarrassed to call back, unable to imagine what they'd even talk about.

She definitely doesn't want to be associated with one of "those women's groups." Still, she admits, her eyes roaming distractedly around her cubicle, the promotions haven't been coming along the way they should. She is working harder than ever. So why doesn't she advance?

At thirty, Jennifer faces a developmental task considerably different from Gwen Allen's, who is ten years older and much higher up the corporate ladder. Although Gwen has spent countless hours in her mind second-guessing her every move at work and home, Jennifer is self-assured, confident, and pragmatic. Where Gwen is stretched between work, family, and the relentless internal dialogue of her own perfectionism, Jennifer is "free" to concentrate solely on her career. But is Jennifer headed for the same identity crisis as Gwen? Is her failure to advance linked to her reluctance to admit that gender matters?

That's Not Very Ladylike

Make no mistake about it: gender has *always* mattered, from cradle to grave, from lonely hilltops in China where female babies are abandoned, to boardrooms on Wall Street where women enter only to serve coffee to the men in suits. For some women, gender is a badge worn proudly. For other women, gender is that uninvited guest who accompanies them on all occasions. Most modern workplaces continue to be occupational ghettos where both sexes know what the "correct" gender for a given job is. Over time, certain behavior has come to be expected in those jobs, precisely because they have been occupied almost exclu-

Figure 2.1. A Woman's Identity.

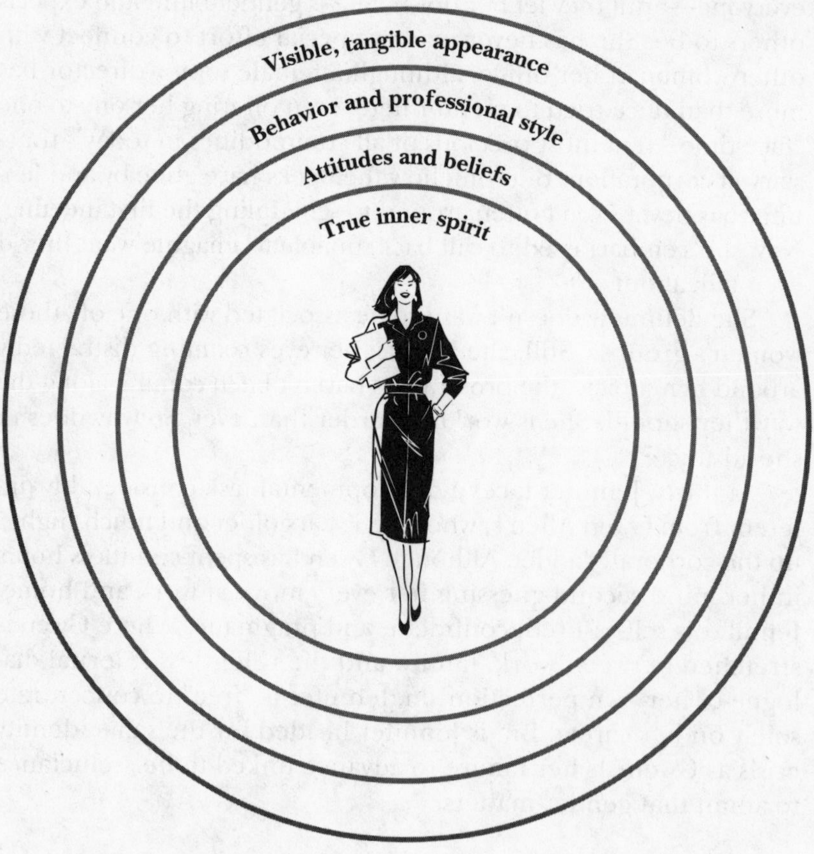

Visible, tangible appearance

Behavior and professional style

Attitudes and beliefs

True inner spirit

sively by members of one sex who, from childhood, have mastered a full complement of gender-appropriate behaviors. When the "wrong" sex enters an occupation, the rulebook disappears, and newcomers must use their own instincts to decide how to manage the tightrope of expectations. It's a lifetime challenge, one that's tough to win—as Jennifer is trying to do it—through simple denial.

Imagine that identity at work is like a series of concentric circles around the individual woman (Figure 2.1). The outermost ring is the visible, tangible appearance of the woman, seen by all. The next ring is also public, but somewhat less tangible, as it constitutes her behavior and professional style. Moving closer to the center ring is the zone defined by a woman's attitudes and beliefs. Finally, in the center of all lies the woman's spirit, the very essence of her workplace identity as an individual.

All women carry their rings with them as they move through their careers. These layered rings become part of the load to be juggled at work since their outer appearance, behavior, and style initially are the means by which women are judged, but women are accepted and ultimately advance for the results they accomplish. Their inner attitudes and beliefs are too tough for others to see and are often ignored during the process. Misalignment among the layers—a disconnect between their public behavior and private thoughts and values—causes many women confusion, pain, self-doubt, and occasionally even self-loathing.

Making Your Third Shift Work for You: Managing the Identity Challenge

To succeed in today's corporate workplace without giving up their true identity, women must consciously examine their multiple rings for congruence. The women I have met through my executive coaching practice who are both personally fulfilled and conventionally successful have learned to manage their thoughts, their appearance, and their behavior in tandem. They are aware, even when they don't wish to be, that how they play the gender card can make all the difference. The trick is to be yourself as much as you can. But until you know who that self really is, you compromise your own chances for true career satisfaction. Here's what you need to do:

- Get real. The first thing people see when you walk into a room is your gender.
- Make a choice, and live with it. Invent your own rules if you have to.
- Assimilate and accommodate—up to a point.
- Analyze your company's stage of gender awareness, and then push the envelope.
- Get on a roll, and keep your career momentum.
- Develop your voice, style, and persona as a woman.
- Strive to leave a personal legacy in every job.
- Remember that the goal for women is to cohabitate, not subjugate.
- Raise your antennae to solicit feedback regularly. Then act on it.
- Hang out with women. Don't worry about what the guys think.

Get Real

The first step begins with the outer ring of your identity, your physical appearance. Whether you're wearing red stiletto heels, muddy hiking boots, or polished cordovan wingtips, others see your gender first—even before registering your race. The trick is to take something of yourself to work every day through your visible appearance as a woman. For some, this means detailed inspections and concern over the minutest aspect of their appearance. Other women may feel silly with personal attention to the superficial; they've heard all this dress-for-success stuff before. But they still don't get it.

Like Jennifer, such women don't want to hear that every time they walk into a room, the men look at their appearance first and make a simultaneous, though silent, judgment. (As women, we do the same with men; it's natural.) Gender denial is well intentioned and understandable, but it's misguided and unrealistic. After all, if Jennifer appeared at work looking (God forbid) too feminine, she might be termed a bubblehead or worse and wouldn't be taken seriously; this is the real root of her decision to downplay her female identity. Women still have to consider the sexual content of their clothes, even though men don't. On the other hand, taking on the appearance of maleness to obliterate one's public sense of self as a woman is an extreme reaction.

I remember my supervisor in one of my first postcollege jobs twenty-five years ago. She was a redhead, taller than anyone else around, who wore only three colors—red, white, and black—and carried it off with the aplomb of a *Vogue* model. Even her glasses—black and white checkerboard frames—were part of her persona. Was she eccentric? Without question. Was she intimidating? Definitely! Did coworkers know her and recommend her for plum assignments? Absolutely, because they wanted to be around her. She positively exuded self-confidence through her unique appearance. She changed what had probably been a painfully awkward childhood image—five foot eleven with carrot-colored hair—into a career asset that set her off from the rest of the pack. I knew that her look was *definitely* not one that I would adopt. Yet it worked beautifully for her, which caused me at a point early in my career to think about what I was trying to say to others through my own appearance. I've enjoyed experimenting ever since, my own needs and preferences changing with the decades until rummaging through my closet is like taking an archaeological dig through women's work fashions.

Few of us need to resort to checkerboard glasses, but the first level of managing a conscious female workplace identity is to intentionally mold the message you're trying to send. Hip and fashionable, or quiet and conservative? I've-made-it expensive, or plain old functional? In my twenty years as a college professor, my female graduate students—many already in their late twenties—brought in more questions about their clothes than I would ever have imagined. One especially bright young woman of twenty-six even asked me if she should cut off her drop-dead-gorgeous blonde hair, which waved magnificently to her waist.

Such questions reflect a basic uncertainty in these young women with high hopes for their careers in an era when the rules are constantly shifting and poorly understood. I have even had human resource directors and senior men privately discuss the inappropriate or unappealing dress of female clients whom I was hired to coach on their leadership style. With the cloud of sexual harassment always hanging over our heads these days, no one wants to say to a woman's face that her dress matters. But women aspiring to executive positions should be crystal clear on this point. The talk goes on, *behind closed doors.*

Therefore, in Jennifer's case, I recommended a personal shopper (available at an increasing range of department stores) who would work only with the budget directions given to her. Because Jennifer seems to have little natural interest in her outer appearance, she can delegate initial steps to improve it. But her first step is to take a moment to define what message she wants to send with her outward appearance. It's not the clothes themselves that are important, but whether they align with the inner woman, and whether they accurately reflect the message she would like to convey to others.

Moreover, Jennifer would be a very rare woman, indeed, if she didn't feel good when she thought she looked good. When we feel better about our outer appearance, the benefits sometimes spill over into our behavior, or even our inner attitudes and feelings. We are likely to call attention to ourselves, seek visibility, and even take risks. Sure, it's only the outer shell, but it's unwise to ignore the public part of personal identity that everyone else sees and makes judgments about.

Make a Choice and Live with It

Obviously, there is more to developing one's identity as a woman than choosing what to wear each day. The real challenge is to make decisions that support one's strengths yet allow further growth and development. In the workplace, the most important visible choice involves your leadership style and the behavior that others see daily and judge you by. Women like Jennifer face choices around their style that most men probably never consciously consider. In my experience as an executive coach, men are much more likely to just follow their instincts and personalities to get the job done because professional and managerial roles derive from the behavior practiced by those who have historically dominated the workplace. I have observed that women face far more uncertainty than men when they decide what is the right style; on this topic, the third shift is a seemingly feminine preoccupation.

The problem begins when outward masculine behavior is inconsistent with our inner attitudes and beliefs as women, which leaves us yo-yoing between self-doubt and self-awareness:

Self-Awareness	*Self-Doubt*
I don't need to pound my fist to get their attention. But I'd better practice projecting my voice more clearly. They're a very loud group.	How can I compete on their level? They only listen to themselves, and they don't even notice how rude they are.
Until I feel more confident, I will just have to prepare more thoroughly for these meetings. I don't like pretending I know something when I'm really not prepared. Over time I will get better if I discipline myself to practice this.	They're always talking off the top of their head. How do they know what to say under all that pressure? Why can't I ever think of the right remark or cite the data at these times?

Oddly enough, the research is clear: women with in-your-face abrasive styles—those consciously or unconsciously emulating a masculine approach to leadership—fare much worse in the workplace than do male counterparts with equally annoying or insensitive styles.[2] More than half of my executive coaching practice with women over the past decade has revolved around women whom others experienced as "too" assertive. In helping these women face their own choices, I'm often certain that they will be damned if they do and damned if they don't—overlooked if they're deemed team players and alienated if they're not. Sadder still, I have seen women with a visibly assertive approach even risk punitive labeling by other women. What, then, is the right choice?

Begin with who you are, and extend the risks you take with yourself. Don't turn yourself inside out to become like someone else. Instead, analyze that other behavior you observe as effective and consider what, if anything, you can apply to yourself. Be willing to experiment, as well as to stretch, change, and grow with your job. Take public meetings, for example. In these crucial information-exchanging sessions, women whose personalities allow greater confidence and comfort with an assertive approach should use their greater "volume" to *share* airtime with the boys. But they should pay special attention to the body language and reactions around them, tempering their approach as necessary, sometimes ratcheting up the volume and at other times holding back and turning it down.

What if you have a reserved, introspective personality or are particularly conflict-averse? Then if you don't speak up publicly in a male-dominated group setting, there's no choice but to do more homework. The homework involves behind-the-scenes selling, extra one-on-one meetings and follow-up calls, or written documents and briefings to bolster a position you may be uncomfortable airing in a group setting. Alternatively, women who like to stay in the shadows or play nice all the time must give up the desire to be put in charge. It isn't going to happen.

Above all, don't deny or ignore the importance of consciously choosing your workplace behavior. Hemmed in by politically correct gestures, women find the workplace war between the sexes subtler than in previous decades, but it grinds on nonetheless. Women who ignore it are choosing short-term silence and safety over long-term progress. Their daughters will end up fighting for the same hill.

Sometimes the choices are small ones, the day-to-day reinvention of practices that are second nature to a man yet awkward for a woman. Should a woman shake hands, give a colleague a hug, or do neither because she is uncertain about the correct form of greeting? One woman from my study gets around this by clasping both of the other person's hands together—kind of a halfway measure between manly handshaking and womanly hugging. Other women give a hug only on the second encounter, offering a handshake at the initial introduction. In short, they invent their own rules.

But often the choices go much deeper. At these times, the real trick is to determine how much risk you're willing to assume at a given moment. Gwen Allen is the perfect example. Her request for a breakaway—particularly if she frames it as necessary to spend more time with her children—can be viewed by men as a gender-specific threat to their decision to live a less-balanced life, or a judgment that women are rejecting or even escaping from the masculine values of the workplace. In her case, Gwen has consciously chosen to temporarily step off the treadmill to regain perspective and rebuild and reenergize her personal life. She has made a deliberate choice to ask for support in a way that most working men don't. She is thereby choosing to behave outside the socially constructed norm. She is inventing her own rules as she goes along. She has calculated the risks and made her choice—not an extreme one that puts her beyond the pale indefinitely, but a choice to take long enough to bring her life back into comfortable equilibrium.

Let's take another example of deeply personal choices that women face: the decision to have children, or to give themselves completely to advancing their career. Not all careers or all personalities lend themselves to both. In *Walking Out on the Boys*, Frances K. Conley, M.D., a Stanford professor of neurosurgery, describes her enormous personal investment in becoming a member of the elite, white, male world of neurosurgery on her campus, only to realize late in her career that women—at least in the medical field—are still judged by their gender first and their abilities second.[3] For some, true sacrifices, not just compromises, are necessary:

> By the time of my tenure review in 1982, Phil and I had decided, without any formal discussion about the pros and cons, that we would not have children. Having children never seemed to fit into our lives. . . . I wanted an unbroken path of credentials and accomplishments, without excuses or absences, a record that would read as having been played entirely by the prevailing (masculine) rules. . . .
>
> At the time of my tenure review I had not produced a child, so I had to be viewed as someone who ostensibly was there for the long haul, someone that was competitive along with the rest of them, someone for whom no given set of rules really applied. Interestingly, for the career women, both childbearing and childlessness are regarded negatively. It would have been far less threatening for many, I believe, had I chosen motherhood, and only secondarily pursued a more leisurely nonacademic career in neurosurgery.[4]

Dr. Conley, at least, made her decision consciously. She was awarded tenure and became Stanford's first full professor of neurosurgery. She is not a mother, and with the passing of time it is no longer even an option. She has made her choice—one that works for her but might not be acceptable at all for Gwen Allen, who has chosen to ratchet down the scale at which she performs both of the roles in her life, rather than choosing a life involving only a single, incomplete identity. Conley's third shift has moved on to other topics, but once in a while her choices haunt her. Trade-offs are not always easy.

Assimilate and Accommodate—Up to a Point

Sometimes the best way to really see something is to step away from it and gain a new perspective. I frame the gender dilemma for corporate women like Jennifer as a classic assimilation drama, a replay of the experience of such groups as Jews, Asians, African Americans, and (most ironically) Native Americans in our country. All of these racial and ethnic groups have faced clear decision points throughout a much longer life cycle of assimilation, each of which involves daily choices: when to adapt and fit in, when to stand out and be different. Within the context of assimilation, women's choices involve several of the concentric rings of identity, beginning with the outer zones that are visible to everyone.

Early in the assimilation process, the first step for Jennifer is clearly to fit in. Over the past century, all but the most ultra-Orthodox Jews have cut off their beards and tossed their skullcaps into dresser drawers, abandoned Yiddish as the mother language, and even undergone plastic surgery on their noses to eliminate what they imagined to be most distinctive about Jewishness from a gentile perspective. Both Asians and African Americans have similarly tried to downplay their differences, in some cases actually bleaching their skin or undergoing eye surgery to "pass." Following this trail of tears, albeit less dramatically, professional women throughout the 1980s sported floppy bow ties and navy suits, as though no one would notice they weren't men. Perhaps this is why Jennifer carefully excises anything obviously feminine from her appearance and behavior. Like many fresh immigrants, she is reluctant to call the wrong kind of attention to herself; she is nervous that it will hurt rather than help her.

In the next stage of assimilation, however, the pendulum often swings backward. Individuals who try too quickly, too overtly, or too completely to submerge their earlier identity at the expense of the new one they are trying to imitate are perceived as counterfeits; on the racial front they are termed "Oreos" if African American, or "bananas" if Asian American. Such pejorative jargon reflects disapproval from both sides, because everyone is threatened when the pace of change moves too quickly. Caught in the crossfire, many simply retreat from the assimilation battle altogether, returning to the safety of their roots.

Later in the assimilation of a group into the mainstream, it is time to investigate closely what should be visibly nurtured and maintained from the home culture, while at the same time adding new elements from the outside culture. Now is the time for Jennifer to perform a thoughtful analysis of her situation and progress from a purely imitative or neutral stance on gender to one involving "coming out" and greater risk. But this is also when the choices can become most difficult, and when the correct choices may seem least obvious. Experimentation is helpful at this stage, to gauge the reactions of others, the true level of risk in particular actions, and also to test one's own comfort level.

For example, I know a female professor at an elite university, Anita Lee, who was deeply interested in researching a topic of interest mainly to women, perhaps the effect of gender on the types of medical and scientific research the government conducts. When she was the lone woman in her department, and untenured to boot, she agonized over whether she should follow her heart with her research. Or should she feign interest in other topics that would be more easily publishable, and that would excite her male colleagues—the very same men capable of granting her tenure when her review comes up in three years? It is the tenured men in her university who control the power positions and therefore define what is important research. If Anita focuses on what they consider marginal "women's research," she risks losing tenure. If she engages in work she's not truly committed to, she is less likely to perform well. What should she choose?

I spent many evenings at professional conferences talking over these choices with her. I told her she should get more information before making a final decision. She should test the water by indirectly asking the colleagues in her department for their opinions—indirectly, because she doesn't want to be perceived as asking permission—and then doing the same openly and straightforwardly with mentors from outside her university, as well as senior editors of journals who might publish her research. She should then take all these opinions into consideration in making her own choice.

Maybe she'll be able to follow her heart without a single career penalty and my cautions to her will seem foolish and unnecessary. From my twenty years in academia, I'd say she is more likely to get a professional cold shoulder if she naïvely rushes ahead. But it's her choice to make. She can leave the university for one that is more hospitable to her research interests; stay and fight an unwinnable, or at least very difficult, battle; stage a campaign to enlighten others; wait to do battle until she is tenured and then fight with larger cannons; or find a stream of research where she can tiptoe into her area of interest, where gender may be one of a number of research variables she is investigating but take a backstage position. She can reinvent, she can compromise, she can fight, or she can secede. Her third shift is noisy with the possibilities: fight or flight, compromise or challenge.

For every Anita out there, the right choice differs because women are more likely than men to integrate their career decisions into the holistic pattern of their entire lives. Anita was a single mother at the time, which made her less of a gambler than if she were childless, unmarried, and geographically unconstrained. If, however, she were in her fifties and academia were her second career, I'd be much more inclined to tell her to kick out the jambs and go after her true interests, no matter what the career risks. The bottom line is that ultimately she will attain harmony only if she actively examines her choices, rather than feeling powerless, fragmented, and diminished.

Analyze Your Company's Stage of Gender Awareness

For workplace choices to be positive, women like Jennifer must rely not only on their own actions and personal choices about appearance, professional style, and behavior but also on the overall gender awareness level in their company. Despite an increasingly dense thicket of federal legislation, there remains surprising variation across corporate America. The groundbreaking research of leadership guru Judy B. Rosener offers one way to view the possibilities (Table 2.1).

Table 2.1. Corporate Stages of Gender Awareness and Action.

Stage	Corporate Message	Corporate Attitude	Women's Response
1	"We're staying out of trouble."	Management (usually men) views women as problems, not resources.	Concentrate on performance and fair reviews; ask for promotions; be alert, cautious; consolidate incremental gains. *Fit in. Imitate.*
2	"We need to react (the world is changing)."	Message to women is that they must think and act like men.	Develop assertive management style; promote junior women and individually mentor; look for male champions and mentors in power; publicize successful women and seek the limelight. *Be patient. Don't move too fast.*
3	"It's a case of survival."	Women recognized as major contributors to bottom line, but company is uncertain how to handle associated issues and difficulties.	Meet informally with other women; discuss issues with HR and then with "enlightened" males; press for concrete actions; demand visible projects. *Analyze when "women's ways" work. Speak out in a reasonable voice.*
4	"It's the right thing to do."	Top-level commitment to eliminate the underutilization of women. Managers held accountable for developing women.	Listen to resisters. Take advantage of training and coaching opportunities; build formal women's networking opportunities; push for promotions before you are ready; ask for support to be successful. *Take more risks. Ask for more. Ask for concrete support to get ahead.*
5	"It's part of our culture."	The ideal organization; employees are judged on their competence, not their gender. Women-friendly policies in place (e.g., flextime, shared work, coaches, programs) and widely accepted.	Build a bench of up-and-coming women; take on visible community roles; push for representation on corporate boards. *Go for it! Go public. Change the rules.*

Note: Stages adapted from Judy B. Rosener, *America's Competitive Secret: Utilizing Women as a Management Strategy* (New York: Oxford University Press, 1995), pp. 142–147.

Women make choices about their own behavior within this complex workplace universe. In less enlightened settings, they may act and dress conservatively and bide their time. They may act like the men around them or be prepared to actively manage conflict— which can either become a powerful force for change or backfire and retard progress for women even further. As with the risks of managing as a stereotypical female (through teamwork and relationships), the risks of speaking out also vary according to a company's willingness to acknowledge and confront gender issues. One size does not fit all in the gender wars. The only way to navigate a sure path is for women like Jennifer to identify what accelerates professional advancement as women in their own companies, and to determine whether it matches the beliefs, attitudes, and behaviors that constitute the rings of their personal identity.

I asked Jennifer exactly what she was and was not willing to do to advance. Would she put up with patronizing behavior from a boss, but no lewd remarks? Would she work on weekends to get a chance at more important projects, even if the guys didn't have to? For how long: forever, or just until she earned a promotion to the managerial ranks? Would she trade in the chance to start a family before she was thirty-five for increasing job responsibility, stock options, and a grand title?

Success has its own metrics at various stages in our careers as women. For Jennifer, a promotion to a position with supervisory responsibility is the most relevant indicator of early career success. As she examines her possibilities in her current company, she may find that only employees with M.B.A.s, no matter their gender, are given such opportunities. If so, she should immediately explore the educational possibilities and perks available to her. Will her company reimburse her for tuition or allow her time off from work to attend classes? Does it matter where the degree comes from, or does she have to attend Yale or Stanford to make it to a corner office? In sum, *what are the rules of engagement?*

Next, Jennifer must face the cold reality that a graduate diploma guarantees nothing. Most of the successful female (and male) executives I know have a sponsor in management who believes in them with or without extra sheepskins. Jennifer asked me whether she should start fresh somewhere else, since she had no sponsor lurking in the wings. But I wondered whether that would really change anything for her. If she hadn't been able to sell herself to others as management material after six years of grinding away in her current company, she might find it even harder to do so with completely new managers in another organization. Her reputation wasn't bad; it was just incomplete. It seemed she could start over without such a drastic change. So we discussed whether she might be overlooking other departments or specific functional areas in the company where women seem to advance rapidly. Could any of these places be an attractive fit with her career dreams, background, and current skill sets?

From the look on her face, I could see that she hadn't given this a lot of thought before. Although a very hard worker, she hadn't prepared her career homework properly. She had definitely overlooked how gender colored her opportunities.

To make her self-reflection process concrete, I worked with Jennifer to draft an actual career "balance sheet" that visually portrayed her trade-offs. This exercise helped her form a true picture of her choices, while eliminating some of her wishful thinking about gender. Her initial draft included these ideas in Table 2.2.

After completing this painful self-evaluation, she began to diagnose her company's stage of gender awareness in great detail, her research including several trips to the corporate human resource department for actual data and evidence. I told her that the more embryonic the stage, the more she needs to actively own and manage her personal success, initiating changes in her behavior rather than waiting for someone else to tell her what to do. For example, in early-stage companies, open sexual harassment may constitute the largest career difficulty. Women are still trying to protect themselves from awkward gropings, especially if they work in company areas historically closed to women such as field installations. In other company environments (such as at IBM), gender awareness is at a much higher level and women's issues correspondingly move to higher ground, involving flex-time, onsite day care, retention of senior female executives, and percentages of women occupying board seats.

Jennifer needs to inform herself about the choices beyond her own company so she has some standard for comparison. Sources such as Catalyst, a nonprofit research organization headquartered in New York City, can help identify the top corporate picks for

Table 2.2. Jennifer's Career Balance Sheet.

Career Positives	Career Negatives
8 years' experience at same company.	No comparative assessment of my worth.
I'm known as solid and loyal.	'Solid' and 'loyal' aren't management material.
Exciting products: I love the industry.	Expertise hasn't led to recent promotion.
	Other companies and industries promote more women.
5 bosses in last 8 years.	No deeper relationship with a manager.
	No "mentoring."
Company has a neutral gender policy; little is discussed or written down on this issue; no obvious problems exist.	Company is out-of-touch and out-of-date on gender issues; no additional understanding or support is likely.
Extremely efficient; can handle more responsibility.	Seen as a "secretary"; tendency to get overloaded with others' administrative projects.
Not perceived as one of "those women"; out of the line of fire (never in trouble).	Not perceived as strong enough to stand up to others; unknown quantity; too risky to promote.

women.[5] For the first time, Jennifer was able to see that her love of working in a high-profile consumer products company must be balanced against the evidence that other companies exist with considerably more enlightened, female-friendly cultures. Those firms could offer executive coaches, internal education programs with grassroots support, women's networks, mentor programs, line rotations for women, diversity consultants, and other outside services providing additional resources to up-and-coming talent. Other companies attained visible top-management support for gender initiatives; created specific, agreed-upon metrics to measure results; and developed built-in communication plans to clearly state how the best diversity practices are linked to business issues and afford public accountability for results. Jennifer was in a daze by the time she read about firms such as Allstate, where succession planning that targeted women produced as many as 40 percent of top, high-potential candidates for the most senior jobs.

The time it took for her to perform all of these steps was instrumental in gradually realizing that her lack of career advancement was partially, though not completely, related to gender. She was not facing outright discrimination, but she initially lacked the sophistication to understand that gender influences one's career advancement in many subtle ways. In our final session together, I discussed how ironic it was that a career marketer like Jennifer would never develop a new product without a carefully researched, planned, and executed product-release process. Yet she had naïvely consigned her own career development to random forces, hoping she'd get the tap on the shoulder some day just for putting in the hours and producing strong results.

Get on a Roll and Keep Your Career Momentum

Rather than simply clocking in longer hours, Jennifer is a perfect organizational candidate to create her own "success syndrome," a self-reinforcing cycle of success that starts with a reputation for solid (even if not exceptional) performance.[6] What she is missing is the next step in the cycle: patronage by a senior sponsor and recommendation for a visible, stretch assignment—a new and challenging job experience that may be a risky promotion because Jennifer isn't quite ready or fully proven. This requires the confidence of her boss and a frank and open discussion with him to plant firmly the idea that she is ready to do more. If, after a short period of time, her boss makes no recommendation about a career move, lateral or upward, she should prepare to create her own stretch assignment, suggesting a visible project that she would like to take on and manage. Before that, however, she should carefully think things through. She doesn't just need more work; she needs *new* work.

The essential elements of a stretch assignment, according to Harvard Business School author and professor Linda A. Hill, are *relevance, visibility,* and *autonomy.* Why? Because work that is relevant to corporate performance is bound to help Jennifer gain expertise crucial for corporate objectives. But hard work alone isn't enough. As she has learned to her detriment, others must recognize it. Visibility therefore would place her matter-of-fact competence in front of powerful people, the very people who control corporate rewards and recognition. Finally, autonomy is important because Jennifer can work at her own pace, leveraging her initiative and creatively shaping where the project is heading, showing others that she can innovate and lead boldly.

As she contemplates her personal career-advancement strategy, she must also ask herself what compromises she can expect over the course of her career without giving up career momentum. Which are acceptable? Mary Farrell, a managing director at PaineWebber and one of the trailblazing senior women on Wall Street (but not a participant in this study), offers a credible perspective on what it takes to succeed in the investment business, arguably one of the toughest industries for women to crack.

Wanting to combine family with career, Farrell actually timed the births of her two children "so they didn't come when earnings were being reported."[7] She faced numerous setbacks, including lower pay than male peers and diminished credibility after bearing her children. Rather than giving in, she focused on winning respect, but without tearing down the men she was trying to impress. "Building outside visibility became part of my strategy in the early days," Farrell said. "If management didn't recognize my worth inside the firm, then I would build credibility outside, so they would be forced to face it."[8] How did she do this? She tooted her own horn, finding out each quarter what the top numbers were for her department, ensuring hers were right up there, and then making certain her manager knew it. She also networked aggressively outside her firm and was invited to speak at important industry conferences. Ultimately appearing as a panelist on "Wall Street Week with Louis Rukeyser," Farrell more than met her visibility goals.

In retrospect, she used strategies that suited her company's stage of awareness and action. In terms of Rosener's framework, Farrell intuitively understood that her company—indeed, her entire industry—was firmly planted in the early stages of gender awareness. Therefore she had to take more responsibility for her advancement than if she were working in a more enlightened company or industry. Her success involved talent, persistence, and alignment of her choices and activities with her company's culture. In the process, she spent many evenings with her third shift at full tilt, wondering if she should continue her battle for acceptance, or walk away to a job that didn't require such painful adjustments.

The real key was the fit between Farrell and her company. The turning point came when she faced the assimilation issue head-on. In her early days, before establishing an enviable track record and credibility in the community of brokers, she concentrated on fitting in, developing close working relationships with clients, and excelling at performance. She refused to take minor disrespect and gibes personally, never allowing herself to feel like a victim or an outsider, even when she knew she was paid less than male colleagues. She kept her eye firmly on her true target: becoming a real player on the street. Here is how Sue Herera, a CNBC anchor who interviewed fourteen dynamic women for her book *Women of the Street*, concludes her chapter on Mary Farrell: "I walked past two guys standing no further than a foot apart, each holding two phones and screaming simultaneously at the top of their lungs. I looked back and saw Mary, standing in the midst of all the insanity, hands on her hips, looking right at home."[9]

Develop Your Voice, Style, and Persona as a Woman

Like characters in a play, one's persona is the public, outer image one reflects to the world. If our outer appearance, behavior, and professional style are aligned with the inner rings of our attitudes, beliefs, and true spirit, our life's choices express our true identity as women, resulting in harmony as well as personal growth. Clearly, we sacrifice harmony if we must deliberately veil ourselves, impersonate men, and hide our femininity at work, as does Jennifer Caldwell.

Women are smart to question exactly whom they are sacrificing themselves for in the quest for an acceptable style. Men come in all sizes, shapes, and attitudes. The truth is that some like smart women who challenge them, while others prefer quiet little wallflowers who help them feel important. Some men like to work alongside women who joke along with the guys. Others like their professional female counterparts to stay aloof from obviously male conversations. And some men don't have a definitive preference at all when it comes to women in the workplace, as opposed to the social sphere. They simply want someone to do the job, command respect from others, be congenial to work with, and not make every issue into a woman's issue.

So, what's all the fuss about? Is there really a single, acceptable, "feminine" leadership style carved as permanently and definitively into the workplace landscape as the lady with the torch is anchored in New York Harbor?

Interestingly enough, Catalyst recently surveyed 1,251 executive women holding titles of vice president or above in Fortune 1000 companies, looking for help with this question. The objective of the study was to identify specific strategies for breaking the glass ceiling. Participants were asked to identify from a list of thirteen career-advancement strategies the ones deemed most effective. The "style thing" came up near the very top of the list! Yet nobody seems clear about exactly what it looks like. Clarity comes in spades, however, when discussing what style *doesn't* work: raising your voice, making waves, expressing your opinion too forcefully, in short alienating the guys. On the flip side, I have also seen first-hand that demure silence buys women nothing either. If there is one answer to building respect for your own ways of doing a job, it is to use your "voice" to stand up for your persona and professional style at work. Thus, for many female executives the first salvo in the gender wars is to use a participative, open style of management rather than the traditional, male, command-and-control style—so long as the job gets done. Nothing commands respect and attention like results.

You have to take it a step further and not only take visible credit for good results but also toot your own horn about the methods you used to get results. Use your voice. Rather than feel marginalized for evolving your own methods at work, stand up and speak up for yourself. Men will not get it without vocal clues from women.

Here are a range of scripts I've culled over the years for this purpose, a "starter set" for women like Jennifer to influence male coworkers that a feminine communication style—one that is facilitative more than autocratic—is valid and effective and, most significant, that it produces results. Each statement presented here is progressively stronger than the preceding one, with respect to the forcefulness of the message and as an indicator of a woman's true beliefs about the right way to manage.

Standing Up for One's Style

Rational information approach	"I know our styles are different, but focus on my results—they're the best in the division."
Stronger statement, to take credit for results	"I worked hard with my team to top last year's results. We made a real difference to this quarter's earnings."
Stronger statements about one's values	"My management style reflects what I stand for— empowerment. It's important to me to develop others on the team."
Linking values to results boldly and explicitly	"Empowering my team has made all the difference. We got the job done because I created a climate in which everyone's contribution was valued."
Broaching the topic of gender when appropriate	"It is not politically correct to bring this up, but I believe we have a clear gender difference in how we are approaching this issue. We are both right, and we should both have the opportunity to solve the problem for the company using our natural strengths. But we have to work together and agree to respect each other's methods."

You may read these scripts over and over again, wondering if you could ever dare vocalize some of these thoughts. Take heed: if you do not stray from your personal comfort zone, you are choosing the status quo.

In addition to selective but vocal editorials for using one's preferred, natural style, women like Jennifer—who are naturally efficient and task-oriented—can help themselves by doing their homework and using this diligent tendency effectively in meetings. To stand on equal ground with men and be heard when decisions are made, it is necessary to outstrategize, rather than outgun, them. At staff meetings or product reviews, for example, Jennifer should come to meetings prepared, planning several specific points to make throughout the discussion, and forcing her turn when necessary. If she has allowed less attentive behavior from her male peers in the past, who thoughtlessly finish paperwork while she is speaking, the occasional direct remark is necessary: "I need your full attention. Please sign your expense reports after the meeting."

Another trick is to sit at the corner of a conference table or at the head of a rectangular assembly, more visible to everyone. Occasionally when speaking, she should stand up to make her point, perhaps even going to the whiteboard and drawing the point she is explaining to others. These tactics are straightforward attention-getters. They represent appropriate behavior to substitute for fist-pounding and yelling, which are practices men may tolerate with their own gender but resent from women. Of course, women who remain completely uncomfortable drawing attention to themselves through the practices I've suggested here need not bother applying for leadership positions in an organization. They should stop worrying about getting into the men's comfort zone, and worry more about pushing the envelope of their own.

Strive to Leave a Personal Legacy in Every Job

Leadership is a dramatic art. It must be performed on stage under the lights, not in the wings. Assimilation is not synonymous with invisibility. Rather, successful assimilation requires broadening one's practices to adopt some—but not all—of the behaviors associated with the new culture, in combination with some (though not too many) of the best practices from the old culture. Looked at from the other end of the telescope, successful assimilation is a two-way process. Let's face it: women cannot successfully assimilate into the workplace without leaving a distinctive trail of practices of their own behind.

Leaving such a legacy requires that a woman develop and visibly express her own point of view on a key issue. Crafting one's voice and persona are empty by themselves. I had a stunningly bright client several years ago, Nicky Green, who was hired away from a competitor for her expertise in brand marketing, an area her new company was just tiptoeing into. During her first year, Nicky skillfully facilitated discussions with her peers at every opportunity but gave little public input. Her genius was in completing projects behind the scenes—on budget and on time.

When her boss was promoted to a new role elsewhere in the company, the CEO briefly considered Nicky for a parallel promotion, but he felt uncomfortable about whether she could handle the job. He didn't know what she stood for, and he questioned her ability to influence others. He was also disappointed that, although she'd been hired to bring a new perspective into the company, her natural reserve and discomfort with public debate kept her from doing so. The promotion went to someone else, and Nicky ended up with a new boss and decreased responsibility, having failed to deliver on her early promise.

Jennifer Caldwell faces a similar risk. She has missed the mark by executing other people's ideas, rarely advancing her own, and becoming known as something other than a hard worker. No one knows what she stands for either. They ascribe no persona to her beyond rapid-fire movement. She prefers to believe that a good idea will sell itself, and that further politicking is demeaning, ugly, or superficial window dressing. She rarely exploits her opportunities in meetings; instead, she makes her point once and then retreats. Nor does she "work" her ideas with others in the company. As a result, only a small portion of her ideas actually get executed, and so she has a reputation as a capable follower of someone else's ideas rather than an initiator of her own vision. A woman (or a man) with a vision is a force to be reckoned with. Jennifer Caldwell, unfortunately, is building a reputation of being little more than an efficient drudge.

Remember That the Goal for Women Is to Cohabitate, Not Subjugate

True appreciation of diversity means that more than one work style is acceptable in a given workplace, not that one model (whether masculine or feminine) is superior to the other. Women should keep in mind that their aim is to promote diversity in style and philosophy, not to substitute their approach for male practices. Both men and women feel their true identities are threatened, and rightfully so, when their approach isn't valued by others. To say it another way, the idea is cohabitation with male work styles, not subjugation, which is probably not realistic anyway.

Translating this concept into practice means that women must pick a *flexible* point on the communication continuum that runs between abrasive, knock-your-socks-off behavior and the demure extreme of Nancy Nice.[10] The tension between these two poles can create a lengthy internal dialogue in a woman's third shift:

Self-Awareness	Self-Doubt
I'm trying to be adaptable and get along with others. But I don't want to take it too far and be a doormat. Or end up with the reverse and become one of *them*!	It doesn't matter what I say. They don't listen because they can tell I don't believe in myself.
It's fun to experiment with some new styles. It's awkward at first, but I can see that I'm getting some results. I need to have faith that it will feel more comfortable after a few tries.	Why should I change my style? Why don't they change theirs? I can't be somebody else, anyway. If they don't accept me as I am, why would they accept a fake me?
I have to keep my eye on the end goal: getting the job done. If that means I'm the one that is the adult and makes some changes, so be it. I'm not changing anything that really defines who I am.	This company has always treated women poorly. How am I going to be able to buck the tide? Is it even worth it? What am I going to get out of all of this?

Communications expert Kathleen Kelley Reardon advises that women must "crack the code" in the workplace, eradicating dysfunctional communication patterns and the language of exclusion. Reardon points out that most women are poor at mastering male scripts. Specifically, women are not as skilled as men at depersonalizing conversations and focusing on substance, rather than emotions, during the exchange. Women are also more likely than men to worry about others' perceptions as they speak, and this often leads to less powerful positioning of their arguments. This is a case of our third shift hobbling us instead of helping us succeed. Finally, women are also less willing to interrupt men than the reverse; hence they can have difficulty regaining the floor, especially if they are soft-spoken.

A realistic approach to getting out of these conversational traps, rather than waiting for men to think and speak more like women, is to identify ways to focus communication on the task at hand while *increasing* the respect and concern shown to others. The emphasis shifts from other-management to self-management, a winning formula. Let's examine a conversation that I role-played with Jennifer, simulating a situation in which she is trying to inch her way into a conversation at an important product-review meeting. But Ryan, an outspoken peer who manages another family of products, keeps cutting her off. In our simulation, Jennifer's boss chooses to listen passively to the interchange, obviously preferring to let them battle it out alone:

Jennifer: My plan will solve this problem. I—

Ryan: You'll never get the resources to even start. . . .

Jennifer: Ryan, I'd like to complete my presentation, and then I'll take your comments.

Ryan: I was only trying to make a point. Our numbers aren't strong enough to—

Jennifer: Hold that thought, Ryan. I have taken your ideas into consideration in this proposal. The spreadsheet addresses our fiscal constraints. My strategy to build up a reserve is. . . .

Notice what Jennifer does during this conversation. She remains in control. She hears and addresses Ryan's concerns. She sticks to the topic. She's concise, firm, and straightforward in positioning what her plan will do for the organization. She uses data to support her position. Notice also what she *doesn't* do. She doesn't back down or get distracted, angry, or annoyed. She doesn't let Ryan bulldoze her. Nor does she humiliate him when she interrupts his interruption. She doesn't ask her boss for help. In short, she holds her ground and gains some. Her boss, watching her in action with a particularly thorny and obnoxious employee like Ryan, knows that Jennifer is able to handle herself in other, even higher-level conversations. If she is to be promoted, she not only has to produce results but has to be able to manage the giant egos of her peers, which can approach the size of the *Hindenburg* as one goes higher up. From this meeting, I'd say Jennifer looks like a pretty good candidate for promotion.

Clearly, cohabitation with men does not mean behaving submissively, accepting slights and dead-end assignments, or becoming an "organizational wife" to keep the peace. For women like Jennifer who enjoy focusing on tangible outcomes, setting limits is crucial. Ironically, I've discovered that the best way to learn limit-setting behavior is to observe how men avoid dead-end assignments they think are unproductive, pointless, or of insufficient status. Tomboys—those "high spirited romping young girls"[11] the likes of Jo March in *Little Women*—have always known how to excel at escaping dreary, pointless work, preferring to be outside exploring in the creek or the woods rather than cloistered in the kitchen with the pots and pans. Such behavior is acceptable in young girls, but it is seen less frequently beyond adolescence.

In the workplace, I see too many women turn to supportive roles in the metaphorical kitchens of the corporation, coordinating and assisting aggressive male peers, rather than driving, directing, and selling. The place for corporate tomboys is out in front with big customers, big deals, and visible assignments. These commissions rarely arise by chance but begin early in one's career as one consistently requests challenging stretch assignments—the visible corporate plums. A certain amount of persistent jockeying may be necessary for an opportunity to strut one's stuff out on center stage. By the way, you need not be a corporate tomboy to land in the limelight. But you do need to actively build a personal web of relationships, particularly with individuals who will take some risks on your behalf. Growing a network not only makes you more visible when the day comes to receive a stretch assignment but also minimizes the risks that accompany the assignment because you have more allies to call upon for support or advice if you sense trouble ahead.

I advised Jennifer that she must be the one to take the first step. She must identify several people she respects whom she thinks she can learn from—regardless of rank within the company—and call them. She must do whatever it takes to get on their calendar. Before the meeting, she should think about what she'll say, and identify several topics or projects she may share in common with these people. Jennifer should anticipate their job requirements. What is first and foremost on their radar screen? Does she have anything to offer them in exchange for their interest in her? At the meeting, she should be herself and openly articulate her reasons for arranging the session. She can learn from them by actively asking concrete questions. For example, if she thinks the other individual is particularly skilled at starting up risky new projects in the company, she can ask how the person goes about getting ideas and finding a coalition they will rally round. At the end of the meeting, if things go well, she should ask whether the person is interested in meeting again, and not feel slighted if the other makes an appointment and then cancels it at the last moment for something more urgent. Jennifer must simply persist, and reschedule.

Until now, I have concentrated on women who are too complacent or too eager to please. What about the other end of the cohabitation-subjugation spectrum? Unfortunately, my practice as an executive coach is replete with women who have simply substituted overly assertive, even combative styles for the quiet, self-effacing approach I have warned against here. I suspect that these women overcompensate, believing that the only good defense is a killer offense. I've very rarely seen this oral pugilism work.

I will never forget Suzanne Williams, one of the first female managers I ever coached. She was convinced that any problems she encountered were motivated by gender discrimination rather than her own limitations. After conducting interviews with Suzanne's coworkers—with her permission—it became clear to me that she was an iron-fisted manager who found compromise difficult if not impossible. She was volatile and demanding, routinely displaying anger or walking out on meetings if she didn't get her way. She reveled in using her woman's voice as a club against all comers, on several occasions even threatening to sue her company for gender discrimination.

The truth was that a howitzer probably couldn't have blasted Suzanne out of her current company. She knew she wouldn't be able to get so satisfying a job anywhere else. Moreover, she was receiving a lot of attention and visibility in her job, although through our coaching sessions she began to see how much of that attention was negative. We worked together on methods first to control Suzanne's anger and then her need to maintain rigid control. Then we spent a number of fruitful sessions refining and damping down her voice without ruining the content of the message she was delivering. A videotape of herself in a crucial staff meeting marked the turning point in Suzanne's behavior. She could finally see in action what her coworkers had been rolling their eyes about for years: a loud, abusive woman who pointed fingers and threatened and was completely ineffective at getting others to go along with her ideas. Yes, she had a voice, all right.

Raise Your Antennae to Solicit Feedback Regularly

As for Suzanne, a great place for Jennifer to begin is with data—feedback from the critical players—since her perception of a given situation is invariably different, and possibly less complete than that of others. If you're clueless, you need clues; feedback provides them. This is a natural for Jennifer because she focuses so narrowly on defining and completing tasks that she often overlooks the subtleties and personalities in a situation.

To elicit feedback, Jennifer can select from several options. A formal 360 degree feedback process involves human resource personnel in conducting a confidential written survey asking her boss, peers, and subordinates (if she has any) to identify and rank her leadership strengths and weaknesses. Some companies do this routinely and include anyone who asks to contribute. In other environments, managers may balk at the request since it's outside the norms of customary practice; in such a case, Jennifer would have to be persistent and knowledgeable about the process if she is to realistically persuade her organization.

Best practice also involves Jennifer in conversations with her boss and human resource representative to identify concrete developmental goals that simultaneously advance her personal growth and development, as well as stated corporate objectives. This type of formal feedback process is commonplace in contemporary organizations for managers who have attained at least first-level supervisory responsibilities. In a company where these practices are not followed, Jennifer can make a special request through the human resource department.

Alternatively, Jennifer can casually and informally spend private time with coworkers she respects—sampling both men and women—asking them to give a candid assessment of her strengths and weaknesses. Whether a formal feedback process or managing casual feedback on her own, I urged her to hold a "developmental conversation" with her boss. In a frank, two-way dialogue, they must openly discuss his perception of her strengths and weaknesses, her unique contributions to the organization, her blind spots, and her most crucial business challenges; they must also articulate likely scenarios for her future advancement.

Throughout the conversation, Jennifer should listen carefully, avoid the tendency to become defensive, and ask clarification questions as needed. Even if the feedback is quite negative, she needs to delay a visible reaction until she is alone and has had time to really absorb the information and get over her first, emotional reaction. This means she must train her third shift to balance self-doubts with the pain of self-awareness. The feedback can stimulate a growth process, allowing her to develop her "flat side," but only if she can objectively hear, understand, and accept the feedback.

She must also help her boss create a conversational climate that includes candor, support, and understanding, and that invites future conversations. In my experience, many bosses actually dislike completing performance evaluations, let alone conducting more extensive developmental conversations. Once again, I encouraged Jennifer to take the lead in this process, being careful not to appear needy. Seeking feedback is *not* looking for approval, but data collection necessary to accelerate and provide focused guidance to leadership development. We worked on several scripts Jennifer could use to frame her request for feedback as developmental. Among them: "I can make a bigger contribution to this company if I understand what I'm good at, and what I need to work on. I'd like to compare my self-assessment with your perceptions, and once every six months or so have another conversation to evaluate my progress."

If her boss agrees to the conversation but then fails to be open and informative, Jennifer can prime the pump a bit: "I can see you're a bit reticent to say what's on your mind. I'm genuinely interested in your feedback, no matter what it is. Shall we start with some specifics? How are my presentation skills? Do you have confidence in my ability to influence the rest of the team? How do you think I could be more effective?"

Of course, having undergone a data-collection process, she must then use the data! The feedback is only the beginning in affording enlightenment. As noted earlier, breakthroughs require visible experimentation with behavioral changes. Jennifer's self-reliance, like her tendency to isolate and not ask others for help, can actually work against her. She needs to focus on one or two tangible practices the feedback process has identified as subpar, and then become an active learner. She could sign up for courses in the behavioral area she has identified as a weakness, and target several new practices discussed in the classes for immediate implementation. I also recommended that she read several how-to books to get ideas about new ways to behave and improve selected management skills. She could interview coworkers who seem especially adept at the skills that are difficult for her, finding out how they do the same things. She can shadow other managers who perform the skills effectively, analyzing their approach from afar. She can even ask her organization to assign her an executive coach.

Hang Out with Women

Two's company, but three is apparently a crowd where women at work are concerned. Many are cautious about visibly networking with other women at work. If "caught" in the hallways chatting with other women, they disband quickly, as though engaged in a conspiracy. Oddly enough, the Catalyst research cited in the last section identifies obtaining a mentor and networking with influential colleagues as pivotal activities for career advancement (numbers four and five on the list, in fact). The study did not specify the gender of the mentor or colleagues. Clearly, it is crucial to develop close working relationships with key players in a company (who are usually male). It is equally important to network with one's reference group: other women. Jennifer, for example, must make an effort to build strong ties to women, not just for career advancement per se but for validation, support, information exchange, and understanding. The two types of networking are related, yet distinct. Men can certainly support, validate, and understand women, but for evolving young managers like Jennifer cross-fertilization with other women can bring a whole panorama of styles and role models, as well as relaying tips over the jungle telegraph on gender-sensitive practices or success stories in the company that pass unnoticed in formal communication vehicles. A woman who spends no dedicated time with other women, fearful of any career risks that may ensue—real or imagined—is a woman without a country of her own or a defining identity. In her recent book, *Becoming Gentlemen,* no less a scholar than Lani Guinier writes of the dangers of "measuring our soul by the tape of others."[12] Women are wise to heed the warning.

Moreover, to the extent that Jennifer is in gender denial and has poorly developed social antennae, hanging around with women more in the know can prove enlightening. But how does she recognize these savvy women when she sees them? In addition to discussing purely work issues, they occasionally—as is appropriate—converse about topics explicitly focused on gender. "Did you hear that they finally promoted a woman over in Direct Sales?" Or "I hear that Toni Lopazzi is the only woman manager who's ever stayed in Customer Support for more than two years." Or "Crystal Ballantine really pissed off the boys at the review yesterday. She called Dick Overstreet a caveman and stormed out of the meeting. Boy, did she blow it!"

At one level, this is gossip, but at another level it constitutes crucial anecdotal data about a company's gender awareness and practices. We talked about why Jennifer had always shunned this kind of discussion. Her first reaction was that they were irrelevant because she was going to get ahead on her own merits. (Never mind that she had been toiling away in the Aegean stables with nary a promotion in sight.) She genuinely believed that gender played no role in advancement or hiring decisions. Armed with data, I gave her numbers about female managers in her company, not to incite her to rebellion but to open an alternative perspective:

Company Level	Female	Male
Rank and file	43	57
Professionals	41	59
First-level supervisors	26	74
Middle management	20	80
Officers (director and above)	4	96

Of course, statistics like this can sometimes mask hidden differences among the seniority, experience, and education level of the participants.

With suitable disclaimers, I handed the table to Jennifer. She studied it and remained silent for a long time. Ultimately the light bulb went on. She recognized that she had always tried to be like the boys because there were mostly boys around her. There were just enough other female managers around for her to ignore the presence of a hard, cold glass ceiling in her company. For the first time, she was ready to admit that she was never going to get ahead without facing the fact that gender did matter in her company, as it matters everywhere, even when no glass ceiling is present.

Women in gender denial like Jennifer are at the opposite end of the spectrum from those like Suzanne Williams, who think *every-thing* is about gender. Jennifer indulged herself with the fantasy that in the nineties "the women's thing" was solved, and her behavior reflected her thinking. Thus, in our coaching sessions, we talked about the need for Jennifer to significantly increase her networking activities, with both men and women. The two types of networking should not be substitutes for one another but considered complementary. If Jennifer socializes only with other women, she may face serious difficulties breaking into the comfort zone of male colleagues. She may either be marginalized or viewed as a threat to the existing order. If she networks only with male coworkers—especially if she displays a preference for senior men—she may be labeled as a brownnoser, viewed askance by other women, and risk ultimate rejection by both groups. In the process, she loses valuable opportunities to learn, as well as to just let her hair down.

Automation or Liberation?

Centuries ago, Thomas Aquinas spoke eloquently about the benefits of work in our lives: "To live well is to work well." Entry, and ultimately full acceptance, of women in the corporate workplace promises a new level of fulfillment, challenge, opportunity, and rewards. But there exists a dark side as well. Work that is not expressive of a woman's true self is barren and joyless. If also accompanied by egregious sacrifices to one's personal life, work becomes ruinous, devastating to one's true identity and self-worth.

Thinking back over these first two chapters, what can we learn from these tales of women in the corporate workplace? How does Gwen's sadness and Jennifer's lack of advancement help us better analyze our own situations and professional identities? Today, 74 percent of all women over the age of eighteen have joined the workforce, many from financial need rather than personal choice.[13] But women haven't yet given up the quest for meaning and enhanced self-image through work. Their third shifts are ever weighing their choices, considering if they should act differently, whether they are taken seriously as a woman, and whether they are getting out as much as they are putting in.

Matthew Fox, author of *The Reinvention of Work,* wonders whether women are more likely to be automated than liberated by the changes around us in the workplace.[14] Internalizing our society's larger disdain for important but unpaid work—raising children, cleaning up one's neighborhood, singing in a choir, tending a garden, organizing youth activities—women have turned their eyes and minds to the paid workplace, expecting to find fulfillment and validation with their paycheck. Yet it is not an automatic process, this finding of oneself through one's occupation. For most of us, work is not a vocation, but the price we pay to live in our work-and-spend consumer society. Our identities, if we are to be honest, come not only from our roles in the workplace but from what we wear, what type of car we drive, what size and style of house we live in, what school our children attend, and—still, at century's end—by the job our husband has.

Fox characterizes it starkly, but probably aptly: "We think that what we buy makes up for all we suffer."[15] Recent polls investigating why women work support Fox's assertion. Fewer than 20 percent of women say they work for "something interesting to do." The rest state they work "to support self," "to support family," or to "bring in extra money."[16] Clearly, our society is completely different from the days when "the disease with no name" drove women from their suburban cocoons into the workplace.

High-achieving and professional women are often at greater risk than those in the ranks below them, because they expect more: more opportunity, more recognition, more challenge, more money, but most important of all more personal meaning. The lack of an obvious visible professional *archetype* also adds to the confusion around women's corporate identities. Without a centralized "organization woman" (the feminine counterpart to William Whyte's 1956 "organization man"), women can be as mystified as liberated by their choices. Indeed, today's diversity of career women includes diversity within categories. Working women in the United States come from every race and religion, every socioeconomic class, and even from countries around the world, mixing ethnic and national nuances into the melting pot at work. The organization man was a white, Anglo-Saxon, Protestant male. Today's organization woman is as likely to be a Jehovah's witness, a member of the Greek Orthodox church, or practicing no religion at all; to come from a local state university, or Yale Law School; to wear Dockers and tennis shoes, or Donna Karan suits with Gucci belts.

After years of work, study, observation, and conversation with all of these extraordinary working women, I have come to believe that the real root of the identity challenge for women in corporations may never disappear. Companies are infinitely better at providing tangible rewards than self-affirmation. As women, we gain satisfaction and self-confidence when we feel recognized and esteemed by others. But we must also turn inward to our own third shift for this precious staple of feminine life. Validation is hollow if it comes only through others and we don't truly believe in ourselves. The workplace offers potential and promise—but not always the reality—for great satisfaction and achievement, financial independence, intellectual stimulation, and even tangible contributions to make the world a better place.

But we must continue to search for the *right* work that enhances our true selves. As Americans entering the next century, it is certainly true that too many of us take work more seriously than we should. We are Calvinists in our hearts, fleeing any unsightly tendency toward laziness as an adolescent self-indulgence, unworthy of our better selves. We have taken too much to heart the realization that people in our culture who lack work tend to lack both pride and hope. In our current era of nearly full employment—even after integrating millions of women and immigrants into the workforce, and expecting that technology would take away, rather than create, jobs—perhaps it is time once again to examine how we can offer *meaningful* work for others and ourselves. Meaning can grow only where there exists a bedrock identity to sustain the roots and system for lifelong growth and development. Without meaning, there can be no harmony, no positive affirmations from our third shift, only self-doubts and incessant anxiety.

For women to find whatever they are individually seeking in the workplace, they must find a distinctively female route, one that sometimes treads the same ground covered by men and at other times strikes out for new territory altogether. But until that glorious day when women stand as full partners next to men, in the workplace and elsewhere, the suggestions here give tangible, action steps in continuing the journey.

What's Ahead

Chapter Three moves beyond this most basic feminine challenge of identity in the corporate workplace, to explore the same challenge in entrepreneurial life. Female entrepreneurs are the new media darlings, the obvious next phase of emancipation for the women of the 1970s who entered medical, law, and engineering schools in large numbers and who joined corporate life in the 1980s. With a new generation of younger women joining in and champing at the corporate bit, a major sociological movement is occurring in America today, fueled by women's collective desire for greater independence and self-expression.

Chapter Three reveals that for a woman building a business of one's own involves much more than developing a product and selling it to as many customers as possible. It involves forging an entirely new identity. In doing so lies all the peril and all the promise.

Notes

1. Judy B. Rosener, *America's Competitive Secret: Utilizing Women as a Management Strategy* (New York: Oxford University Press, 1995), pp. 129–130.
2. See, among others, Deborah Tannen, *You Just Don't Understand: Women and Men in Conversation* (New York: Ballantine Books, 1990).
3. Frances K. Conley, M.D., *Walking Out on the Boys* (New York: Farrar, Straus & Giroux, 1998).
4. Conley (1998), pp. 57–58.
5. See *Advancing Women in Business: The Catalyst Guide to Best Practices from the Corporate Leaders* (San Francisco: Jossey-Bass, 1998). This volume cites specific women's programs and initiatives from companies that earned prestigious Catalyst awards for their practices on behalf of women. In 1997, winners were Avon Mexico and Allstate; in 1996, Texas Instruments, Knight-Ridder, and Hoechst Celanese earned acclaim.

6.   A term first coined by John Kotter in *Power and Influence* (New York: Free Press, 1985), *success syndrome* is discussed in depth in Linda Hill's Harvard Business School 1995 Teaching Note no. 9-494-082, *Managing Your Career.*

7.   Sue Herera, *Women of the Street: Making It on Wall Street—The World's Toughest Business* (New York: Wiley, 1997), p. 4.

8.   Herera (1997), pp. 8–9.

9.   Herera (1997), p. 14.

10. Kathleen Kelley Reardon, *They Don't Get It, Do They? Communication in the Workplace—Closing the Gap Between Women and Men* (New York: Little, Brown, 1995).

11. Christian McEwen (ed.), *Jo's Girls: Tomboy Tales of High Adventure, True Grit, and Real Life* (Boston: Beacon Press, 1998), p. xii.

12. Lani Guinier, with Michelle Fine and Jane Balin, *Becoming Gentlemen: Women, Law School, and Institutional Change* (Boston: Beacon Press, 1997), p. 101.

13. These statistics come from the Bureau of Labor Statistics and are cited in Sally Helgesen, *Everyday Revolutionaries: Working Women and the Transformation of American Life* (New York: Doubleday, 1998).

14. Matthew Fox, *The Reinvention of Work: A New Vision of Livelihood for Our Time* (New York: HarperCollins, 1995).

15. Fox (1995), p. 41.

16. Bickley Townsend and Kathleen O'Neil, "American Women Get Mad," *American Demographics,* Aug. 1990, p. 29.

CHAPTER THREE

A Business of One's Own

Who Are We When We're on Our Own?

*Perhaps women were once so dangerous that
they had to have their feet bound.*
MAXINE HONG KINGSTON, *The Woman Warrior*

Gloria Adams has left corporate America to start her own business.
"All of the women there are gone," she says, referring to her last
company, a prominent high-tech employer in Silicon Valley. As an
experienced senior executive, Gloria left "because there was no
place for me there anymore. I got shoved aside. I just got tired of
arguing with the men all the time. I'm smarter than them. I'm
more experienced. I got tired of trying to convince someone else
of what I want to do. . . ."

Unfortunately, Gloria knows more about what she *doesn't* want
than what she does. In our early conversations, the dialogue cir-
cled around the myriad frustrations of corporate life that she had
experienced. Some were generic workplace evils—constant politicking, coworkers taking credit for her efforts—while other com-
plaints were tainted by gender issues, as in the sense of being an
outsider in a male-dominated work culture.

Like many other women I've met professionally who are
unhappy with corporate life, Gloria thought about running her
own show for years but was slow to take the leap. Organizational
psychologists term her type an "analytical" personality, an individual who makes decisions after considered and thoughtful intake
of data. But the lure of doing her own thing wasn't quite strong

enough to entice Gloria to step off the financial and psychological cliff of entrepreneurship. Forging an entirely new identity as an entrepreneur involved too many uncertainties and factors beyond her control.

Ultimately, her creative impulse drove her to action. "I wanted to build a product," she said, her voice calm and decisive now that she wasn't talking about her frustrations anymore. "I wanted to have a company." We discussed the fact that she could have easily gotten another job but chose instead to become a consultant, which she really enjoyed. She took whatever came along and got into some new situations, learning a lot—including how to work alone. She met countless people and created a name for herself. But in the end, she emphasized, "I wanted to be building a product."

Still, Gloria had difficulty seeing herself as a real entrepreneur. As she recalled, "I had an idea and wrote up a little business plan. At the same time, my husband had something he wanted to do. It seemed like neither of us would be successful unless we teamed up. Then I joined a forum for women entrepreneurs. I really liked those women. They weren't trying to impress you. And I realized that I wanted to be an entrepreneur. And everyone believed me. But you know, even after we raised $1.5 million in capital, I still had trouble taking myself seriously."

I was stunned by her admission, although I had heard this lack of self-confidence before, over and over again, from outwardly successful and competent women executives and professionals. I stared silently at this strong and determined forty-six-year-old, her eyes clear and intelligent, her hair shaggy and turning that indeterminate color between brown and truly gray. With an M.B.A. from MIT and more than twenty years' experience in the computer industry—the last seven in the executive ranks—she still voiced concerns about taking herself seriously as an entrepreneur. Why was this transition so hard?

Reinventing Yourself

Gloria's transition was made difficult in part by her loss of a sense of who she was. Her decision to leave corporate America to run her own show was right, but she was unprepared for the difficulty of reinventing herself as a woman entrepreneur, and it caused her to obsessively question herself and her decision.

The Identity Challenge

Hours of discussion with Gloria and other women I interviewed to learn more about specifically female approaches to entrepreneurship taught me that the shift to an entrepreneurial identity represents far more than a change of job and lifestyle.[1] It involves forging an entirely new identity. A sense of oneself as a "businesswoman," "executive," "manager," "professional," or just plain "worker" depends first and foremost upon the *employee* status implied in these roles. When a woman launches a business of her own, she is moving from being dependent upon others for a paycheck to living by her wits. It is an act that requires supreme self-confidence. Those women who have been badly battered in corporate life are often poor candidates for entrepreneurship. Like women who have suffered physical abuse at the hands of spouses, they are not yet whole; the entrepreneurial leap, like the rebound into a new marriage, can be premature.

In addition, the entrepreneurial identity also requires a strong self-image as a leader, in this case defined as the ability to get others to follow—whether investors, customers, or prospective employees. Entrepreneurs must show unstinting initiative and exert control and mastery over their environment. Women passed over in corporate life because they are either too passive or overly self-deprecating may find it particularly difficult to develop a successful business outside of a known structure. Such women are often highly vulnerable to pernicious self-doubt. But former corporate women who men thought were too assertive—as in Gloria's case—are also vulnerable to self-doubt because no matter how hard they have worked they felt they could never win acceptance from their male peers.

Either way, in the early phases these doubts can swell into a full-blown entrepreneurial third shift, a continual inner expression of the fear that something is wrong with *me* rather than wrong with the workplace. The problem strikes even successful and independent-minded women like Gloria, for whom it may take a surprising number of years of pain, rejection, or boredom to conclude that corporate America is a poor fit. The statistics from a recent national study on women entrepreneurs bear this out. When asked about the biggest barriers to entrepreneurship, nearly 40 percent of the women across the country chose "being taken seriously."[2] Male and female entrepreneurs face similar hurdles: lack of capital for start-up costs, unknown customer reactions to new products, absence of a seasoned management team, and competition with entrenched rivals. When asked what worries them about launching a new venture, male entrepreneurs do not typically voice psychological barriers or concerns about being taken seriously.[3] As a group, they are quite likely to focus on the utilitarian fears accompanying life without a paycheck, such as whether the business concept will attract enough customers to be viable.

In the four years I served as the executive director of a community mentoring organization for women entrepreneurs in Silicon Valley, I discussed obstacles to entrepreneurship with hundreds, and maybe thousands, of women. Again and again, I heard the outward voices of a woman's inner third shift, focusing all too often on self-doubts rather than self-awareness. Moreover, the duration and intensity of the third shift prior to leaping into the entrepreneurial life was surprisingly high. A number of factors may explain this.

First, the lure of conventional success in corporate America continues to be surprisingly powerful and seductive for contemporary women. "There's gold in them hills!" admitted one woman working out of her home these days but clear eyed about what she'd traded in for her current life. Corporate life yields large, visible rewards for many of its faithful. For baby boomer women in particular, who have struggled for years to get *into* the executive suite, it can be very disconcerting to admit one day that they want to get *out* and leave those rewards behind. Moreover, on the surface at least, career corporate women have instant identities as "female managers" or "female employees." Even if they feel discriminated against or misunderstood, the women I talked with often continued to identify closely with the company that employed them, particularly if their employer was a visible, national Fortune 500 company whose products and services were household names. The skills and business experience they had built up over the years would travel nicely from corporate to entrepreneurial life. But their identity would not.

A second aspect of the entrepreneurial third shift was feeling guilty about wanting to leave the corporate workplace. After all, the feminist revolution in the workplace is far from complete. Many saw their own corporate careers as bricks in the wall of progress for women, necessary if larger social change is to occur. Senior women were more susceptible to these tweaks of conscience. "I know it's a cop-out to get off the bus," said one female executive who'd enjoyed all the corporate perks but knew the time had come to try a different career path. "I put in the hours—I put in the years—and I thought I could change things. But I just got tired. Let somebody else take over."

Despite an increasingly loud third shift, like millions of other wannabe female entrepreneurs Gloria remained with her corporate employer a full two years beyond the point of serious pain and unhappiness. She felt stuck. Her inner third shift focused alternately on self-confidence and self-awareness, giving her reasons she could leave her situation and start fresh on her own, but then self-doubt and uncertainty would arise and keep her from in fact taking action:

Self-Awareness	Self-Doubt
I'm too sensitive. Just because I don't like my job doesn't mean every problem stems from gender discrimination.	It's pointless to continue here. They just don't want women around in the best jobs.
I could be jumping from the frying pan into the fire if I start my own business. It may take me a while to understand what I want as an entrepreneur and what direction I should try.	I don't even have a decent business idea. How can I make it on my own if I don't know what I want to do? Am I just going through some midlife transition, or do I really want to be my own boss?
It might be sensible for me to stick it out here a bit longer. I can crack the glass ceiling if I stick it out. But I'm not certain if that's what I really want any more. This is a painful time for me. I've never felt so uncertain before.	Every day I have a different idea about whether I should stay or go. How can I start my own business when I'm waffling so much? I'm not ready to do this, I'll just be unhappy without a paycheck coming in.

Gloria suffered in her third shift because she could identify what she wanted to leave behind but was struggling to pinpoint where she should go next, since her sole professional identity was as a corporate executive. She was also uncertain that the skills and experience she had developed in a corporate setting would be sufficient for her to effectively launch and manage a business on her own. My interview with Gloria came a full two years after she had left her corporate job to run her own company with her husband, but she still barely felt herself to be an entrepreneur. Her old identity was no longer serving her, but a new one still hadn't formed. Gloria's story teaches us that escape from pain is definitely a first step, but it can never build an identity on its own.

The Tsunami

Only a few years ago, few corporate women personally knew another who had left her day job for an entrepreneurial pursuit. (Of course, everyone knew of Debbie Fields and Anita Roddick.) These days, between the heady economy and troll-like bosses straight out of the pages of Dilbert, it's the rare woman executive or professional who doesn't browse *Inc.* rather than *Working Woman* while she kills time at the airport newsstand. Joline Godfrey, author of a pioneering soliloquy on women entrepreneurs, likened the millions of American women who are launching their own ventures to a sociological tidal wave: "Like a tsunami, women are rumbling up from their quiet invisibility and making their mark on the land. Like a tsunami, [they] are coming."[4]

Women are starting businesses today at a rate double that of men.[5] With more than eight million American female role models out there launching their own businesses, why would any woman still hesitate? What else should she know if she is contemplating a leap to entrepreneurship? How should she diagnose whether this is the right personal and professional step to take? And if it is, how should she build a new entrepreneurial identity that is crucial to economic health and psychological well-being—and that fits her distinctive needs as a woman?

Hijacked!

As in the prior chapters on the identity challenge in the corporate arena, this chapter concludes that men and women are likely to be searching for differing goals along the entrepreneurial path. The female quest most often includes validation, meaning, and self-expression through the new business she is launching, and only secondarily visibility and money. Moreover, women are seeking an entirely different identity, not just a new job. They are also seeking better working conditions—first and foremost, enjoying being in charge. Finally, women are seeking to elevate employee satisfaction for others (not just themselves), to better balance work and family life, and to make genuine contributions to society through their entrepreneurial endeavors.[6]

Of course, men may also be looking for these things. But they are much more likely to be seeking high growth and profit as their primary objectives. Like women entrepreneurs, male corporate exiles may also face difficulty acquiring an entrepreneurial identity overnight, but the depth of the disorientation is clearly different. Moreover, many men tend to think about launching a new business as a grand adventure, a game to win.

For example, in Jerry Kaplan's story of the founding of GO Corporation, a Silicon Valley darling of the eighties, there is little discussion of self-doubt or inner psychological difficulties.[7] Instead, he writes about the external competitive challenges and the opportunity to get on the Silicon Valley high-tech marquee: "Early in 1981, *everyone* in sight was starting companies." He concluded there was no reason he couldn't go for the gold also. The only vexing question apparently was how to summarily crush the competition. The entire book has the flavor of an extended duel,[8] with a noticeably self-confident swordsman at the helm.

Stepping into this entrepreneurial game—so similar to the corporate gamesmanship she had left behind her—ultimately proved intractable for Gloria, who had left her employer in search of something different and more meaningful but found instead much of what she had left behind her in her prior job. As our interview continued, I was therefore stunned when she voiced a wrenching twist in her personal entrepreneurial drama. She felt that her company had been hijacked.

The Internet start-up Gloria and her husband launched was enjoying its first trickle of financial success when it became evident that more capital was required. The husband-and-wife team had clearly struck a marketplace nerve with their concept. Hits to the Website were overloading their personnel; unlike the case for many competitors, their hits actually involved credit card purchases from consumers. Revenue flowed into their firm, albeit not at the rate needed to manage expansion.

The pair arranged for not one but two rounds of venture capital, first for seed funding to get started and then to fuel rapid expansion. The first round of capital, acquired from Gloria's contacts rather than her husband's, was accompanied by active managerial direction and focus from the venture capital firm. A senior partner kept an eye on results and stayed closely engaged with day-to-day management of the business. The second round of funding came through another venture capital firm, accompanied this time by a brand-new executive who was placed in the company as CEO so the venture capitalists would feel completely comfortable with what was an investment in comparatively unknown entrepreneurs.

At first the trade-off of control for money seemed fine, even though as founders Gloria and her husband both stepped down from the chairmanship and presidency to vice presidential roles. But nine months later, in a Kafkaesque twist of the very politics and masculine culture she had tried to escape in her day job, Gloria once again found herself an outsider. It had nothing to do with her title:

> Every time he [the new CEO] sends me an e-mail, it's to manipulate me. He complains about me to my husband. I'm trying to find a way to get my stock out. My peace of mind is pretty important to me. . . . We've lost control. I would rather have failed with control than have succeeded without it. The second round VC [venture capitalist] was very negative on women. Even though I'm the CFO, he only worked with my husband. . . . All of a sudden, it's changed. I don't know what to do now. I created this company, but I don't like to work here anymore.

Gloria left the start-up she had created with her husband to cofound a new one. It is smaller, but she feels more successful, more involved, and considerably happier. Her husband remained with the start-up, and their marriage—a second attempt for each of them—has safely weathered the transition. She realizes now that she somehow failed to see herself as an entrepreneur in her first venture with her husband. In retrospect, she felt she had joined efforts with him because it was the best option available to her at the time. Even though she was excited about the generic idea of entrepreneurship, the first company they founded was never truly hers. Like everyone around her, she jumped on the Internet bandwagon. But it wasn't right for her.

The identity challenge—expressing yourself as you really are versus trying to be accepted and fit in—clearly caught up with her. She had changed jobs, but nothing else changed. But Gloria managed her internal third shift effectively. She never allowed her self-doubts to keep her from trying again. The second time around, she used her self-awareness to think quite differently about her needs and identity. The next section can help you avoid the mistakes that Gloria made at first.

Making Your Third Shift Work for You: Managing the Identity Challenge

In my study of more than one hundred entrepreneurial women, conducted over a three-year period in the mid-1990s, a handful of ingredients for entrepreneurial success for women emerged over and over again:

- Assess your true readiness for the entrepreneurial life.
- Take hold of your finances *and* your emotions regarding money.
- Be realistic. Entrepreneurship is not for everyone.
- Develop a personal vision. See yourself and your new business before you take the leap.
- Design your product, service, and company culture to express what makes you unique.
- Learn before your leap, but don't wait forever.
- Enjoy your success. Take only those risks you can live with (no matter what other people think).

These ideas can only guide rather than guarantee entrepreneurial success for women. Several are obviously useful for men as well, but women should persistently question what they need specifically as women to make the transition to this exciting way of expressing themselves in the workplace. Keeping Gloria's story in mind, let's systematically work through the list.

Assess Your True Readiness for the Entrepreneurial Life

Launching a business of her own demands that a woman run an emotional gauntlet. The course involves a complex blend of openness, adaptation, and flexibility, coupled with fierce stubbornness, resolve, and plain toughness. One woman I talked with described her transition from corporation to cottage as an "emotional roller coaster." In her first two years on her own as a fire-protection engineer, she'd gone from asking a former business professor whether she should open a separate checking account for her business to signing a six-digit, five-year office lease to house the growing number of employees. She was even contemplating the launch of a second office in another part of the state.

Although she appeared outwardly successful, this woman's internal self-image was in turmoil. At the root of her disquiet was the unexpected emotional transition from a salaried, career employee in a "safe" public utility to a one-woman band working out of her laundry room with a laptop computer and fax machine. An experienced fire-protection engineer accustomed to creating elaborate plans and drawings to ensure safe egress and ingress in public buildings, this budding entrepreneur drafted a detailed business plan to guide her start-up efforts. But the plan failed to prepare her for the real psychological work of turning herself into an entrepreneur.

In the frantic scurry to make her new business produce monthly cash flow comparable to her old paycheck—which is the most common early yardstick of success for an entrepreneurial woman—there was precious little time to properly grieve the loss of a clear career path, enjoyable colleagues, and the structured identity she had enjoyed as a public utilities employee. Thus, for more than a full year she was continuously caught unawares by the peaks and valleys of her inner third-shift dialogue. She vacillated between healthy self-awareness and fruitless self-doubt:

Self-Awareness	*Self-Doubt*
It's hard to budget when I don't know how much is coming in. Thank God, the phone just keeps on ringing. Somehow we'll make out. I imagine it will get better over time.	It's impossible to live like this. How will I ever make my house payments? I have no idea if my clients will ever call back.

Self-Awareness	Self-Doubt
Thank God I don't have to be in that bureaucratic maze anymore. I feel free! But it's also scary to be out on my own.	I don't have the personality to run my own business. I'm too volatile, up one day and emotionally wasted the next.
It was a real struggle for me to be the only woman at my level. Now I can see that it's a difference that makes me stand out and might even bring me new business.	Who's going to hire a woman for the job? I'll never break into their club. I should never have left my job to try this.

I wasn't surprised at all by this emotional ping-pong, so common to new entrepreneurs. After spending more than a decade in the trenches with them, I have seen the need to manage three distinct yet related types of entrepreneurial readiness for women: (1) emotional, (2) business, and (3) financial.

Defined simply, *emotional readiness* involves self-awareness of the psychological changes that entrepreneurial life represents. A woman should give some thought to how she will feel in her new role as a business owner. To increase self-awareness, time for reflection is crucial, as is contact with others experiencing similar emotions. Acknowledging that the transition to entrepreneurship has an emotional as well as a business component is often the key. Your lifestyle changes, and your professional peer group is no longer in the next cubicle. It may not even be obvious at first who the new peer group is.

Emotional readiness therefore requires the extra step of enlisting personal support from others. The support must be over and above mere resources—the growing array of online and real-time newsletters, magazines, courses, and financial programs deemed especially suitable for women entrepreneurs. True personal support can come from individual female mentors, who are available through formal mentoring programs in major metropolitan areas across the country. When experienced women entrepreneurs volunteer to pair up with fledgling mentees, the resulting personal relationships can offer everything from specific contacts, business advice, and war stories to close sharing and friendship. Spouses and friends undoubtedly offer useful support to women starting out. But anyone who has ever personally experienced the electric feminine energy in a crowded roomful of women entrepreneurs understands why it is so important for women to spend time with others who are feeling the same pressures and uncertainties.

Business readiness, on the other hand, involves straightforward knowledge and application of business know-how in a given industry and marketplace. A woman must be an expert, at some level, on her own business. She should have a unique business vision that is valued by the marketplace. Business readiness can often be accelerated through degree programs and coursework, but the best way to improve one's concept and understanding of the market is to work in the business. For example, if a woman is a successful public relations specialist in a consumer products company and has always yearned to start her own restaurant, she may already have a basic understanding of how to compete with visible rivals, or how to advertise and launch an ad campaign. But does she understand the restaurant business from the ground up? I have met many a woman with a mouth-watering stack of recipes and a love of fine cuisine who is convinced she'd be able to succeed as a restaurateur.

For these women, I recommend a test drive: taking time out to work as a waitress or assistant manager in a food establishment. With such hands-on training, especially if paired with coursework in specialized food-service management programs, a fledgling business owner has a proper chance to understand the business better.

Another important tactic in previewing entrepreneurial life is to amass tangible leadership experience. This can be especially important for women who have not held corporate positions with managerial responsibilities. Volunteering as an officer on the board of directors of a nonprofit agency, running a visible special project for a school, or taking on a soup-to-nuts task force that requires decision-making, organizational, and marketing skills builds entrepreneurial muscles (while unearthing potential new contacts). Women also boost self-confidence through these practices, thereby accelerating entrepreneurial readiness.

Take Hold of Your Finances *and* Your Emotions Regarding Money

Financial readiness is the third important category that women must face head-on; they must focus first and foremost on such practical issues as cash flow but realize that money also comes with tremendous emotional baggage. Like it or not, money is one of the most emotionally laden of all topics. The problem for many women is not holes in the balance sheet but self-doubt arising from their third shift around managing money. A great many women possess strong professional identities, yet they manifest distinctly unhealthy attitudes about money, even to the point of "moneyphobia"; so say numerous financial experts.[9] Throughout my study, it was certainly clear to me that the majority of the women I met were less conversant about money and financial strategies than on any other aspect of their entrepreneurial idea. Even women with undergraduate or graduate business degrees visibly lacked confidence in their ability to accurately interpret financial statements and intelligently manage the financial aspects of their business.

Hence, financial readiness for aspiring women entrepreneurs must involve psychological as well as practical preparation. The first step is to face one's true emotions about money. Karin Abarbanel, founding editor of *Executive Female* magazine and a career guidance expert for women entrepreneurs, puts it this way: "As an entrepreneur, your emotional relationship with money is going to be more intense and powerful than it was when you were an employee."[10] Even more so than males, women entrepreneurs face substantial financial difficulties when starting a company. Superficially, the problem seems to be shortage of capital, a dilemma that hobbles budding entrepreneurs of either gender. But women are much more likely to use personal financial resources—such as home equity loans, personal assets and savings, credit card advances, or loans from family and friends—rather than the institutional sources preferred by men, such as bank loans and funding from investors.[11] This can leave them psychologically vulnerable to failure if the business goes south, because family members may suffer financial losses also.

When all is said and done, the subject of money arouses negative, not positive, emotions in most women. It may be an "inert substance" with no intrinsic value of its own,[12] yet it stimulates enormous discomfort for many women. Some of the individuals I interviewed equated money with power, which made them feel apprehensive. Others saw money only as a scorecard. But if their score was too low, they were left with negative self-esteem, even when money per se was not their driving motivator. For other women, money represented their darkest fears about success and security.

Perhaps a new way to look at these fears is helpful. I recall a defining moment in my own confusion about money. Many years ago, I attended a local women's leadership function. The sponsoring group, the topic, and the other women in the room have long since faded in my memory, but I never forgot the definition of financial security I heard that day in the crisp Australian accent of the luncheon speaker: "Financial security isn't having money in the bank; it's knowing that you can make money."

Our lack of self-confidence is a curious vestige of the Victorian era, when ladies were deliberately kept ignorant of and distant from any type of practical money management. It is true, of course, that many women today are highly paid and increasingly sophisticated about the topic. But the media have greatly overblown how widespread this trend really is by giving a few visible role models a disproportionate amount of attention. The fact is, fewer than 1 percent of American women actually earn more than $100,000 annually.[13] The trick to psychological well-being regarding money, then, is to face it head on—examining one's emotions, certainly, but also gaining hands-on, practical experience.

At a minimum, financial readiness for entrepreneurship requires the ability to draft a detailed, written monthly projection of cash going out and cash coming in. There is no other way to identify whether an exciting new concept is feasible without outside financing. In addition to creating accurate numbers, the financial community is comfortable with specific financial terms and jargon and accustomed to a somewhat narrow visual depiction of data on conventional financial statements. If you can talk the talk and your figures appear in this conventional format, you have won half the battle—with yourself as well as with others—in earning credibility. You don't need an M.B.A.; just check with your local Small Business Administration (SBA) office and community college schedules. Numerous evening and weekend courses focus on the basics of developing and interpreting financial statements.

In addition to the financial needs of your business, you need to identify your personal financial requirements. Again, Gloria is an excellent role model for this discussion because she was able to depersonalize her thinking about money and thereby make meaningful financial decisions. The first thing she did was to calculate the amount of financial resources that were within her control. Gloria had been married eleven years, but she always worked, keeping her own checking account and making a solid monthly contribution to the family coffers. She would have felt extremely uncomfortable with the idea of complete financial dependency on her husband, even though they were going to launch their new company together. Fortunately, she left her high-tech employer with enough seniority and rank to earn a handsome amount of stock. Gloria calculated how much of this hard-earned capital she was willing to invest in the fledgling business, and how much she wanted to hold back in the event that she had no other income for several years. Her personal level of financial readiness required that she be able to pay herself two thousand dollars a month for three years, in the event that the new company couldn't afford a salary for her as a cofounder. This amount still left a sum untouched so that Gloria and her husband could protect a portion of their joint holdings from financial risks should the new venture fail.

Before arriving at the two-thousand-dollar figure, Gloria did her homework. She calculated her minimum monthly needs on the assumption of making reasonable sacrifices in her daily spending but staying in the same house and keeping a similar, but somewhat downsized, lifestyle; she continued to plan on shared payment of regular obligations with her husband, as they had always done in their marriage. This helped her combat "paycheck anxiety," the visceral fear new entrepreneurs typically experience on the first and fifteenth of each month because they no longer have automatic paychecks. Few escape this anxiety altogether until several years pass and income from the new venture assumes more of a taken-for-granted quality, as the paycheck previously did. The practice of actually drawing a fixed sum from savings once a month— no matter how small—helps ease this anxiety in the early days. Because Gloria and her husband were childless, they had relatively greater resources than other couples of their age and fewer regular obligations. Other women without Gloria's stock cushion would have to wait and save, borrow if possible, or take the personal risk of financial dependency upon a spouse or other family member.

These decisions are highly individual and emotional. A finance primer that recommends drawing down no more than 25 percent of one's savings misses the real point for many women. The married women I spoke with had the most resources but struggled acutely because the discussion about money became a proxy for a discussion of the power distribution in their marriages. Many women who had been competent earners were loath to give up their financial contributions to the family till because they were afraid they would end up with more housework, child care, or other new obligations as a result—the infamous second shift. Working-class women in my study were at greater risk than were middle-class and educated women. In particular, working-class women faced the most difficulty in taking advantage of their largest financial asset: accumulated equity in the house. These women were two to three times more likely than the other women to face resistance from husbands to taking out second mortgages. California, the location of my study, is a community property state that requires two signatures on mortgage loans. Spousal refusals to assume such loans derailed nearly 10 percent of these women from accessing *their own money*.

I was surprised that there was not one case in which, as a result of this impasse, a woman elected to end her relationship with a spouse to extract capital for her business. These women consistently made choices that supported the existing family structure and norms, rather than risking choices that would aggressively support their own professional needs. Several women voiced the same concern, that they could not—emotionally or financially—handle a divorce and a start-up at the same time. I concurred but was saddened by these women who simply shrugged and concluded, "I don't have enough money now to fund my dream."

Clearly, financial readiness highlights one's true feelings about risk, control, and even power. A general rule of thumb is to accumulate adequate financial resources, but to take some monetary risk. When risking money, nearly all of us leave our personal comfort zone. We undoubtedly feel anxious; this is to be expected. But unless there is absolutely no other choice, no woman should expose herself to financial ruin in the event her business fails. Better to wait, or save more money, or figure out Plan B. It is similarly unwise to err on the side of too much conservatism. Financial readiness that requires an inordinately large amount of backup cash in the bank and complete financial security signals an unrealistic attitude about the true financial risks of entrepreneurship.

Entrepreneurship Is Not for Everyone

After thinking through these three types of entrepreneurial readiness, a woman may conclude that building an entrepreneurial identity is more important and more difficult than she had previously imagined, and that entrepreneurship is not a realistic choice for her. In my study, two difficulties were the most common roadblocks to the entrepreneurial life: difficulty in acquiring resources, and a personality unsuited to the uncertainties of entrepreneurial life. The first problem, acquiring funding, is easier to overcome, though still quite difficult. Let's look at the practical steps that must occur by focusing on Gloria Adams, who was able to network her way into investment in the business concept she and her husband first developed. We can learn from her efforts, although only a minute percentage of start-ups attract venture financing.

Like many aspiring entrepreneurs, Gloria was initially reluctant to network and socialize with people she didn't know for the express purpose of extracting money from them. Moreover, she knew no venture capitalists personally, but at the suggestion of a friend she attended a women entrepreneur's forum where she met numerous interesting and highly educated female professionals. Some were in business for themselves already; others were, like her, merely contemplating a change. All were generous with their contracts and personal support. As a group, these women reminded Gloria that entrepreneurship is a perfectly reasonable career path for women, and that it is possible to overcome whatever barriers exist on the way to success by turning to other women. Men are not the only ones who can provide support and resources.

As the new idea for that first company firmed up, Gloria wrote a business plan and then went out of her way to circulate through her new contacts until she met someone who could introduce her to investors. The first fourteen—all men—turned her down cold, but at the end of each meeting she asked who else they would recommend she talk with next, a deliberate snowball strategy to increase her reach. Throughout this exceedingly difficult process, she forced herself to phone at least one new contact a week; this gradually increased her self-confidence, which was a great help when it came time to negotiate terms with an investment group.

Gloria overcame financial barriers that have stopped thousands of other women. She first recognized her feelings about money; then she managed those emotions; and finally, she acted aggressively and decided how to use the money that was available to serve her business and personal goals. Before moving on, we may find it useful to contrast Gloria's bold moves with a much different type of woman, one for whom entrepreneurship is not a realistic career option because her basic personality rejects the personal or financial risks that are central to a successful entrepreneurial venture.

I recall an experienced and intelligent accountant in my study, Lucy Cannon, who had labored away for nearly two decades as an employee and then began speculating that she could do much better on her own. She knew as much about her industry—accounting—as Gloria knew about the computer business, but her experience by itself was insufficient for a successful outcome.

Lucy arrived at a dinner forum for women entrepreneurs one evening virtually aglow with her decision to leave her employer. The circle of women around her listened intently at first and then slowly drifted away to other conversations. It was as though they knew that Lucy was never going to make it as an entrepreneur, and they were afraid her shortcomings would somehow become contagious.

Lucy spoke with little self-confidence and was clearly risk-averse. Her ideas for promotion were narrow and self-limiting, and she was visibly unrealistic. "I don't want to advertise because I'm going to work from home," she said. "I don't want strangers to walk up to my door. I'd rather start with someone I know. And I sure don't want to go all out in case something happens." On the other hand, Lucy had pie-in-the-sky ideas about what success would look like—five hundred thousand dollars a year in income!

Her naïveté sounds extreme, yet in my experience it's far from rare. A full 25 percent of the women I tracked for three years as part of my research could be classified as hard-core wannabes, permanently aspiring entrepreneurs who would either never take the leap or, if they did decide to move forward and launch their business, fall flat on their faces because of personal shortcomings. A common theme pulled these women toward entrepreneurship: their strong desire to create meaning as well as profitability by starting a business around something they loved. Significantly, every one of these women possessed clear talent and a working knowledge of the business she wanted to start.

But desire and experience are not enough. Research study after research study isolates high needs for achievement, control, independence, and tolerance for ambiguity as the very hallmarks of the entrepreneurial character, independent of gender.[14] One can understand how individuals with these traits hardwired into their DNA easily and quickly build successful entrepreneurial identities for themselves. Such women can actually *see* themselves in new roles, taking risks and succeeding. One's first entrepreneurial venture is no place to assume a new personality. The personal and financial costs for failure are too high.

The bottom line, then, for women? Be realistic. You may be ready to leave the boss-from-hell, a company that underpays you, or a job that bores you. But that doesn't mean you can make it on your own. On the other hand, as every Little League mom tells her kids, you'll never hit a home run unless you swing the bat. Thomas Edison tried more than ten thousand experiments before coming up with a light bulb that worked properly. Develop your personal vision as an entrepreneur. See yourself and see your new venture before you take the leap.

Develop a Personal Vision

Alas, persistence without a clear entrepreneurial vision gives you blisters but little else. For years, I've watched women—and men—search for the silver bullet that might shortcut the journey to their personal entrepreneurial Mecca. Some people think an MBA degree will move them into the fast lane. Others think it's personally knowing at least one venture capitalist or "angel," the private investors who back others' entrepreneurial dreams. Most experts will tell you that a successful venture begins with a hot idea, one so exciting that others can actually see it before their eyes. But for women, it can be particularly difficult to sort out good ideas from mediocre or even bad business concepts, let alone to publicize them. And if *you* can't fully see your idea, how do you expect anyone else to do so?

This is where the third shift's litany of self-doubts can mentally flay a woman into inaction, even if her entrepreneurial idea is solid. Sometimes the blockage is straightforward fear of failure; *What will everyone think?* Other times women stymie their own entrepreneurial impulses through inexperience and indecision. Either way, what can be done to help women visualize and then act on their personal visions?

They must turn inward to themselves, beginning with appraising their own behavior and identifying when it becomes self-defeating. If the literature on adult female development holds true, women entrepreneurs are somewhat less likely than men to openly trumpet their ideas, because this draws too much attention to themselves. It simply seems immodest and conceited to do so. Yet developing an entrepreneurial vision requires exactly these self-publicizing behaviors. Moreover, a world-class vision does not drop from the sky like a blazing meteorite. Rather, it typically forms quietly over time, gradually coming into sharper focus with sustained thought and research. Too many women I met were reluctant to offer an early rendition of their vision publicly, feeling that it was too unformed to withstand the critical eyes of others. But a winning vision must be tested early, so that new thoughts and possibilities can enrich and improve the idea without fundamentally changing the initial concept.

When women hesitate to voice their embryonic visions, they place an unrealistic burden on themselves, creating a great idea from scratch, all alone. Given the sophistication of business today, the multitude of competitors for any idea, and the relative ease of starting a new business—especially from the home—the bar has been raised for entrepreneurial visions. No one can succeed in the marketplace without soliciting feedback on her idea before she begins. It is only one idea in a thousand that is so proprietary that complete secrecy is required. In general, the best source of feedback is from potential users of the product or service or other business people. Spouses, friends, and family may be convenient, but they're too often reluctant to extend honest feedback, and they may be ill informed.

Of course, going public with a vision (even if public means an informal chat with a single coworker) may make a woman vulnerable to criticism or ridicule. It can be quite a trick to get others to see a new and different idea that may be only half-formed in your own mind. In this case, soliciting feedback is a true test of belief in your idea. Witness the story of Kat Albrecht, a policewoman turned pet detective. A seven-year veteran of a local police force, she looked for lost children as well as criminals with her highly trained bloodhounds. Along the way, Albrecht saw firsthand how a missing pet caused profound feelings of loss in its owner. When an injury forced her into taking early retirement, she used her convalescent period to research whether she could launch a viable business using her skilled tracking dogs to search for other people's missing pets.

She began by gathering data on the money our affluent society spends on pet supplies, wondering how much owners of a lost pet would pay if only they could find competent professional help to guide the search. She moved from tracking for free for acquaintances to charging a modest hourly fee. Yet when she started talking her idea around, "people laughed." "Not out loud," she said, "but the response was discouraging: 'A pet *detective?*'" Still, increasingly caught up in the excitement of her own idea, and buttressed by the knowledge that she couldn't return to police work, she persevered, talking with anyone who would listen. Because she knew she'd been a successful search specialist in her prior career, it was easier for her to *see* herself in this new role. Her vision gave her clear direction, which she was able to translate into concrete objectives over the course of her first year—finding several advisors to help with the business side, performing a certain number of searches each month, and so forth.

Her idea took shape over her first year away from the police force. It was during this period that she refined her vision to incorporate nonprofit status for her organization, believing this would open new sources of funding. By now, Albrecht's vision had truly come alive for her, and she was able to make it vivid for others who could visualize it as well, all of which set up a true success cycle.

In an interview one year after she first launched her business, she reflected, "I've learned to stop worrying about what other people are thinking about what I'm doing." She transformed her third shift from self-doubt to self-awareness by adroit use of the feedback around her when she decided to start her own venture. She solicited feedback openly, paying special attention to the part that buoyed her self-awareness and her vision of her dream. She ignored the feedback that nibbled away at her self-confidence but listened intently to the feedback that helped hone her business concept. Ultimately, she successfully transitioned from policewoman to entrepreneur. We should not minimize how huge a shift in Albrecht's identity this was. In law enforcement in particular, one develops strong and bounded self-images, even to the extent of socializing only with other law enforcement personnel. Successfully creating a new identity as an entrepreneur—even if the daily work content remains substantially the same—only occurs if the woman creates a clear inner vision of the new role.

Design Your Product or Service to Express What Makes You Unique

By definition, a strong personal vision expresses the distinctive thoughts and values of its author. The opportunity to build a new company, whether a sole proprietorship or a start-up that will one day employ thousands, is an opportunity first and foremost to express what is important to a woman, even if it goes against popular definitions.

Gloria Adams is an example of a woman who took a detour from the entrepreneurial mainstream. The company she started with her husband was cited in a leading business magazine during its first year of existence as one of the hot new Websites. But The Big Idea, with all its outward trappings of success, wasn't necessarily what she wanted, at least not at the cost of feeling like an outsider in her own company. Thus, in her second entrepreneurial effort she started much smaller to better control the outcome.

Some will argue that other women start small because they are discriminated against by financial institutions. Studies clearly show that women are more likely than men to start new businesses with expensive credit card debt rather than other types of financing. Recent research also indicates that only 1 percent of women businesses employ more than one hundred employees. Also, women are still much less likely than men to start businesses around products or manufacturing than services or consulting.[15]

To understand why these differences between male and female start-ups exist, I argue that it's necessary to look beyond the statistics, which can never fully explain behavior. Rather, I prefer to supplement the statistics by listening to the voices of women entrepreneurs. In my study, the women who reported the most satisfaction with entrepreneurial choices and who felt successful measured themselves by whether their entrepreneurial ventures became satisfactory vehicles for self-expression. (This is why Gloria felt something was missing as a consultant; she wanted to develop her own product.) It was not that the scent of money and conventional success wasn't pleasant and alluring; it just wasn't enough. Before she left to start her own second company, Gloria confided:

> To me, there's a big difference between doing a high-tech start-up like this thing—you know, raising venture capital—and opening a dry cleaners, which is a mom-and-pop business, more a lifestyle kind of thing than a big business idea. We wanted to be in our own space. Worldwide, we had this vision. I guess I think that an entrepreneur is someone who has a vision of something she wants to do and who goes out there and does it. . . . We define our success as making enough money to have more flexibility.
>
> But it all comes down to—we just don't want to be in that rat race. If we achieve that, and have cash in the bank—we talk about it all the time, how to get the cash out—that would do it. You know, this is our big chance. You don't know how hard it is to work in the high-tech industry. Where's the payoff? What do you have to give up? Maybe I could have gotten married earlier and had kids. You know, you get caught up in this high-tech thing and think you're doing something important.

Gloria gave up a lot in her old day job, although superficially her big job with a big-name company was the very essence of conventional professional success. Her first experience with entrepreneurship was also a disappointment, clearly failing to meet her expectations for self-expression. The third time around, she wanted it to be completely different. She wanted to be doing something she loved that allowed her to be who she was. When she realized that she was well and truly back in "that rat race," it took her less than a month to announce her resignation and begin her entrepreneurial search anew. She knows that her new venture may not grow as quickly as the one she is leaving behind, but she doesn't care. She recalls a saying from her M.B.A. days that sums up the scramble to get ahead for its own sake: "The higher you go up the ladder, the more people can see your ass." Gloria is definitely looking for a different view this time. But how will she get it?

Her first step is to concretely identify how she uses her talents and experience to develop a new product. The first decision concerns whether to leverage her e-commerce[16] experience or fall back on general business knowledge. The decision turns upon how she can best build a sustainable competitive advantage, biz-school-speak for the differentiating points that might be tough for others to copy and that would give her an edge to break into a market already populated with strong competitors. Because she lacked a solid idea as a starting place, beyond her desire to "do something on the 'net'," she fell back on an analytic approach to locating the entrepreneurial muse. She began by researching this list of questions, hoping to stumble upon an idea that would offer a different (yet not *too* different) experience for her online customers:

1. Think creatively about *where* you sell your product (remember Avon).
2. Reinvent the way you *package* your product. (Remember when soup-in-a-cup first came out?)
3. Develop a new idea for *what* your product looks like (how about the market reception of Apple's new teal-colored computer?).
4. Rethink *who* uses your service. (How about personal shoppers for women too busy to shop?)

Following this guided and linear process, Gloria gradually identified a solid idea to attract funding and begin to build her new company. Her search for self-expression was difficult and emotionally strenuous; other women may arrive at new business ideas more quickly and intuitively. In my research with women entrepreneurs, I listened to a remarkable variety of business concepts that express the unique personalities and interests of their creators. In most cases, the impetus to move from secure employment to entrepreneurship involved a single common theme: transforming a beloved idea, hobby, or homegrown product that they had been thinking about for years into a money-making proposition. In my sample of women, ideas ranged from doll-making (customized creation of a personal doll to express the client's life, business, or values) to frozen food just for children, to a drive-through bagelry, to a new type of spectrum analyzer for computer chip equipment makers.

In follow-up interviews conducted two and three years later, it was clear that not all of the concepts survived the test of the market. But all of the women who attempted to build a business around a concept that was of personal interest to them felt rewarded for their efforts. Roughly 20 percent of the women had met or exceeded their initial goals. Their lives—psychologically as well as financially—had greatly improved, as had their self-confidence, business acumen, and personal sense of well-being. Approximately 30 percent of the women were struggling. Entrepreneurial life was more difficult than they had foreseen, yet these women continued to remain optimistic, still excited by the chance to make a living from a product or service concept having particular meaning to them. Another 20 percent of the women had returned to corporate life, or never left it, teased by a dream but unable to implement it.

Learn Before You Leap, But Don't Wait Forever

Entrepreneurship is as much about self-confidence as it is about experience. A woman is wise to wait until she has adequate levels of both before starting out on her own. But the typical American workplace can make it difficult to acquire self-confidence in parallel with experience. In fact, the reverse may even occur if a current work situation is inhospitable to women, as is the case with many companies in such growth sectors of our economy as medicine, finance, and high technology. In my mind, Joline Godfrey's tsunami of women entrepreneurs constitutes a veritable "Dilbert backlash." Poor workplace conditions, the indignities of downsizing, the stupidities of inept or uncaring managers, and years of

trying to prove themselves to men help to ignite women's entrepreneurial ambitions.

I heard the details of corporate discontent over and over again
during my interviews with these women. When anger combined
with the dawning realization that "I can do it better myself,"
women approached their personal entrepreneurial flash point. I
remember the tense body language of a visibly angry woman who
told me, "I first thought about starting my own business two years
ago when I checked into my retirement. I found out that I'd get
$360 versus $260 a month if I worked another ten years. Boy, was
that ever an eye opener. How stupid do they think I am?" She felt
betrayed.

I also conversed with women whose entrepreneurial epiphany,
if there was one, came through quiet moments of reflection, as was
the case with forty-five year old Rita Alwether, a self-described army
brat reared with constant change in her life: "I'm at a point beyond
the ego. I don't need to have a title, I don't need to prove anything
from that standpoint, and I don't want to operate there. . . . I see
myself evolving, kind of recognizing my own demons, my own
shadows, and the things that get in my way. I'm beginning to be
able to believe in myself, and trust that it's all going to come
together. . . ." This woman felt calm and strong, but again this
alone is insufficient for entrepreneurial success.

In both these cases, I counseled the women to stay with their
current jobs until they accomplished specific goals or developed
more skills that would help speed them on their entrepreneurial
journey. Together, we identified what each woman needed most to
succeed. The first woman, for example, decided she would spend a
final year with her employer consolidating general business contacts,
learning more computer skills, and identifying potential partners
or associates for her new business (she was interested in starting
an events planning service, work she had done in a prior job
and enjoyed). During that final year of preparation to launch her
company, she worked evenings and weekends, taking on just a few
clients at a time so that once her paycheck stopped completely she
would already have the beginnings of an entrepreneurial income.

Rita's situation was more problematic. She was bored with her
current job and ready to take on something new. She had read a
number of books lauding the entrepreneurial life for women, and

she was in the early stages of defining herself as stepping into that role. Unfortunately, she had absolutely no business concept in mind, no personal vision of what her own business could be. All she knew was that launching "my own thing," as she termed it, felt increasingly vital to her well-being. Her quest was to narrow the field, and together we embarked on an investigative path. The spare time and energy that she was no longer putting into her work went into investigating specific career options and actual new-business opportunities. During our conversations, I asked her question after question to accelerate her thinking process:

- What's missing for you professionally?
- What do you really love to do? Could you make a decent living at it?
- Why do you think you'd be effective at launching and sustaining your own business?
- What bothers you most about going out on your own?
- How much flexibility is there in your financial situation?
- What sacrifices would you make to start a new career or launch a start-up?

Our patience paid off. Gradually the entrepreneurial mist began to clear up for Rita. Following in the footsteps of many a California entrepreneur, she borrowed forty thousand dollars in equity in her house, still leaving a comfortable amount untouched. She then arranged to downshift her job to twenty-five hours per week, leaving a financial cushion acceptable to her and her husband, who was nearing retirement and didn't want to put it off any longer. Initially, Rita wanted to use her nest egg to open a florist shop. She adored working with flowers, growing them, arranging them, developing new hybrids, and so forth. With help from a coworker, she mastered two software programs that helped her draw up financial projections and a budget. Much to her chagrin, she learned that there was absolutely no way that she would be successful opening a florist shop. Rents in her metropolitan area were simply too high. The advertising costs to announce her presence and compete with existing rivals would suck up every cent she had. It was back to the drawing board. The only thing that got her through this disappointing period was the emotional and practical support of other women facing the same situation. Personal advice from a formal mentor in a woman's entrepreneurial program was instrumental to her sanity.

Eight months later, she virtually flew into my office one afternoon, dumping a stack of seed catalogues on my desk. "I did it!" she announced triumphantly. She explained that she had paid to become an independent distributor in a specified territory for a line of esoteric flower and vegetable seeds. The business deal was structured in accordance with her existing financial resources and projected income needs. An attorney she trusted had supervised the contract. As an independent franchiser, she was turning a respectable profit after three months, and learning as much about herself as about the bulbs and shrubbery she was selling to others. She was planning to give notice to her current employer after three more months, waiting to be certain her initial success could be sustained.

In Rita's case, a delay into full-scale entrepreneurship for eighteen months paid off. Other women might chafe badly at stretching out the transition for so long. The secret is to set measurable, achievable goals for the twilight period left in your day job: build up a certain capital reserve, attend workshops, and locate your first customers. Learn before you leap.

Take Only Those Risks You Can Live With

Financial risks make the headlines, but they are only one kind of gamble for women thinking about starting their own business. Women who make a serious emotional investment in a business idea are betting on their very identity because they are likely to take failure personally. Men don't like failure, of course, but they don't tend to turn it inward. Communication theorists, in fact, have amassed solid research pointing to this difference between the sexes.[17] Men are much more likely than women to explain a particular failure as the result of external causes: "a bad spell in the economy," "lack of investment capital," "consumer indecision," and so forth. Women are more likely to point to themselves, explaining failure by saying "I didn't work at it enough," "I misjudged the market," or "I didn't take enough risks."

These voices form the very essence of the entrepreneurial third shift. In the sample of women I talked with, they ranged from fully self-punitive comments ("I am disgusted with myself for not getting my business plan done yet") to factual self-assessments of mistakes ("I didn't have a clue about how to figure out how much market research I could afford"). Not surprisingly, in these two cases the former woman wasn't experiencing any of the "magic" of entrepreneurship that she had envisioned as a by-product of self-employment. In some ways, the process of starting her own business was even more psychologically painful than the frustrations she had endured in corporate life. The second woman, on the other hand, had moved from self-doubt to self-awareness, learning from her many mistakes. Her personal third shift actually helped to accelerate her progress with her new business because she was better able to see where she needed help, and where a simple boot in the backside was needed to get her to try something she had never done before.

I often tell women entrepreneurs in the early days of their launch that "a little bit of denial isn't such a bad thing." The sheer number of things they must do to get a business off the ground can traumatize women. If they worry about every single thing at once, they'll shut down emotionally and physically. Yet newspaper articles, women entrepreneur organizations, and all the recent self-help books on entrepreneurship seem to promise that women will experience an entrepreneurial *euphoria,* a blissful emotional state in which self-empowered women valiantly march off to do their own thing.

The reality can be joltingly different. Moments of euphoria clearly occur for all entrepreneurial women, but they are moments only, interspersed with periods of doubt and anxiety ("What will I do if I don't get a new client by next week?") and pure boredom ("If I have to stuff one more envelope for this direct-mail campaign, I may shoot myself"). The emotional road map for new entrepreneurs involves a personal emotional process not unlike the cycle that mourners go through after the loss of a loved one.[18] Like any important transition, the early phases can be the most painful. In her book *How to Succeed on Your Own,* Abarbanel discusses how releasing the past in a type of grieving process may be necessary before a woman can step forward to envision her new future as an entrepreneur.[19] The emotional state during this phase of entrepreneurship is likely to be particularly fragile, involving far more negative than positive emotions, such as hope. Success seems so far over the horizon at this stage. Women having low emotional resilience will crank up their third shift, wondering over and over again if they are really making the right move. Over time, as the new venture is actually launched and then builds momentum, many women become too busy to feel quite so anxious. The balance of positive to negative feelings, however, naturally begins to shift. No matter what is happening with the business, at least these women have acted on their dreams. Most days, they feel damned good about it!

I have also observed that a placid and contemplative sense of success—as opposed to intermittent euphoric moments—never occurs overnight but often takes well over a year. Women begin enjoying their entrepreneurial journey once several things click into place. The first milestone is the experience of moderate financial independence. For many of the women I met, the scorecard that matters is when cash flow from the new venture equals income from the last paycheck. One woman I talked with was waiting for the day when she ran out of deposit slips before needing to reorder checks! Over time, of course, financial goals typically ratchet upward from these understandably unambitious levels.

A second milestone bringing deep enjoyment is when difficult customers are landed, or an early client requests repeat business. Joan Kee, a buoyant and successful accountant-turned-entrepreneur who left a solid, safe job with an accounting firm after nearly a decade to start her own practice with a partner, described the unique way she celebrated her success with her employees:

> We have a lot of image goals. We're really having fun at this office. We have this orange bell. When we get a new client, we ring the bell. And if we get a client from the old office [the former employer], we ring the bell twice. And then we also have this jar. We're putting these beans into a jar because we're bean counters, you know. We put the names of our clients on white beans, and

our goal is to try to fill the jar by the end of the year. Twenty years from now, we're going to look back and say that was our first jar. And we're going to have a party when we reach our goal.

Joan truly earned her beans. She opted for her own practice only after being turned down to become a partner in her current firm. Rather than wallow in numerous early self-doubts, she ignored the negative voices in her third shift and concentrated on getting clients. She taught herself new skills, including how to effectively make cold calls, and she phoned every former client she had ever done work for. A somewhat reserved second-generation Asian, she forced herself to attend every local business function she could, never leaving until she had spoken with at least three prospects for her new accounting practice. These activities began to pay off, and the self-confidence she gained helped her actually begin enjoying these self-marketing activities. At the end of the year, she had a lot more than a jar full of white beans. She had a viable business and a brand new identity. She was over the hump, and she was never going back.

Coming Home

The metamorphosis to entrepreneurship is strikingly different from any other professional change in a woman's life, so it is all the more illuminating that literally millions of women are checking their own entrepreneurial pulses. Women's large-scale interest in entrepreneurship is a collective bid for independence and self-expression; most of all, it is a search for something different that feels right. Women willing to take the risks of launching their own business share common motivations as they craft new identities and develop new skills. They are looking for validation, for more meaning, and for more control over their professional lives. Most important, they are using entrepreneurial careers to continue their personal development and to stop feeling like trespassers at work. They are coming home, metaphorically as well as literally—70 percent of women-owned business are home-based—to forge a workplace of their own where they can make the rules.

It is no accident that the age group most likely to start off on its own—women in their mid-thirties to mid-forties—is approaching, or has arrived at, midlife. I joke that these women are "young enough to have lots of energy but old enough to know something." For this crowd, entrepreneurship involves reshaping one's identity and building a self-structured life, one in which the individual woman identifies her own rules and daily disciplines for success, the outcome enhanced by the wisdom and experience gleaned from decades in the corporate trenches.

A forgiving economy has also helped. Since 1994, in Silicon Valley and elsewhere across the nation, the economy has revved close to redline, making conditions nearly ideal to chuck corporate life and seize any lurking entrepreneurial opportunities. For women like Gloria Adams, the problem is often one of zeroing in on which idea is best to inaugurate entrepreneurial life. The statistics are clear. Millions of women who would never have dreamed of starting their own business ten years ago are now reading, thinking, and talking with each other about new choices. The waves of the entrepreneurial tsunami build quietly, steadily, creeping inexorably toward the beach, one woman at a time.

We might ask why these women aren't sticking it out on the corporate front, although (as earlier chapters highlight) women can use myriad strategies to experience both inner and conventional success. But knowing when to cut one's losses is key to preserving self-esteem. As workplace communications expert Kathleen Kelley Reardon points out, "More important in the long run is knowing how to find a work environment that doesn't require credibility-saving efforts all day long. . . . There is nothing to be gained from women wasting their time to change organizations that don't get it now and never will."[20]

In today's do-everything-be-everything-you-can-be world, it may even seem de rigueur to seriously contemplate entrepreneurial life. How ironic it would be if women felt forced into an entrepreneurial mold that doesn't really suit who they are, just as many corporate women experience the futility of trying to become someone they are not so as to match the corporate temperament around them. Gloria Adams, or any woman who has ever taken the entrepreneurial journey, has experienced personal moments of terror and loneliness, as well as instances of exhilaration and profound contentment. These feelings are not unlike being lifted high off the ground, out of control, with no sense of where one will land. It must feel like being part of a tsunami reaching shore.

What's Next

For women seeking freedom, independence, control, and validation, there is room for great optimism on the entrepreneurial path. However, as we begin to explore in the next chapter, many women today—most with children, but an increasing number without— are opting out of both the corporate and the entrepreneurial games. In essence, they are refusing to play and are taking a lengthy time out. Some women are making permanent changes, finding that they have no desire to leave a stay-at-home lifestyle that works for them. Like the transition to entrepreneurial life, the decision to stay home or work in the community shapes the identity of women in a new way. It also places women at risk because our society—men and women alike—can sometimes view a move home or out of the conventional economic sector as a retreat rather than a win. The women I interviewed formed two basic groups. One was happy and feeling lucky that they were able to be at home. The second group felt shelved and sidelined, even if they wanted to remain at home with their family. The next chapter explores what divides these women, and it offers suggestions for thinking and acting for each group.

Finally, beyond the entrepreneurial tsunami another swell is beginning to form up and take on a shape of its own: the movement of corporate "retreads" to the ministry and to community posts, where salaries and recognition are demonstrably lower but increased meaning and satisfaction are higher. Women have always been large-scale participants in social agencies and community or educational organizations. Obviously, they have always stayed at home. What is different today is the growing number of experienced corporate and professional women who are deliberately choosing these paths. *Reentry,* as it were, is assuming a whole new meaning for these women. Their decisions reveal quiet courage in an era when women staying at home are often suspect, even if it is the green-eyed goddess of envy speaking.

Notes

1. Most of the women I interviewed transitioned to the entrepreneurial life from corporate employment, but the transition from the home front can involve just as significant a switch in identity.

2. "Credibility, Creativity and Independence: The Greatest Challenges and Biggest Rewards of Business Ownership Among Women," *National Foundation of Women Business Owners,* 1994, p. 6. The report is based upon a 1992 survey of nearly four thousand women business owners; an impressive 28 percent of questionnaires were returned. The top five challenges of business ownership for women were maintaining growth and competitiveness (21 percent); proving capability and credibility (18 percent); competing and succeeding in a male-dominated atmosphere (13 percent); balancing work and personal life (12 percent); and overcoming sexism, discrimination, and stereotypes (8 percent). This study did not involve a matching sample of male entrepreneurs for direct comparison. For a good overview of other research that has compared male and female entrepreneurs, see Robert D. Hisrich, "Women Entrepreneurs: Problems and Prescriptions for Success in the Future," in Oliver Hagan, Carol Rivchun, and Donald Sexton (eds.), *Women-Owned Business* (New York: Praeger, 1989), pp. 3–32. This study cites as key differences that women, not men, experience the glass ceiling in corporate jobs, that women have greater difficulty in attracting capital for their start-up venture; and that the level of self-confidence is typically greater in male entrepreneurs.

3. In a landmark 1994 study conducted by the National Foundation of Women Business Owners in Washington, D.C., "Styles of Success: The Thinking and Management Styles of Women and Men Entrepreneurs," clear differences were found between male and female entrepreneurs, particularly in their thinking and management styles. The study involved 127 entrepreneurs. Women are less decisive, taking longer to make a decision than men. They are more likely to combine feeling with logic, are more likely to gather more information before making a decision, are more likely than men to ask for additional opinions from others, and are also more likely to consider the effect of their decisions on others. Their goals also diverge, with women describing success as having control over their own destiny, building ongoing relationships with clients, and doing something worthwhile from which they can derive fulfillment. Men define and describe success in terms of achieving goals.

4. Joline Godfrey, *Our Wildest Dreams: Women Entrepreneurs Making Money, Having Fun, Doing Good* (New York: HarperBusiness, 1992).

5. The best and most up-to-date data compiled on women entrepreneurs may be found in the annual *Fact Sheets* from the National Foundation of Women Business Owners, titled "Women-Owned Businesses in the United States." The statistics cited here were published in the 1996 report.

6. Numerous recent surveys of women entrepreneurs have concluded that entrepreneurial goals differ for men and women. An excellent new resource on this topic is Dorothy Perrin Moore and E. Holly Buttner, *Women Entrepreneurs: Moving Beyond the Glass Ceiling* (Thousand Oaks, Calif.: Sage, 1998).

7. Kaplan's story may seem reflective only of a single man, but research conducted by the National Foundation for Women Business Owners finds clear differences in orientation between male and female entrepreneurs. The 1994 NFWBO study on this topic mentioned in note 3 above is cited again in the conclusion of Chapter Six of this book.

8. Jerry Kaplan, *Startup: A Silicon Valley Adventure* (Boston: Houghton Mifflin, 1994).

9. See Annette Lieberman and Vicki Lindner, *Unbalanced Accounts: Why Women Are Still Afraid of Money* (New York: Grove/Atlantic, 1987). These authors make an excellent case that women have varying types of moneyphobia.

10. Karin Abarbanel, *How to Succeed on Your Own: Overcoming the Emotional Roadblocks on the Way from Corporation to Cottage, from Employee to Entrepreneur* (New York: Henry Holt, 1994), p. 215.

11. This parallels other differences between male and female entrepreneurs with respect to resource and support structures. Females, for example, consider their spouses as their most important advisors, while men are likely to use outside advisors such as lawyers and accountants. These differences continue today and were first explored systematically in the seminal research on women entrepreneurs by Robert D. Hisrich and Candida G. Brush, *The Women Entrepreneur: Starting, Financing, and Managing a Successful New Business* (New York: Lexington, 1986).

12. Abarbanel (1994), p. 235.

13. Catalyst Census of Women Corporate Offices and Top Earners, New York, 1999.

14. Kathleen Allen, *Launching New Ventures* (Chicago: Upstart Publishing, 1995).

15. "Women-Owned Businesses, Breaking the Boundaries: The Progress and Achievement of Women-Owned Businesses." (Report.) Washington, D.C.: National Foundation of Women Business Owners and Dun & Bradstreet Information Services, Apr. 1995.

16. E-commerce is the current buzzword for electronic commerce and Internet-related businesses.
17. Julia T. Wood, *Gendered Lives: Communication, Gender, and Culture,* 2nd ed. (Reading, Mass.: Addison-Wesley, 1997).
18. Abarbanel (1994).
19. Abarbanel (1994).
20. Kathleen Kelley Reardon, *They Don't Get It, Do They?* (New York: Little, Brown, 1995), pp. 183–184.

CHAPTER FOUR

From High-Rise to Hearth and Home
How Do We Thrive?

If there were no girls like them in the world,
there would be no poetry.
WILLA CATHER, *My Antonia*

Laurel Andersen loves her job. Her cell phone. Her company car. Her expense account and her customers. And the global travel she'd only dreamed about before she took this job. She's a product distribution manager for a major biotech company, responsible for order placements for all customers in North America and the growing Asia-Pacific regions. The company's growth curve is a rocket ride. Every day brings a new challenge, a chance for action and recognition. It's heady stuff.

Every day also usually brings at least one phone call from her baby-sitter. Fourteen-month-old Sammy, the youngest of three, has recently been diagnosed with a rare skeletal dysfunction that regularly produces high fevers, muscular pains, or an unnerving lethargy. The illness is not fatal, thank God, but it is persistently debilitating. The doctors say that he will grow out of it, but they won't commit to anything more definitive. They also say that the care he receives now will make all the difference to his ultimate recovery as he grows older.

Laurel's husband, Ben, is a firefighter with a rotating schedule. He's home half of each week, but the days vary. Ben takes care of Sammy's doctor visits on his off days but can't do anything from the station house. At a huge financial sacrifice, and by cramming their three kids into a single bedroom, Laurel and Ben have hired a live-in babysitter to make certain that Sammy gets the extra care he needs. What with his constant fevers and attendant problems, conventional day care simply won't work out. Besides, someone has to be at home when Laurel travels.

Everyone always congratulates her as being a supermom. Her husband is "enlightened" and quick to pitch in without being asked. But she always feels the crunch. She's ultraefficient and rarely sweats the small stuff. Still, at work she's finding it impossible recently to make up the six to ten hours each week that Sammy's care consumes. She's falling further behind in a work climate where no one else has the time to take up the slack. Yet she doesn't feel right about delegating this responsibility to a paid baby-sitter. Ben has offered to quit his job, but it makes no sense. He's just received a promotion to captain; with just four more years at this rank, he'll be entitled to a generous retirement pension that will give everyone in the family new choices and flexibility.

These days, Laurel has no downtime, not even one hour a week. She reserves all her extra nonwork hours for her two other children. Why should they suffer because of an ill sibling? She knows she can't keep going on like this. She's tested the waters at work about a part-time role, but the response has been discouraging. "Make a choice," her boss urges her. He claims he's supportive, yet he offers nothing but words.

Without the baby-sitter and the extra hidden expenses—designer suits, take-home dinners, and dry-cleaning bills—Laurel realizes that they could live on Ben's income, decently but not extravagantly. The problem is not really the money. It's her ego. She loves the thrill of "the working life." But lately the phrase has turned into an oxymoron. When the pediatric specialist tells her that Sammy needs daily, intensive massages, she knows the game is up. What she doesn't know anymore is how she really feels. Relieved? Or a sense of failure?

Who will she be without her job?

Two Kinds of Mothers

At thirty-eight, Laurel is not just exhausted; she is suffering from an identity crisis. For the past eleven years, she has been a career woman with a family, her self-image defined primarily through her work rather than her children. Transitioning to stay-at-home status is an enormous adjustment, one she never thought she'd have to make. Laurel grew up with the confidence that her generation would be different—smarter, stronger, better than the women before her. Naturally, she'd have a family. (What "real" woman wouldn't?) But naturally she'd also have a meaningful career.

The Identity Challenge That Never Dies

What Laurel didn't bank on was the unending confusion she would feel over her maternal role, angst that is a full-blown epidemic for modern working women. Effective parenting is theoretically a gender-free obligation, but good mothering seems to carry more psychological baggage for women than good fathering does for most men. It invokes the third shift big time. As I listen to woman after woman discuss her feelings and accomplishments, it is clear that how (or if) one mothers greatly influences a woman's core identity, even for women who work upwards of sixty hours a week, *and even for women who have no children.* Very few women seem to me free of the internal third shift or the visible public debate about maternal identity. The senior corporate women I have spoken with who deliberately opted for careers rather than children continue to struggle with their choices, a fine thread of self-doubt buried deep beneath their elegant professional veneers. Of the entrepreneurial aspirants I interviewed, more than half were researching self-employment to gain more flexibility for their families, convinced their corporate careers were unhealthy for themselves and their loved ones. Even the stay-at-home moms succumbed to unending anxieties or outright apologies for their decision. Not one woman felt completely confident—in the dark of the night—that she was doing it right.

This chapter explores how a new generation of stay-at-home moms are faring in a world of inconsistent expectations and silent pressures that they should be doing more in corporate or entrepreneurial life, yet fulfill their maternal roles fully and competently as well. Every woman knows in her heart that we expect more from women than men. The presence of the third shift suggests our complicity in this cultural trap: we expect more of ourselves. Every woman—like Laurel—also knows that our cultural practices and workplace support systems have not yet adjusted to fully support these heightened expectations. It is not mere multitasking at stake here, the ability to talk on a cell phone to clients while little Johnny is playing in the sand. At issue is the difficulty of carving out a clear, focused identity rooted in multiple roles that are equally demanding and rewarding. Further, as women we are expected to figure this all out on our own, and when we can't, our third shift clicks in, reminding us that we—not society—are somehow falling short.

Based on the women in my study, I conclude that anxiety over maternal identity for working women is increased by the mind-numbing psychological and physical activities connected with raising children today, at least for middle-class families. It's cruelly ironic that in an era when working women have less time to mother and manage the home front, the duties of "housewives" have actually expanded since the days when suburban moms played mah-jongg with the girls.[1] We live in an era of missing children's faces on milk cartons, which makes the second shift considerably more complicated. We press a great many structured experiences upon children. Few mothers permit their kids to walk home alone from school, or just hang out in the house without adult supervision. After-school hours are crammed with computer school and Little League, art classes and gymnastics. If women were once bored to tears by ladies' bridge clubs and lawn parties, today's women often face carpool and after-school overload. For women on the run from the corporate grind and slavish schedules, it can be daunting to discover that it may be no easier at home. For many, the pace is scarcely slower. Happily, many women report that the rewards of close participation in their children's lives make the frenetic pace meaningful, though perhaps no easier.

For today's power moms, the M word means they are expected to do all of the societal tasks, from home and school club to volunteering at homeless shelters, that their counterparts at work—"the suits"—just can't get to. There is also the sickening sense that stay-at-home moms have to continuously prove themselves by doing more to justify their existence (an insidious theme, incidentally, that rings with deja vu from the corporate sector). Thus, many women don't stop at extracurricular excess for their children; they are convinced that if they're going to stay at home they should fully enrich their children's lives with activities and experiences. In my study of entrepreneurial women, I felt certain that at least half of the women launching home-based businesses were taking on their projects as a way of justifying staying at home in a vigorous economic boomtown such as Silicon Valley. Many women confided to me that in the privacy of their third shifts, as well as in the public eye, stay-at-home motherhood in the 1990s can be viewed with enormous ambivalence. It's desirable, but is it enough?

Undoubtedly, mothers come in all flavors, but as I dug deeper into the data my study showed two general types of stay-at-home mothers. The first group, distinctly smaller in my sample, was completely committed to full-time parenting. Even if they were career women, these individuals had always counted upon stepping back from their careers while their children were young so there would be no tug-of-war between job demands and those of family. They were clear, rather than ambivalent, about the primacy of their maternal role.

The second group, which includes Laurel Andersen, either did not think through in advance how children would work into their careers or assumed that they would combine both spheres of their lives, yet somehow avoid the supermom syndrome. Several of these women privately admitted that their careers were too important to them to give up for anyone, even their own children. The latter group, not surprisingly, faced many more difficulties if they transitioned—even temporarily—to at-home status. I have devoted this chapter to this latter group of women, whose third shifts rumble with conflicting messages, while recognizing that millions of American women are completely satisfied with their at-home lives. Indeed, many such women feel highly fortunate that they can participate full-time in the lives of their children. They face little psychological conflict over their choices and maternal identities and therefore find the third shift doubts more muted in this realm.

For the other women, who face varying degrees of third shift uncertainties, it helps to recognize that it is difficult to stand back and see that the standards for good mothering are completely culturally derived, subject to change in every era. At one extreme, an expert tells us that today's standards are so "formidable, self-denying, elusive, changeable and contradictory that they are unattainable."[2] Psychologists warn us that there is no second chance for children. If mothers don't do their thing effectively when their children are very young, irreparable harm occurs that can never be reversed.

But many in the profession disagree, wondering if we have all been deluded by our own cultural myths. Shari Thurer, author of *The Myths of Motherhood,* writes, "The all-importance of mother love has been fueled by a giant collective wish for perfect mothering. It is bolstered by a religion that gave us the Virgin Mary, nursery tales that supplied us with fairy godmothers, and a psychology that failed to question many cultural assumptions. . . . The modern mother [has become] a life support system."[3] Working mothers who subscribe to this view are left with residual self-doubt and guilt—their maternal third shift—that they are selfishly feeding their own professional needs at the cost of their children's psychological well-being. Susan Chira, a journalist attacking the problem in her best-selling *A Mother's Place,* notes that we are captive to a single vision of motherhood, a "kind of June Cleaver vampire: no matter how many times you kill her, she never dies."[4]

Hence, women like Laurel have packed their tents and curbed their ambitions, turning to sequencing—stepping off the career ladder while the children are young and hoping for an effective reentry later—to solve their motherhood issues. But they remain ambivalent and struggle with the transition. They may feel as though they are sacrificing economic and bargaining power in the family while giving up challenging work that they love. Significantly, they are uncertain what they receive in return, because they may have a limited or skewed perspective of the maternal role. They have never previously performed it full-time, and their role models may amount to out-of-date portraits in the form of their own mothers.

We shall see that what this group of women receive in return depends upon the clarity of their identity as well as how they spend their time at home. Stated differently, stay-at-home women who feel fulfilled by the role have learned to meet both basic and higher-level psychological needs through their actions and activities on the home front.

Fulfillment: The New F Word

You may be familiar with the work of the eminent psychologist Abraham Maslow. More than fifty years ago, he envisioned a hier-archical pyramid of human needs. In his theory of human moti-vation, Maslow noted that satisfaction of higher-order needs (affection, self-esteem, self-actualization of one's full potential) occurs only when earlier, lower-order physiological and safety needs are satisfied.[5] The women in my study arrived at stay-at-home motherhood from divergent locations on this psychological pyra-mid. Some, like Laurel, began their stay-at-home life on the lower rungs, dealing with their children's medical complications. Others viewed the at-home life from the perspective of self-actualization. Such women are clear in their belief that they can fulfill themselves and their children only through full-time parenting. Of course, many other women in the study were prevented by financial con-straints from living out the choice they would actually prefer.

A woman's third shift around work and mothering can be loud and demanding if there is a disconnect between her "Maslowian needs" and her day-to-day reality. In addition, some of the women in my study were unrealistic about what the full-time mothering role involves, because they had never experienced it or had so inflated the standard for good mothering. Hence, of all the emo-tions I catalogued from the interviews conducted for this book, most stunning is the raw *guilt* that pervades the entire topic of mothering. Laurel's feelings were perhaps more extreme than most. Every time she visited her son's pediatrician, she felt on trial—even though the pediatrician never once mentioned that Sammy would be better off if she didn't work. "It's nuts, I know," said Laurel, twisting a much-used tissue around and around her fingers. "But Sammy's like a walking guilt machine. Every time I hear him cough, I feel guilty. I know it's not my fault that he's sick. I know I haven't done anything wrong. But I just don't feel right."

During the interviews, I also learned that the guilt and self-doubt about mothering could be present even if a woman chose to stay home. The object of the guilt simply transferred from self-reproach about the time spent with one's family to a sense of betrayal of one's education or the women's movement. Looked at from the perspective of Maslow's pyramid, these women seemed to feel guilty because they weren't self-actualizing. No wonder they fall far short of true fulfillment when they come home.

Self-Awareness Versus Self-Doubt

At the root of the identity dilemma over the maternal role is the feeling that women like Laurel are trapped in a vicious crossfire of self-doubt and self-awareness. Laurel's third shift is an alternating litany of rational, detached objectivity and punitive self-criticism, without resolution and seemingly without end. It may be helpful for us to explicitly call out this painful internal dialogue, even though you may not have experienced the particular pain or guilt that accompanies a critically ill child:

Self-Awareness	Self-Doubt
I love the mental invigoration I get from work. But I love my children also. Sammy needs me more now than my customers do. No decision is forever. I can go back to work later.	I must have my head screwed on wrong. My priorities are backwards. How can any job ever be more important than Sammy getting well?
In a perfect world I could do a better job of managing both my family's needs and my needs for professional growth and development. In the real world I have to make a choice and I'm resentful about it. I feel powerless. Life can be unfair, can't it? I shouldn't be so hard on myself.	Why did I bother having children if I don't want to stay at home and take care of them? Ben doesn't torture himself with this question over and over. He thinks he's a pretty good dad. And so do I. So why do I feel so lousy about my own parenting?

When the third shift moves to the right-hand column of self-doubt, it is scarcely surprising that women like Laurel feel confused, anxious, and even cut adrift from their core identity as women. The professional, workplace identity can be an easy, default self-image because it poses few psychological complications, offering the freedom of comparative objectivity, as in the left-hand column above. A woman's worth at work may depend on both task accomplishment and satisfactory professional relationships with others,[6] but the emotional ties to success draw less upon who she is than upon what she does to earn money. A woman may feel bad but still walk away from a failure with her boss, her customers, or her peers. She can start over. But if she loses on the home front, if she deems her children's problems as an outcome of inattention or neglect, she may find it difficult to recover from the pain of self-reproach.

When there looms too great a distance between the self-doubt and self-awareness in a woman's third shift, it becomes challenging to fuse a satisfying integrated identity that encompasses both career and motherhood. Instead, identity becomes lopsided and never expresses the whole woman. In my study, when women face changed life situations, such as the serious illness of young Sammy, the transition in status from working mom to stay-at-home involved significant decompression anxiety—the working woman's "bends" from swimming up too quickly from the depths of the other identity. In this lopsided model, the portion of one's life and identity that was overly demanding (professional life) now becomes the one that is completely excised. A new identity must be rebuilt quickly from the very part of the woman that has been neglected and that is most subject to self-doubt. It is a perilous process indeed, yet many women in my study practiced useful techniques to accomplish it.

Coming Home

Clearly, women who transition from corporation back to cottage face major personal adjustments. These days, *reentry* has new meaning, and coming home has become an issue for an increasing number of women affluent enough to have a choice. The press has been quick to jump in. Major magazines and newspapers are awash in stories about career women who have abandoned their posts for their *real* job, motherhood. This is Susan Faludi's backlash all over again. In some circles, it has become the in thing to give up the big career in search of personal, down-home fulfillment. For women who have experienced true success on the job, the logical sequencing is to experience that same high at home, where it really counts.

As mentioned, the stay-at-home women from my study include two basic populations, one a struggling group comprising Laurel Andersen and others (for whom this chapter is especially targeted). The second group includes women whose journey home stems from disenchantment and lack of fulfillment, rather than necessity. I saw how relieved, even delighted, some of these women became—those who could afford the transition. In this second grouping, I also spoke with younger, gen X women who grew up on the receiving end of feminism, with mothers who had tried to do it all and whose legacy to their gen X children was indigestion. Many of these younger women are unconsciously turning back the clock. They have absolutely no intention to squeeze in their children around their jobs, or defer a family until their careers are better established. They assume they will figure out the career piece later, if at all, and they see little risk in their decision. Additional members of the second group were corporate retreads, senior women retiring from the fast lane to offer their experience in the nonprofit, educational, and community sectors. Having made it, these women want to give something back to others; they are looking for personal fulfillment as well as accomplishment. Finally, I spoke with women who desperately wish they could stay at home with their children but can't afford to do so. With low-paid, blue-collar jobs and limited educational backgrounds, these women aren't worrying about the ground gained since Betty Friedan's day. Nor are they unduly concerned with what their neighbors think. Or whether their kids are unhappy in day care. These women are trying to keep food on the table and reasonable shelter over their heads. As the have-nots in the Magic Kingdom of Silicon Valley, these women simply feel left behind.

Making Your Third Shift Work for You: Managing the Identity Challenge at Home

Regardless of why the women I talked to decided to stay at home or leave the corporate or entrepreneurial rat race for nonprofit work, I found a number of common threads in their experience, and several lessons about what to expect and what to do to improve harmony and satisfaction:

- Be a positive role model for your choice.
- Be yourself—*now.*
- Be clear about your expectations; take charge of fulfilling them.
- Enjoy your nurturing side.
- Stop proving yourself over and over.
- Recognize the difference between compromise and sacrifice.
- Strive for parity with your spouse.

The practices I recommend here focus on what to think, not just what to do. They concentrate on the attitudes, beliefs, and values that need to be in place so that the self-awareness, rather than the self-doubt, of the third shift guides a woman to act upon the identity right for her. These recommendations offer a starting place for women to use to begin their inward journey, looking first to themselves for guidance.

Be a Positive Role Model for Your Choice

Women who expect others to applaud their choice to stay at home must start with themselves, visibly demonstrating confidence in their decisions, even if they are pursuing a path different from those of women around them. Women may need something different from men, and they don't need to apologize for it. Yet women often hold themselves to an unrealistic standard, one that imitates the linear, conventional male worklife. If they don't follow this well-traveled route, they pay a harsh price in reduced self-confidence and loss of respect from others.

Studies of college reunions illuminate the issue. In one sampling of Harvard Business School female graduates, *exhaustion*—not *satisfaction*—topped the list of terms these so-called successful and intelligent women use to describe themselves. A full 25 percent of the respondents had left the workplace entirely; these incredibly high-achieving women were unable or unwilling to combine motherhood with the fast track.[7] A recent polling in *Fortune* of the "most powerful women in America" showed significant differences between Harvard's class of '73 and '83, with the latter women obviously feeling much freer to choose entrepreneurial, part-time, or stay-at-home lives than the older career women.[8] On the other hand, the '83 grads may simply be more realistic that they can't do it all anyway, since 70 percent of them are mothers, compared to only 53 percent of the '73 alums.

The women in my study—a number of whom boasted M.B.A.s from Stanford, MIT, Columbia, and Harvard, but some of whom had no college experience at all—expressed continuous ambivalence about their choices. One woman I interviewed initially framed her decision to leave after seventeen years with a fast-track high-tech company as a personal failure and then realized that she was actually profoundly relieved to leave it behind her. The day-to-day grind was literally melting her down. She had lost nearly fifteen pounds in the prior year, a combination of worry; back-to-back travel among Korea, the Netherlands, and California; and a new boss she disliked.

"I've never run away from a challenge," this woman said, making certain she looked me straight in the eye as she offered this important admission. At forty-three, she had no husband to please and no children to care for, the legitimate excuse for turning her back on her corner office. She had several years of "running money" saved up, a rental unit she could sell if she ran low on funds, and the hope of a modest bequest at her mother's death to help tide her over if necessary. She had no immediate plans to return to work, or even to immerse herself in community service. She developed a somewhat brusque script to reply to people who clearly were surprised or threatened by her decision to turn her back on corporate America, without a specific replacement for her time and personal energy: "Bears hibernate every winter, and no one thinks twice about it. Why should I kill myself to prove that I can work as hard as everyone else?" Despite her bravado, at the very conclusion of our interview a hint of the uncertain inner woman emerged: "I've earned my time away, haven't I?"

Our culture deems these individuals who defy conventional practices to be corporate dropouts, a value-laden term in our Calvinist culture of work-develops-character and a term laced with envy as well as disapproval. Mothers leaving the workplace to concentrate on child-rearing may face equally negative metaphors describing their choices: "on the shelf," "stepping off the ladder," "sidelined," "on hold," or "downsizing the self." These terms share a second-best quality. As women repeat these seemingly innocuous phrases, they risk making the negative message part of themselves

and their identities. Such messages are also delivered unconsciously to one's children, especially one's daughters. The point of
staying at home is to live one's espoused values; to parent deeply
and in a hands-on manner; and to be a positive role model every
day for one's children.

In a recent study of more than twelve hundred American
women who have developed successful careers and are also happy
with their personal lives, Sylvia Rimm and her research team found
that children may ignore messages from mothers who are full-time
homemakers unless the mothers themselves are positive about
their role.[9] "Your daughters are watching you," Rimm concludes.[10]
You must consciously consider the kind of role model you are
enacting, both with your words as well as your actions.

Hence the first step for women who are returning to the home
front is to consciously select a term for their choice that expresses
confidence and positive energy, rather than doubt, yet does not
disparage the life forgone. Laurel Andersen, for example, might
say, "I want to take care of my son." Or "It's time for me to develop
a part of myself I've neglected." Or "I feel good about being with
my family." In saying these words, she isn't denying her other feelings ("I still miss my job"; "I don't feel as important anymore";
"Sometimes my children bore me"). But what she is doing is learning to concentrate more on—and to practice verbalizing aloud—
what she has, as opposed to what she doesn't have. At first, this
takes concentration and sheer discipline. It literally means teaching yourself a new attitude. But I've seen it work.

Those making this transition can also benefit from taking time
to be with many kinds of women. Exposure and openness to others who are living out alternative choices are essential to clearly
perceiving and understanding your own needs. Like the first suggestion, this route takes patience and motivation. For women who
have only hobnobbed with other career women, it is not obvious
at first what to talk about with stay-at-home-moms (and vice versa).
It takes genuine willingness to bridge the surface differences and
to inquire about the other's experience, to share one's own story
openly, and admit aloud the uncertainties of the transition. Questions at this stage are often more helpful than anything else, along
with nonjudgmental responses. Above all, remember that you're
not alone. Many other women with strollers in their Cherokees and

tubes of diaper rash ointment falling out of their pocketbooks were once successful working women like you. Now they feel equally successful in a new way: as a full-time mother. Some are actually happier than they were as working mothers. Either way, they understand how you feel as you move through your own transition.

Be Yourself—Now

I've noticed that many women who elect to stay at home seem happiest if they are busy and ever on the go, enriching their family life. I've also talked with other women who would truly like to slow down and smell at least a few of the roses, yet who don't do so. They defer their needs in the belief that "my children need me now" and that they have little choice. Or they sometimes ignore their own needs because our society increasingly looks down its collective nose at anyone who isn't moving a million miles an hour. I wondered if at least some of these women at home who are in constant motion were unconsciously competing with their working counterparts.

Think about it. If it's de rigueur in your set to be a crazed working woman, up at five to exercise, checking voice mail messages at six, dropping off kids at eight, and careening into your first staff meeting a half-hour later, there's a certain adrenaline charge that accompanies the start of each day. Your life is endless movement, running from one thing to the next, multitasking your head off. Like Air Force pilots bragging about how many missions they've flown without being shot down, women today take great pride in their ability to manage multiple roles. "How do you do it?" "You're so capable." "You're so organized." "How do you get so much done?" Unconsciously, women staying at home may feel that they too need to "get so much done."

These are probably the wrong questions to ask, but most of us are too polite to offer an alternative inquiry: "Why are you doing this to yourself?" "Is this how you want your life to be?" "What do you get from running around like this?" Caught within the psychological and physical spell of this working woman's high, it can be difficult to actually understand what you're truly feeling underneath. Take your personal psychological pulse, and answer these questions:

- Is the high masking satisfaction, or despair?
- Are you feeling happy and content to be needed by so many, or empty and burned out because everyone is pulling on you?
- Are you simply too busy to think about what you really want from your life?
- Do you chase away your feelings that something is wrong?

Like Gwen Allen in Chapter Two, who needed a breakaway from work, we all need a sabbatical from our lives on occasion to ask the important questions *before acting*. In particular, we each need a new perspective to look at our current life and see if we are sacrificing it to an abstract and nebulous future—"The Waiting Place," as Dr. Seuss[11] terms it: "a most useless place . . . for people just waiting." How many of us have deferred our needs with plausible rationalizations? Do we recognize ourselves in any of these sentences?

- When my kids are grown, I'll take more time for myself. . . .
- When my kids are out of school, I'll buy myself a decent car. . . .
- When soccer season is over, I'll wind down. . . .

Working women have their own litany of deferrals:

- After we ship this product, I'll take some time off. . . .
- When my husband retires, I'll switch to part-time. . . .
- When my boss moves to corporate, I'll try for his job. . . .
- After I get my M.B.A., I'll quit this job I hate. . . .
- When I get promoted, I won't work so hard. . . .

We all have our own personal variations. While writing this book, I must have said to myself (and others) a hundred times, "When I've finished writing this book. . . ." As healthy adults or as parents, naturally we must defer gratification of some of our needs on behalf of others, or of goals crucial to us. The question is whether we overdo this, following a persistent pattern throughout our lives that results in a perpetual holding place defined by others' needs and expectations. Historically, women at home can be particularly vulnerable, as though they have to earn the right to live for themselves rather than others. Some women even need a life-threatening illness such as breast cancer to shock them into placing their own needs higher on the family list.

Other women benefit from the help of a professional counselor, a resource useful to all women at times but especially valuable for women at home who may be isolated and thus vulnerable to the self-doubt in their third shift. A new, professional perspective on their lives can be prove very enlightening. As the millennium arrives, understanding between the sexes has greatly increased from the time when Sigmund Freud pejoratively asked, "What do women want?" But many women still find true benefit and validation, as well as a new language for expressing their needs, by turning to professional help rather than friends or family. Most communities offer low-cost professional counseling through nonprofit, religious, or educational institutions that is designed expressly for women's issues. Taking the first step to seek help is key because it acknowledges the problem. Our most profound strength as women comes when we acknowledge our personal vulnerability. We fail not because we are weak or need help but because we forget how to use our third shift.

One woman in my study who illustrates this point is Juliet Dowling. She was a successful pharmaceutical salesperson in her past life, as she called it. She traveled extensively with her job and earned enough to more than cover her needs as a single woman. Cautious about men after an early heartbreak, she married somewhat later than her contemporaries. She didn't even meet Rob until she was thirty-eight; their nuptials occurred a year later.

When I first interviewed Juliet, Rob had just left academia for a new career as a research scientist in an up-and-coming biotech company. His hours were much longer than anyone had expected, but she genuinely didn't seem to mind how much of the parenting responsibilities fell on her shoulders. She had been waiting for decades to be a mother, and their oldest was born less than a year after she and Rob were married; their second and last child arrived scarcely two years later. Although she had always enjoyed working, Juliet left her job in the eighth month of her first pregnancy and never looked back.

Now her principal identity centered around parenting two young girls, Tracie Anne and Tori. She wistfully thought on occasion that it would "round things out" to have a boy also, but the mere thought of a third pregnancy at age forty-three made her molars ache. Besides, when would she even find the time to fit the activities of a third child into her routine, or give that child the personal, individual attention she loved to lavish on each of her girls? At nine and eleven respectively, both Tracie Anne and Tori were bright and imaginative and possessed seemingly limitless energy. They wanted to be involved in everything! And Juliet wanted to be involved with them, not just sitting on the sidelines cheering, or chauffeuring to and from tennis tournaments. She liked to be involved as a team coach. She liked to volunteer hands-on time in the classroom, and she felt especially fulfilled by leisurely mother-daughter chats with each of her girls, on topics from boys and music to how to deal with schoolmates who acted snobby and disinterested.

For Juliet, the essence of the at-home mothering role was these in-the-trenches talks and special moments with each of her girls. In contrast to Laurel's expectations, Juliet's stay-at-home model envisioned parenting as a set of significant psychological activities that were tremendously rewarding. They more than compensated for the physical needs—chauffeuring and the like. Mothering both girls was a full-time job, not just because Tracie Anne was in a private middle school twenty miles away while Tori was down the road in the local elementary school, but because Juliet didn't want to miss anything. She was busy, yes. But she was content. In her mind, raising her daughters was her true vocation. "But I'm not one of those women who are trying to live my life through my girls," she assured me when I inquired about the overflowing schedule she lived with to be sure Tori could play soccer and piano while Tracie Anne took advantage of art lessons, after-school tennis camp, and band practice. "By waiting so long to get married, I was able to exercise genuine choice. I *chose* to be single. Then I *chose* to get married. I *chose* to work. And now I'm *choosing* to do the mommy thing. I may go back to a career. I may not. My head is somewhere else right now."

Analyzing her transcript, I unconsciously compared it to Laurel's, noting immediately that although Laurel continued to struggle with her transition from career to the at-home life, Juliet made it look easy. Both had supportive husbands and were in a similar income class, once the switch to a single salary was made. Both genuinely enjoyed their lives as career women. The key difference, of course, was in the exercise of choice. Sammy's illness forced Laurel's hand, while Juliet knew for years that she would shelve her career once the kids started coming. Juliet wakes up every day trying to make the most of mothering (even the tedious aspects), completely focused on what she *has,* while Laurel spends the same energy worrying about what she has given up, and what used to be. Moreover, her parenting experience is seriously marred by profound worry about the ultimate prognosis for her young son. Her transition remains painful because she hasn't yet fully accepted it.

Be Clear About Your Expectations; Take Charge of Fulfilling Them

Both Laurel and Juliet came on line with *Fear of Flying* and *Dressing for Success.* But Laurel is more vulnerable to social expectations for a successful modern woman. She can only imagine one kind of satisfying life, which includes full-time, challenging work. It took more than a year for her to reexamine this somewhat rigid model and open herself to other possibilities and their unanticipated rewards. In contrast, Juliet realized her life could encompass both types of satisfaction, but not necessarily at the same time. Juliet and Laurel are different, in part because Laurel was "forced" home by the severity of young Sammy's illness; but they also differ with respect to their innate flexibility. Juliet's life and overall perspective favors shades of gray, while Laurel's depiction of her choices involves starker trade-offs.

In our conversations together, Laurel was always candid about the days before she quit her job: "I thought my life would fall smoothly into place if I just asserted myself, seized opportunities, and stayed organized." This may be a reasonable supposition on the surface for someone raised to believe she could do anything she wanted. But to me, the costs seemed high. Laurel ran her life like an Excel spreadsheet. On Sunday nights, she made lists to manage the following week, discussing with her husband their joint responsibilities according to her travel schedule, his station duties, Sammy's physical therapy visits, and her other kids' after-school activities. The list was posted on the refrigerator, as a kind of central processing unit for the week. Every activity had a name next to it, assigning responsibility. Nothing was left to chance. Organization, not serendipity, ruled the Andersen family in a tight grip.

Faced with the decision to resign from her job or watch her youngest child's health spiral downward, one of Laurel's first tangible fears was that she would inherit the entire refrigerator list. "That damned list gave me nightmares," she admitted; "it became the entire symbol for what I was giving up and what I was getting myself into." Clearly, Laurel possessed an unrealistically narrow picture of the stay-at-home life; in her own words, it was a black-and-white vision. Additionally, her expectations were way too low. As a working mother, she rarely found time to provide more than the most basic of Maslow's physiological or safety needs for her children. The psychological parenting that resides on the upper rungs of the pyramid was usually performed by her husband, who had a more flexible work schedule and was often around at the very moment when the kids needed his willing ear. Laurel had limited insight into this side of parenting. She was in denial, seeing only what she wanted to see, unconsciously denigrating the true, rich panoply of maternal activities that awaited her and seeing little more than the drudgery. Because she suffered continuous third-shift guilt about her own parenting, she convinced herself that life as a full-time homemaker would be boring and unappreciated and hold minimal attractions. She needed to learn for herself just how inaccurately she used to picture the stay-at-home life from the outside.

Along with the need for a broad and true perspective, missing from Laurel's new life was a tangible way to meet some of her own needs in the context of a stay-at-home role. To help her learn from the experience of other women in the study, we discussed how she could rectify this. At the beginning of her transition, the only context Laurel had for meeting her personal needs was her former identity as a career woman. For her entire adult working life, the job challenges themselves, recognition from others, travel, assorted perquisites such as a secretary and spacious office, and satisfying financial remuneration had given her both a well-defined self-image and enough complementary positives to make up for what she was trading away: a leisurely lifestyle and personal time for herself and family.

Now everything changed. Deep inside, she remained resistant to her new life, stuck with the awful feeling that her freedom to choose was actually being stripped away from her. Liberty may be particularly precious to contemporary women, who have fought hard for it. It became clear to me that Laurel's unhappiness was with the sudden tug on the reins, more than the actual choice itself of staying-at-home. Now she was going to have to put all her eggs in one basket, so to speak, and gain satisfaction and meaning from an entirely different source. But where to start? How could she raise her expectations?

We started with her need to express expectations openly, in conversations not only with Ben but also with her two older children, who, at ages six and ten, were old enough to understand that if their mother's role changed, so would their lives. I impressed upon her the importance of focusing on the positive aspects of this change, while admitting to her children that all transitions involve uncertainty and struggle. With Ben, Laurel began by voicing her fears. His reply surprised her. He didn't expect her to take over everything because she was leaving her job. He was already assuming he'd continue managing the child care and housekeeping responsibilities—for starters, fixing dinner twice a week and picking up the older kids from school on the weekdays he wasn't at the station house. They could negotiate the rest. Then they discussed a reasonable budget to fit their new circumstances, identifying what would be available to spend strictly on herself: baby-sitters for time to get away, tuition for classes she might take, materials that might be needed if she took up a hobby, and so forth.

Like any of us experiencing a transition, she needed time to bury the past before she could envision an entirely new future. As another woman described it to author Elizabeth Perle McKenna, "I had to mourn the loss of my dream life."[12] After several months, things finally began to click into place. Laurel's worst fear—that she would be bored—never materialized. Instead, she started taking advantage of the newfound time for herself. She began swimming for exercise four times a week. After a while, she filled a newly vacated interim position on her local school board when a neighbor suddenly resigned; she came to enjoy the new responsibility of the school board, her skills, and articulate leadership evident to all. Best of all, she was now able to complete her assignments thoroughly and on time, something she had never managed to her satisfaction when she was working long hours and traveling. In fact, doing one thing well was not just a novelty for her; it was practically a spiritual awakening, the very tonic needed to accelerate her transition to stay-at-home mom.

Ultimately, she began to hit her stride as a stay-at-home mother, understanding its true depths and joys. With the older kids, she became a trusted counselor and confidante, a silent but supportive presence nearby at other times. She became much more adept at anticipating when her children wanted to spend time with her, and when they preferred to retreat to their own rooms. With Sammy now an active preschooler, she was able to accelerate his long-term recovery, taking increasingly longer walks every day to build up his muscles and carrying him home when they overdid it. Reading quietly or folding laundry, she, not Ben or a baby-sitter, was the one lucky to be at home and receive Sammy's prize-winning smile when he woke up from his nap.

By the time of our last interview together, fifteen months after she left her job, Laurel had a new frame of reference from which to evaluate the fit of her new life. She was still building new expectations for herself as her view of the maternal role expanded. The turning point came when she stopped trying to pinpoint when she would return to work, realizing that she would have to wait and see how Sammy's progress continued. Essentially, she began to believe in the present again, even though it was offering her something very different from what she expected, or even wanted, before. She still doesn't know if she will resume her career:

> I had to let that go, or it would just drive me crazy. I'm amazed at how much energy I have. I didn't realize how tired I was all the time. Or how tense. Not to mention worried. Sammy isn't shaking off this thing as quickly as I'd hoped, but I feel so much better that I'm more involved in his care. I've been reading about his condition on the Internet, and I think I've actually turned our pediatrician on to some new ideas. . . . I went to a Christmas party last week for my old boss. You know, I never realized that those people don't talk about anything but work. Was I ever that way?

Enjoy Your Nurturing Side

Our deepest need is for connection to others, yet the nurturing issue for women involves several complications. First, and all too often, women are deeply ambivalent about how to express this need openly in a culture oriented toward wealth, material gain, and tangible accomplishment. Money is important, and people who earn it doubly so. We value by extension whatever work is performed that results in high salaries. The corollary is that unpaid work—nurturing children in the home, for example—has only marginal value beyond the boundaries of an immediate family. No wonder high-achieving women like Laurel Andersen struggle to reinvent core identities as nurturers rather than breadwinners when the choice becomes an all-or-nothing proposition.

Moreover, devaluation of nurturing is more than feminist hyberbole. Consider this: in the thirty-year period beginning in 1945, the birthrate per woman in America plummeted from four children to two.[13] Shari Thurer interprets this trend as widespread disillusionment, the gradual devaluation of a maternal role as burdensome and psychologically perilous when mothers are blamed for problems of today's children. The maternal influence has been overstated with regard to child development;[14] the media at times have demonized working mothers, reviling them as selfish and materialistic. All of this has been fueled recently by reports of inadequate, even dangerous, day care in this country. Headlines in credible magazines blaze a warning that poor day care can actually stunt a child's brain growth![15]

This climate has ignited a new epidemic of third shift second-guessing by working mothers, notwithstanding a definite uptick in the number of women who are leaving the workforce to return to the home front.[16] I can't help but conclude that Thurer's view about motherhood is extreme, but even if she is not entirely correct and some women are unconsciously having fewer children as a partial response to this cultural subtext, the real problem lies elsewhere. Women are cutting themselves off from the very aspect of their lives that can produce the most lasting meaning. Experts advising women to have only one child in this era of superparenting are missing the real point.[17] Women's power and progress are connected to experiencing *true*, not deep, choices. For many of us, being told to have only one child constitutes an outrageous misassignment of responsibility for the rigidity of a patriarchal working world, as well as forfeiture of our very soul as women.

The freedom to love and nurture one's children closely and fully is one of life's greatest joys, even as it remains among its most significant challenges. Stay-at-home mothers have no monopoly on such activities, but we could argue that the opportunity to influence their children's development may be greater than for their working counterparts in terms of time available. On the other hand, many working women have learned exactly where and when these critical nurturing opportunities occur, making time available at those moments specifically. Of course, it's impossible to predict and orchestrate such times perfectly. But it may help to cite a personal example.

Our son, Evan, now eleven years old, is an enthusiastic, knowledgeable, and usually talented baseball player. He is loyal to his team to a fault, but he is also prone to surprisingly punitive self-attacks when he performs below his own expectations. I learned about the depths of this self-recrimination only recently, when I observed a negative pattern of behavior following many of his ball games. Because baseball is so important to him, it has become increasingly important to me, and I have scheduled even critical business meetings around his games and practices. I have also learned that it is never enough to be a sideline parent, merely showing up to watch a game or practice session and then heading back to the office. It is at the end of the game, and even later, that Evan may need parental nurturing the most. If he is having an off day and hasn't batted, pitched, or fielded to his satisfaction (sigh), he can feel tremendously alone when he comes off the field and throws his glove and bat into the trunk of my car. On the way home, I've learned (the hard way) not to say a word until he's ready to talk. Yet I also recognize that my simple physical presence can be useful as he works through his negative thinking. Although I respect his silence, I'm convinced that parenting involves strategic parenting moments and interventions because eleven-year-old boys have a limited range of knowledge and perspective to solve their problems.

Ultimately, Evan and I perform an instant replay of his experience, including not just his actual plays on the field but his thoughts and feelings as well, to the extent that he will share them.

In the end, my husband and I turn to techniques from the field of sports psychology to offer him practical mental drills and affirming statements he can actually use during a game to counter his negativity. We have seen marked improvement to date, although realistically this self-critical behavior is undoubtedly something we will all be dealing with throughout Evan's life. But I feel best about our role as parents when I see my son's self-confidence improve and translate into more enjoyment of this sport he so deeply loves. It doesn't get any better than this as a parent.

This portion of the chapter on nurturing is not meant to be a comprehensive discussion of parenting per se, but scanning my interview transcripts did reveal a significant finding about maternal identity and the third shift: the one area where self-doubts do *not* poison the thinking of women is when they are involved in conversations or actions with their children that help their kids enhance their self-confidence and self-esteem. I might add a corollary: if we can leverage our children's self-confidence to help them make wise choices and manage the dilemmas and trade-offs they face on the road to adulthood, we not only diminish our offspring's self-doubts but also travel a far piece down the road ourselves toward reducing our own negative thoughts.

Stop Proving Yourself Over and Over

Stay-at-home women learn that they can face time shortages just as acute as those of working women. For her first six months at home, Laurel unconsciously substituted for the frenetic pace of her work life an equally overzealous load on the home front. At times, her new life veered as wildly out of balance as her old lopsided existence. But what did she really gain? Where she used to put in that last hour to finish up a project report for her boss, or volunteer to take the red-eye to the East Coast to make an early morning meeting in Boston, Laurel was now schlepping kids all afternoon from one activity and "play date" to another and then racing home on the days Ben was on duty to pull a meal together for her hungry kids. While waiting outside her daughter's piano lesson, she now used her car phone to call appliance repairmen rather than customers. She was clearly missing the real possibilities in her new life.

It is impossible for anyone to create meaningful identity from a smattering of moments between shopping, homework, and doctor visits. In our discussions, Laurel began to see that she was still hell-bent on proving her worth, to herself and to others, filling the void in her life the only way she knew how, by endowing her life with movement, a habit perfected over years of managing both home and career through brute force and disciplined organization.

Taking time one day to lunch with another mother while Sammy was at physical therapy, she listened attentively to a peer close to her own age who hadn't worked since her oldest son was born ten years earlier. Like Juliet Dowling, this woman had enjoyed working but didn't really miss it. She was confident that when and if the time was right she would initiate the transition back into a career. "I really loved nursing," she told Laurel. "I had a lot of responsibility, and I was good at it. I was used to hard work and long hours, so when I first came home I think I tried to fill the void with nonprofit work. After catering to demanding surgeons all day, taking care of one little baby boy wasn't really too demanding. I needed stimulation and interaction. I didn't feel like I could just stay home." She reflected: "Of course, it takes time to find your way. You need to give yourself some time. And some space." But it was her final comment that sent the zinger to Laurel: "I don't work so hard at not working anymore."

Two final suggestions to reexamine and refocus your days at home may prove useful. Talk with your own mother if she's alive, and try to get a better understanding of her life, particularly if it was spent at home. Focus on what worked about her life. You may be surprised—in our post–Stepford Wives world—about what you can learn. Second, if you're a mother with children at home (whether you are a working parent or not), ask your kids what they like about their current regimen and what really isn't such a big deal for them. It can be a pleasant shock to find out, while trying to cram everyone into the van for the latest Disney movie, rock-climbing party, or basketball tryout, that the kids just want to stay at home and be with you.

Recognize the Difference Between Compromise and Sacrifice

A healthy adult life (for either gender) requires regular compromise, what the dictionary calls the ability to settle differences through mutual concession. On occasion we are also asked to sacrifice, to give up and surrender our position or needs to serve some other goal or relationship. Prolonged self-sacrifice and persistent subordination of one's own needs and identity is most assuredly not desirable; it is usually the last refuge of the powerless. But in practice, it can be exceedingly difficult to distinguish between compromise and sacrifice in advance.

Juliet Dowling remained single because she hadn't met "the right man." She was making a compromise, although she desperately wanted children, and she actually would have preferred to bear them when she was much younger. (She also knew that she didn't want to be a single mother.) Compromise about when to have children was acceptable to her. But after she met and married Rob, she knew that returning to work would be a deep personal sacrifice. She was prepared to fund her life at home, if necessary, with her savings of nearly twenty years. All the time she was working, she never stopped thinking about starting a family, and she prudently set aside a portion of her paycheck every month so nothing would stand in the way of her being home with her kids. Determined and practical, she knew the difference between compromise and sacrifice.

Tina Wu was another woman who understood this distinction. When I met her during this study, she was trying to figure out a way to become a full-time mother. She was also unemployed. Her dream seemed impossible at first, because in addition to having no sure source of income she was single, the divorced mother of Louis, a seven-year-old. Although she received small monthly checks from her ex-husband, they never quite covered the true expenses of raising a quickly growing child. At the time, she had just moved back into her parent's house to save on rent money.

Unlike Juliet, Tina had no substantial savings even though she had worked for most of her adult life. She was laid off when a local cannery shut down. Her severance package gave her several months to figure out her next move, but she was reluctant to "blow it all, then be stuck at home with no money, no job, and no prospects."

I met her as she attended a program at the Center to Develop Women Entrepreneurs. She was looking into self-employment, wondering if she could jump-start her dream through a home-based business. But she didn't have a business concept, and she lacked business skills and acumen.

Six months later, after intensive work with a mentor from the center, she enrolled in a local community college as a court reporter, using the money from her severance package to fund the program. Once she completed it, she would be able to set her own hours. She could work as little or as much as she wanted. In the meantime, she would have much more time to spend with her son than she did previously as a cannery worker. Although she would have little financial security in the immediate future (after her severance package ran out), she was willing to borrow from her family, ". . . despite all the strings. I have to listen to what my mother thinks I should do, which is pretty annoying since I'm thirty-one years old, but it's a worthwhile compromise. And it won't be forever."

Tina was able to attend classes during the afternoon while her son was at school, so her compromise of living at home was a good one, "although some days my mother gets on my nerves. She doesn't understand why I don't get married again. She says I can stay home with Louis if I get remarried. She puts a lot of pressure on me to get remarried. She thinks that way I would have more children. More grandchildren for her. But I don't think I want to be married again. Now, *that* would be a sacrifice I'm not prepared to make. At least, not right now."

In the end, the difference between compromise and sacrifice is an individual choice, and a matter of the true dialogue in one's inner third shift. Here are two excerpts from comments by working mothers, as opposed to stay-at-home moms, but the contrast between the two voices of self-awareness and self-doubt is illustrative for everyone. Note that when the voices of self-doubt are too negative, they may signal a needless sacrifice that is too painful and can't be sustained, as is the case with the first woman:

> Every time I have to schedule a trip for work, my husband complains so much about the disruption to the family that I cancel it, or send someone else. I hate fighting with him all the time. I feel like I can't ever win. Besides, there's an energetic new guy on my team, J. J., who really loves these customer trips. He's much better with the customers anyway. But I think I might have screwed up. Last month, my boss reorganized my group, and guess who is

running the whole show now? When I asked my boss why he put
J. J. in charge, even though I have seniority, you know what he said?
"You didn't act like you wanted to manage." So I gave the hard job
to someone who did. I didn't know what to say, so I just left the
room, but now I'm wondering what I can do about it.

Now contrast this self-doubting voice with that of a self-aware
and positive woman. It is not just that the second woman is more
self-confident. Her life involves a useful compromise (in her existing job) rather than a pointless sacrifice (of the time she most likes
to spend with her family):

I'm supposed to get to work by eight o'clock because my boss likes
to start the day with a quickie staff meeting. But that means I have
to completely kill the idea of breakfast with my family or ever taking the kids to school. I don't know why, but somehow I feel like a
real mom if I start off the day with more family involvement. It's
important to me, and I think everyone else likes it also. So I've
told my boss that I can't make those early meetings, and I send
someone else instead. If this is going to be a career-limiting move,
it's better to find that out now. I'll live with the consequences,
or find a new job with more flexibility. But I'm not giving up my
mornings with the kids so I can listen to a bunch of nerds discuss
why their product is over budget.

Strive for Parity with Your Spouse

As a practical matter, most stay-at-home moms or women with low-
paid or unpaid jobs in the community are married (there would
be no income to support the family otherwise). Hence the final
area of discussion on the stay-at-home life is the role of the spouse.
Women are kidding themselves if they think all the changes must
be on their side.[18] The transition from career woman to the stay-at-
home role involves adjustments for everyone. In Laurel Andersen's
case, it was helpful that her husband did not assume that she would
automatically end up doing everything just because she no longer
had a paid job to fill up her weekdays. She did not have to give up
all her bargaining power just because she wasn't earning money.

Many other women are not so fortunate, and I have seen the
problem surface in the transition from career to home *or the reverse*.
Marlene Casey, a homemaker-turned-minister in my sample,

began questioning her overly compliant role in the family when her husband's confusion, resentment, and outright resistance to her emerging new needs completely broke down the communication and trust between this couple of thirty-some years. Because he was used to her managing all of the household chores, he was naturally very unhappy to discover that he had to make a personal adjustment—whether he wanted to or not—or else leave the marriage, something he assuredly didn't want.

As Marlene moved from divinity school to the complete responsibilities of a pulpit minister with a congregation, her husband had to completely change his life: beginning to do grocery shopping, cooking on occasion, handling repairmen, and the dozens of other details and annoyances that she had skillfully and invisibly been managing for him for twenty years. At the same time, he felt like an innocent bystander in her identity crisis. Marlene no longer seemed to gauge her worth as a mother or wife. From where he stood, she seemed to be creating from scratch an entirely new identity, and her work in caring for her flock was competing directly with his work—and therefore his own identity—as a surgeon. They had to force themselves to sit down and negotiate—twice and sometimes three times on the thornier points—who would be responsible for what, how flexible the arrangement could be, and what it all said about what they meant to each other. Indeed, they discovered that flexibility was more important than anything else during their transition period because it was rarely obvious in advance how they would feel, or what would work out well in practice.

In the case of the Andersens, Ben's supportiveness helped ease the daily frictions and confusions that quickly ensued when Laurel came home full-time, but it still wasn't an easy period for anyone in the family. He was not only willing to hold onto some chores even though Laurel was now the one with more free time but also willing to give up control over the duties he had previously managed and performed in a certain way for several years. He also purposefully and gracefully moved aside as she took on more of the rewarding, psychological-parenting activities he had quietly performed in the past. He was quick to recognize that she was never going to make it at home if all she had to contend with was household drudgery every day.

Laurel chuckled when we discussed her first three turbulent months at home. "It was a nuthouse, and I was the head nut. Fortunately, Ben stood back and gave me some space to work it all out. I was still so resentful that I wasn't working, and so busy pretending that everything was fine, I was making life a living hell for all of us. I was completely rearranging everyone's schedule and creating havoc in a system that had run perfectly well before I stepped into it. Naturally, I assumed I could do everything better, and without all of my energy going into work I threw myself into 'perfecting' the home front."

At this point, Laurel rolled her eyes while shaking her head in despair. We laughed together, realizing that a sense of humor was indispensable to the learning process. "I remember clear as a bell one night when we were fighting over [our oldest daughter's] flute lessons. I wanted them changed to Tuesdays or I said I wouldn't take her, she'd just have to switch to another instrument. Ben wouldn't even fight with me about it. He stood his ground and said in the calmest voice, 'Are you prepared to die on this hill?'"

That fight was the turning point. It is still not perfect for Laurel at home; as she admits, she has her good days and bad days, but the proportion is better balanced now. In her household, the trick is to respect each other's role, responsibilities, and decisions. She can see that it is not so very different from work after all. A good manager needs to have her own ideas but also has to let the team members do their own thing. Her job is to get out of the way, provide support and resources, listen carefully to others' needs, and then to celebrate on occasion.

In her final interview with me, I noticed that Laurel wasn't talking about work anymore. Instead, she was toying with returning to graduate school. At first she found this desire "too much of a cliché," and she was hesitant to make a decision prematurely, admitting that she still surprises even herself by beginning to enjoy her relatively relaxed routine at home. Moreover, she's still in the dark about what field particularly appeals to her, but knowing Laurel's energy and commitment level to whatever she takes on I have confidence that she'll find her way, without compromising Sammy's care. She's one of the lucky ones. She'll have her family behind her 100 percent.

Sophie's Choice

As we grow older as women, our needs and desires change, as does our perspective on our lives. Accomplishments and activities that fed our sense of self in our twenties may feel barren or irrelevant to our fifties. Because our lives are cumulative studies of thought and activity, the choices made in earlier years always inform and impact later ones. Thus working women who transition, temporarily or permanently, to stay-at-home status may feel relieved or dejected, euphoric or apprehensive, depending upon how the stay-at-home role fits into and builds upon earlier choices.

We can also learn from women such as Laurel Andersen that we are too often quick to prejudge a lifestyle in which we have no firsthand experience. The choice to return home is a no-brainer, a windfall, for someone like Juliet Dowling, but it may take a surprisingly lengthy period for newcomers like Laurel to fully understand and appreciate. Women who have always known that they would stay at home with their children must try not to judge others who struggle with what "comes so naturally" to them. And vice versa.

Independence of thought and deed is the very hallmark of contemporary American women, at times threatening to be our undoing rather than our haven. Our trade-off for this freedom is confusion over who we are and uncertainty about the women we would like to become. These four chapters on female identity—identities that sustain us in corporate, entrepreneurial, or domestic life—inform us that we take ourselves wherever we go. The tactics to better develop our identity in each of these spheres are not really so different after all, except in the precise details. But in each sphere, I have emphasized the need for women to begin with *reflection,* followed by *experimentation* with activities and actions (some of which involve moderate personal risk), which in turn leads to further *analysis* of results and then loops back again to further *reflection.*

In my years of study and work with women, I have learned that, above all, women are starved for reflection even though surfeited by the loud demands of their internal third shift. When we listen to our third shifts without pausing to digest varying perspectives, or ask ourselves questions we haven't considered before, we are taking the risk that our inner voice will lead only to self-doubt rather than self-awareness, an unhealthy and lopsided combination. The stay-at-home choice has its deep pleasures, but in terms of identity it can pose the greatest risks of the three arenas for some women (though not all). Whereas the corporate or entrepreneurial life is externally validated and recognized as a legitimate—if not *the*—modern choice for women, the stay-at-home path can be undervalued and is often misunderstood, even by other women.

In the final analysis, the goal is to give ourselves permission to choose our own paths freely as we each deem best, to follow the route that illuminates our souls. We must not forget how fortunate we are as modern American women to entertain such choices, no matter how vexing and uncertain we experience them as modern working women and parents. We might do better to recast our perspectives on choices for women by remembering both history and literature. Two literary examples suffice. In Toni Morrison's Nobel Prize–winning novel *Beloved,* the African American mother, Sethe, kills her daughter rather than place her in slavery. In William Styron's piercing novel *Sophie's Choice,* a young Polish mother is forced to name which child will live, to be sent to a concentration camp, and which will die, sent to his immediate extermination.

We must also remember that fewer than 10 percent of American women are staying at home today because millions of our sisters simply cannot afford the luxury of this choice. For those of us able to do so, we know that a clear identity may not pop up for everyone overnight, transforming one's career self-image into a satisfying maternal identity. We must actively manage our third shift and its powerful tool of self-examination to continue and accelerate our individual development as women. If nothing else, I hope that this section has taught us that we must sometimes stop, step back, and teach ourselves how to enjoy the great gifts and opportunities we have as women.

What's Next

In Part Two, we continue from the *identity* challenge and untangle the myriad dilemmas inherent in the *task* challenge: getting the job done versus worrying about how everyone feels. At home or at work, in a corporation or in one's own business, we can lose ourselves to these twin demands. Or we can enhance our lives, our identity, and even our productivity all the more.

Notes

1. See Glenna Matthews, *"Just a Housewife:" The Rise and Fall of Domesticity in America* (New York: Oxford University Press, 1987), which leisurely explores housewifery and female domesticity in the context of history and feminist thought. The word *housewife,* as opposed to the modern term *homemaker,* has a long and honorable history, with the latter arriving on the scene about the time domesticity began to be widely devalued. When most goods required home manufacturer, the home and the person in charge of domestic tasks were highly valued.

2. Shari L. Thurer, *The Myths of Motherhood: How Culture Reinvents the Good Mother* (New York: Penguin Books, 1994), p. vxi.

3. Thurer (1994), p. vxii.

4. Susan Chira, *A Mother's Place: Taking the Debate About Working Mothers Beyond Guilt and Blame* (New York: HarperCollins, 1998), p. 254.

5. Abraham Maslow, "A Theory of Human Motivation," *Psychological Review,* 1943, vol. 50, pp. 370–396.

6. This topic is addressed in detail in Chapter Six, which covers the task challenge at work.

7. These studies are reported in Deborah J. Swiss and Judith P. Walker, *Women and the Work/Family Dilemma: How Today's Professional Women Are Confronting the Maternal Wall* (New York: Wiley, 1993).

8. See, in *Fortune,* Oct. 12, 1998, Anne Faircloth, "The Class of '83," pp. 126–130, and Betsy Morris, "Tales of the Trailblazers: Fortune Revisits Harvard's Women MBAs of 1973," pp. 107–122.

9. Sylvia Rimm, with Sara Rimm-Kaufman and Honna Rimm, *See Jane Win: The Rimm Report on How 1,000 Girls Became Successful Women* (New York: Crown, 1999).

10. Rimm (1999), p. 16.

11. Dr. Seuss, *Oh, the Places You'll Go!* (New York: Random House, 1990).

12. Elizabeth Perle McKenna, *When Work Doesn't Work Anymore: Women, Work and Identity* (New York: Delacorte Press, 1978).

13. Thurer (1994), p. 249.

14. This trend owes much to the pioneering research of a British psychiatrist, John Bowlby, who observed that orphanage babies with limited cuddling who didn't form attachments and bonds with their nurses failed to thrive. The World Health Organization published a document in 1951 that concluded infants deprived of a mother's

care were at "high risk of lifelong emotional difficulties," and further that many forms of neurosis and character disorders could be traced back to a baby's separation from the mother. The rest is history.

15. Betty Holcomb, *Not Guilty! The Good News About Working Mothers* (New York: Scribner, 1998), pp. 22–23.

16. If nonemployment is chosen voluntarily by one spouse (as opposed to unemployment, forced layoff, etc.), the conventional nuclear family describes a relatively small number of total American families, hovering below the 10 percent mark. The sustained economic recovery in the United States over the past several years has probably helped fuel this trend, at least for middle-class women.

17. This is the view taken by Joan K. Peters, *When Mothers Work: Loving Our Children Without Sacrificing Ourselves* (Reading, Mass.: Addison-Wesley, 1997).

18. In Rhona Mahoney's book *Kidding Ourselves: Breadwinning, Babies, and Bargaining Power* (New York: Basic Books, 1995), the additional point is made that "what women do at home matters a lot outside the home" (p. 4). That is, we kid ourselves as women if we think that we can achieve economic equality with men, unless we let them do half the work of raising children. "Whether or not that happens," says Mahoney, "depends on whether men can be tender and competent hands-on parents and whether women will let them do it." We should be aware that our choices to remain the primary parent at home must involve ongoing negotiations about the sexual division of work, to keep choices alive for both men and women.

PART TWO

The Task Challenge: What Are We to Do?

Getting the Task Done Versus Worrying About How Everyone Feels

*He's teaching me to be strong. You just say
yes and no and don't apologize.*
ELLEN GILCHRIST, *Starcarbon*

In Chinese philosophy and religion the world is divided into two forces, the yin and the yang. The yin relates to so-called feminine principles, drawn as the negative, dark side of the circle, while the masculine yang, the positive and bright side of the circle, is said to influence the destinies of creatures and things.

The task challenge involves its own yin and yang, and a corresponding blend of two seemingly irreconcilable foci: getting the job done versus worrying about how everyone feels. Each alternates with, reinforces, and gives substance to the other, but it can be especially tricky for women to make a satisfactory whole out of the yin and yang of the task dilemma. This dilemma haunts women, whether they choose a corporate career, an entrepreneurial start-up, or a stay-at-home life to focus on family and the community. Because women typically have stronger relational needs than men, managing the task dilemma invokes third-shift doubts as they struggle to strike an appropriate balance with the task dilemma, more often than not overemphasizing their yin at the expense of the job to be done.[1] In the corporate world, they may hold back from pushing a team too strongly so as not to ruffle feathers. In entrepreneurial start-ups, women may overly placate customers or even provide too much service relative to the price they charge. Both such strategies are ways to subordinate the actual task to the feelings of others who are involved. Finally, for stay-at-home women, the task challenge highlights even more fundamental issues: the importance of parenting and nurturing children (the central task), coupled with ambiguity about how to measure its value. Is taking care of others a task in its own right, with the attendant rewards and pleasures? Or is it sacrificing oneself to worry only about the needs and feelings of others?

My perspective on the task challenge comes from the voices of more than one hundred women in my study, as well as many years as a management consultant listening to women voice their inner third shifts. But my thoughts on the task challenge stem also, and perhaps even more profoundly, from the memories and role models of my own past. My reflections on the task challenge actually take me all the way back to my two grandmothers, Rose Shandel and Florence Berman, each of whom would be slightly over one hundred years old if still alive, and each of whom offers me a completely different lens through which to view the dilemmas of the task challenge.

Florence was a stereotypical Jewish immigrant from Lithuania who braved a third-class boat voyage by herself as a twelve-year-old to join an older sister in Boston just before World War I began. She married a handsome young pharmacist after the war; they owned a small corner drugstore in Cambridge, Massachusetts, long before it became a hip, yuppified neighborhood. Florence helped out in the store as much as she could, fitting her assistance to shopping, housecleaning, and care of their two daughters, the older of whom was my mother, Evelyn.

Florence never earned her pharmacist's degree, but she could often be seen in the backroom of the store with the heavy brass mortar and pestle used to grind and blend the various pharmacological powders prior to placement into their appropriate capsules. My grandfather was often to be found out in front, smoking a cigar and schmoozing with customers and his friends. I grew up in the fifties. I remember my grandmother standing behind the long stainless-steel counter, making mouth-watering sundaes and creamy vanilla frappés. She would frequently leave her post to see if my grandfather needed anything. In the words of Patty Montgomery's mother (to be introduced in Chapter Eight), "I can never remember her sitting down."

But my major memory involves the spectacle of Florence bustling in the doorway at lunchtime with a large, steaming iron skillet held in a pot-holdered hand, under which could be found huge portions of meat knishes, kasha and bowtie noodles, cheese blintzes or rich briskets, hearty food necessary to fuel a working man like her husband. Somehow, no one even really noticed when she slipped out of the store every day to "just run home" (approximately a one mile walk) shortly before the noon hour, and jog back as quickly as she could so the food would be hot. Grandma Florence measured her effectiveness in two ways: the temperature of the food, and the size of the portion that my grandfather Abe ate. Her "task" in those days was crystal clear: prompt, complete satisfaction of *any* needs of her husband—in the business, or on the home front (a distinction was irrelevant because she was always on call for either). Using the language of the task dilemma, I can unequivocally say that Florence always got the job done, but the real point for her was worrying about others.

Still keeping the task challenge firmly in mind—getting the job done versus worrying about how everyone feels—let's contrast this scenario with my second early role model, my paternal grandmother, Rose. A few days after graduating from the Columbia University Dental School in June 1919, my father, Seymour, was born, the elder of the two children Rose and her husband, Meyer (also a graduate of the Columbia Dental School), would have together. The couple practiced dentistry side by side in their Manhattan apartment until the mid-sixties, when my grandfather died. Rose continued to see a few patients until shortly before her own death in 1984. I grew up half in awe of her (I was so proud of having a grandmother who was a dentist). But I was also half in terror of my unconventional grandmother (who knew when she would decide I needed to have a cavity filled?).

Rose had a remarkable influence on how I think about the task challenge because she would never have gotten through even the first day of the very first course of her dental education if she had worried too much about what others thought. In contrast, Meyer was freer to concentrate on the task at hand, without a steady deluge of self-doubting, inner voices. Even understanding the underlying differences between them and the contrasting career expectations for women, Rose forced herself to learn from her husband's objective detachment to his work. She had no choice but to focus on the task at hand, a choice that undoubtedly caused her to feel quite alone with her inner third shift at times.

Even after graduating, Rose faced slights all of her life, doubts from others that as a woman she could be as good a dentist as a man (or even as good as her husband). But she never let others' judgments keep her from continuously striving to excel at dentistry, slowing down her practice as her children were born, enlarging it somewhat after my father and aunt grew up. Rose used her third shift to her advantage, dampening her doubts and playing up her self-awareness, even to the extent of using her maiden name professionally—a virtually unknown practice in those years. *Dr. Rose Shandel, D.D.S.,* was proudly engraved on a smart brass plaque in the vestibule of their office-apartment. Just above her plaque rested her husband's: *Dr. Meyer Kremen, D.D.S.*

For many years, I thought of my grandmother as an authentic trailblazer, the lone woman who had somehow injected herself into a sea of men in white lab coats—my very own task-challenge heroine. Imagine my delight when one day she pulled a sepia-tinted photo from an old album in her closet. In it, staring out at me were seven women in prewar-vintage clothing grouped around my grandmother, each either a dentist or a medical doctor. The caption underneath was scrawled in a delicate, spidery hand: "Dr. Fox's Afternoon Tea."

Today, I routinely recommend to contemporary women that they find others like themselves and enlist their support to improve managing their own task challenges. It is not always possible (or realistic) to experience all of our needs for connection to others just in the workplace. My grandmother unconsciously compartmentalized her relational needs, forging meaningful lifelong bonds with other professional women. She always poured considerable energy into her dental practice, but she often curtailed her hours to be with her family, actively and intimately. She worried only about the individuals around her whom she could influence, ignoring or overlooking the rest.

As we shall see in the following chapters, the essence of the task challenge is to effectively blend concern for others with concentration on the task at hand—a difficult undertaking at times, one that may demand lifetime effort for full mastery. But as for my grandmother, the attempt makes you a much stronger woman than you would otherwise be. Managing the task dilemma properly does not mean aiming for a Confucian middle, concentrating 50 percent on the task and 50 percent on people's feelings. Rather, it requires a subtle, if not seasoned, situational approach. Techniques to master this are described in greater detail in Chapter Five, which helps women explore the nuances of the task dilemma in the corporate arena. At the heart of the difficulty is the unhealthy tendency to perform a mental instant replay of your decisions in your third shift, a persistent, inner questioning of your actions that ultimately weakens your attention to the task. In Chapter Six, I discuss how the focus of the task challenge in entrepreneurial life switches from emphasizing your boss and coworkers to worrying over how your customers will react to you or your product. Finally, in Chapter Seven I examine the particular vulnerability of stay-at-home women in a society with vacillating understanding and respect for this crucial role.

As with Part One on the identity challenge, each of the three chapters in Part Two is rich with suggestions for women who face the task challenge in their respective spheres: corporate, entrepreneurial, or domestic life. The strategies discussed come from the numerous women in my study, those who have successfully managed the many challenges of the task dilemma, as well as their sisters who are still struggling. We can clearly learn from the lessons of each; as I specifically point out in exploring corporate life in Chapter Five, the real trick is to give yourself permission to fail and then recover and move on.

Note

1. Naturally, for many women this generalization is *not* true. In my experience over the course of this research as well as in two decades of consulting and teaching, women are consistently more likely than men to err on the relational side. This tendency is consistent with gender research on adult development patterns discussed in earlier chapters.

CHAPTER FIVE

Management 101 for Women
Doing What Matters

*A woman can be demolished just by
her own opinion of herself.*
PENELOPE LIVELY, *Heat Wave*

Amy Rosen sits in front of her fireplace, balancing a glass of Chianti on one knee and a squirming terrier puppy on the other. Superficially, she seems relaxed. Trevor, her significant other of many years, is telling her about a new novel he thinks she'd enjoy reading. Every so often Amy nods, but she offers no eye contact. It's clear she's deep into her own reverie.

Amy is thinking about work, even though she's been home for hours and Trevor has made a special trip over to spend the evening with her. Specifically, Amy is replaying in her mind—over and over again—that morning's staff meeting. As director of customer support for a rapidly growing young telecommunications firm, she has moved from an individual-contributor role to a visible and demanding leadership position. Her job is much more complex than she ever envisioned. Every day she must balance the straightforward, heads-down, damn-the-torpedoes approach that her male coworkers exemplify and value with a participative style directed at gaining buy-in from her team members. Amy has been promoted over her male peers, and as the youngest in the group she is painfully aware of how enormous her new responsibility is.

She obsesses endlessly about whether she is pushing her team too hard to meet the formal customer-service directives that are so important for the company to achieve its ambitious market-share targets. Amy never knows when she should back off and encourage the team, versus driving them even harder as they approach the goalpost. In this morning's meeting, she listened patiently to three of her subordinates, one after the other, give excuses for missing an agreed-on milestone. After the third presentation, she completely lost her cool and blurted out, "Damn it, guys! This is completely unacceptable, and you know it! I don't care if you're up all night, I want to see a solid plan on my desk tomorrow morning to turn this thing around."

Coolly and deliberately, she then stood up, shoved her papers into her briefcase, and left the room. If she had a dollar for each time she'd run through that scene in her mind, she'd be halfway to Bora Bora by now, instead of sitting in her own living room wasting a perfectly nice evening with Trevor. Of course, on her good days she is the first to agree that she's her own worst critic. Her boss has been telling her for months that she worries too much about how everyone feels. But she can't help internalizing others' reactions. She feels responsible for achieving high-performance results as well as building strong morale. Isn't that what a good leader is paid to do?

Much Ado About Nothing

Amy is not a classic workaholic. This evening aside, she fervently believes in balancing her intellectual and professional side with her personal life. Nor is she a perfectionist. Rather, like numerous professional women I've met, she suffers from the inner turmoil of her third shift. Unlike the women described in Part One, her self-doubts revolve less around her core identity and more around the task challenge. She is clear about who she is, but her third shift winds into high gear when she faces the ongoing demands of getting the job done versus worrying about how everyone feels. Let's take a closer look at this challenge for so many women.

The Task Challenge for Corporate Women

For women like Amy Rosen, equal concern about both people and results can be a true strength at work, leading to outstanding performance, promotions, and increased responsibilities and rewards.

But it can also become a crushing nightmare at times. As one high-octane female executive puts it: "Sometimes I feel like the ever-ready bunny [sic]. I have to have all the answers, be energetic and enthusiastic, and keep everyone moving. People are always amazed at how much I get done. But it's not the work that gets me. It's worrying about all the people. . . ."

Interestingly, the core of the task challenge is not a gender-specific dilemma but rather a well-researched theme at the heart of contemporary leadership research and practice. These days, most managers—from shop floor supervisors to executives in the inner sanctum—have probably attended at least one training seminar where they were introduced to a concept known as "situational leadership."[1] Using this much-touted model, managers can diagnose a given supervisory situation and decide how much emotional support employees need to do a job effectively versus how much guidance they need to properly perform the task itself. The balance depends upon the situation and how seasoned the employees are.

In Amy Rosen's situation, it's probably not fruitful for her to agonize endlessly in her third shift about how to stay on top of her team's results as well as their feelings. If she emotionally detaches herself from the situation, she can use the situational leadership framework to analyze it. The underlying assumption of the model is that managerial effort depends on the maturity level of the individual worker and how far along the worker is in his or her own development. The model groups employees into four development levels and recommends a management style for each level: directing, coaching, supporting, or delegating. The least-experienced employees require strong directing. Managers of newer workers should provide frequent feedback about their performance but worry less about how they're feeling. As employees gain experience over time, solid direction continues to be necessary, but increasing attention to their emotional needs is also helpful. (Amy shouldn't just direct; she can coach her employees at this stage, praising, encouraging, and involving them in decisions to build commitment.) As employees continue developing, the situational leadership model recommends that managers shift to an emotionally supportive role: facilitating and listening, and encouraging self-reliant decision making with less emphasis on specific guidance about the task. Finally, those managers supervising the most seasoned employees can relax their efforts even further through broad delegation. With the most-experienced workers, supervisors like Amy should empower the team to act independently, making necessary resources available for the task but distancing themselves somewhat from both the people and task concerns.

Amy is right to worry about both task and people concerns, but the situational leadership model can help her eliminate some of the self-doubts stemming from her third shift. Because her team is fairly seasoned, she can look to the model for direction and feel comfortable standing back to let her employees do their own thing. In leadershipspeak, she should "manage by exception," setting and consistently communicating the group goals, providing requisite resources, and then letting the team do its work—without undue concerns for emotional support. They know what they're doing, so they don't need confidence building, rah-rah pep talks, or special attention to how they're feeling. No third shift here for Amy, right?

The team hasn't met its stated goals, so it's appropriate for her to ratchet up supervision. Despite the members' years of experience, the team is apparently less seasoned with respect to the current task than she originally diagnosed. So she needs a supportive supervisory approach appropriate for workers further back on the development continuum. The model signals that Amy should tune in to her employees' emotional needs. The way to do this is through a participative style, inquiring into her group's concerns and frustrations, helping them with problem solving and working out whatever the difficulties are.

It appears that her leadership instincts are sound. She actually *should* be worrying about both the task and the people aspects of her team's performance issue. In gender terms, is the task dilemma much ado about nothing? Doesn't any manager, male or female, have to consider both? Or is it just Amy who's a worrywart at work? In broad terms, the research says that she follows the norm for female managers. Let's probe a bit further to understand why this is the case.

If Not Now, When?

The task dilemma is daunting for women because they often internalize interpersonal issues at work, rather than view them objectively and impersonally using guides such as the situational leadership model. Research on gender differences has found that women are highly likely to blame their own deficits for performance problems of the group; men tend to point to external circumstances when things go awry.[2] This behavioral pattern undoubtedly stems from the feminine developmental cycle discussed in Chapter One, the cultural conditioning and social expectations that reward girls for their understanding, acceptance, and empathy for others. It also makes them vulnerable to what others think, causing acute self-doubts, as in Amy Rosen's third shift:

Self-Awareness	Self-Doubt
These guys don't get it. They aren't getting the job done on time. I need to be even clearer about the importance of deadlines.	These guys never listen to me. I can't ever get it right with them.
It's possible that they still resent a woman being promoted over them. That's not the battle I want to focus on. If we can get them to ship a product, no one will care who's a boy and who's a girl.	Maybe I'm just too nice with them. Or maybe I'm not nice enough. Can a woman ever make it here?
I overestimated their ability to focus on the deadline. I think I'll increase review meetings to twice a week and see if I can scare up some temps to help them out. If we talk this through, I think they will feel encouraged.	I'm afraid to ask my boss to hire some more help. He'll think I don't know what I'm doing. Maybe he's right. I never know if someone else would have better luck with these guys.

The third shift about the task dilemma can be acute for younger women, who take so much longer than young men to trust themselves and cling to their concerns about what others think. Many bright young women I've coached have been troubled with indecision about the best way to manage. They seem to feel particularly vulnerable when most of the supervisors in their workplace are male. I especially remember Sheila Davis, a fast-speaking, outwardly assured young assistant store manager in a women's clothing chain. After three years as a salesperson, she rose over others and was slotted for further advances, according to her boss (a man). But it was much tougher than she thought to supervise store employees. People would nod their heads and then go do whatever they wanted to. Her boss wasn't very helpful, since he was never good at giving feedback or specific guidance; he just kept telling her to "follow your instincts. You'll be fine."

But she wasn't fine. She felt it was her fault that her employees weren't performing satisfactorily. She worried endlessly about whether she should be even nicer to them, or whether she should just put her foot down and give people warnings if they didn't follow through as promised. Her boss had earned a special degree in retail management, so it was easy for him to "follow his instincts"— they were buttressed with hundreds of course hours of theory and practice about how to manage in the retail environment. But Sheila had never completed college, though she did earn an associate degree. In her case, lack of experience coupled with lack of formal education fueled indecision and self-doubt. We eventually decided upon an evening business program that included practical coursework in supervision and would lead to an undergraduate degree in three years.

Once enrolled, her third shift on the task challenge calmed down considerably. She had a new perspective to inform her efforts at work, and she felt increasingly confident. Her boss agreed to get her into a company tuition-rebate program; this helped her feel valued, and she began to take more risks with her supervisory methods, being less quick to blame herself if they didn't work out.

Not everyone wants to go back to school to tone down the third shift. Besides, I've talked with women with multiple graduate degrees who still suffer indecision about the task dilemma. What can be done to alleviate the third shift on this challenge? Where should women start?

Making Your Third Shift Work for You: Managing the Task Challenge

As for the identity challenge discussed in Part One, my experience with corporate women has distilled a number of recommendations with proven effectiveness for managing the task challenge at work:

- Learn how to compete as a woman.
- Control your thoughts.
- Build respect from men in power.
- Act "as if."
- Decode your boss.
- Line up your players.
- Give yourself permission to fail, and then recover.

Every woman identifies one or two of these recommendations as hard for her to implement consistently. As with all other personal growth, the first step is often the most difficult. Sometimes it helps to know that others share your fears.

Learn How to Compete as a Woman

Despite burgeoning growth in the presence of women in the workplace over the last three decades, most of them, whether senior managers or rank-and-file employees, are uncomfortable with visible exercise of power, particularly if it involves intense competition. Indeed, until recently it was the rare woman who could take pride in openly acknowledging her competitive spirit, even if she wanted to win. Marian Burton Nelson, a former college athlete at Stanford and later a professional basketball player, surveyed thousands of women nationwide to better understand how women perceive competition. Her results show that too many women confuse "conquering" with "competing," although female athletes in her study were nearly twice as comfortable with competition as their nonathletic peers. The words of one of the athletes Nelson surveyed are worth repeating here: "So we pretend not to compete. Or we try not to compete. But just because competition can be difficult and confusing and painful doesn't mean we should retreat into a world in which no one's allowed to keep score. She who never plays the game never wins. We need to compete. But competition doesn't have to be cruel or destructive or hateful. Games don't have to be battles. Opponents need not exhibit 'killer instinct.' Winning doesn't have to be the only thing."[3]

The point, of course, is that competition by itself is neither good nor bad. Rather, competition is a heady drug that can devastate self-esteem and destroy relationships, or it can enhance confidence, relationships, and performance. Women's ambivalence about competition is understandable. As Nelson says, "Society was not designed to accommodate or reward female winners."[4]

The situation is clearly changing. In 1971, only one in twenty-seven girls played high school sports, compared to one in three in 1996. According to Nelson's logic, when these young athletes arrive in the workplace, they are not only more comfortable with competition but may even be stimulated by it enough to attain high performance. But for now, there remains a large population of working women out there who view competition negatively. Nelson concludes, "When I find competition painful, it's usually because I'm losing. Often, I'm losing a game I didn't realize I was playing."[5]

Many women discover somewhat belatedly that their workplace efforts are always a kind of competition, and not just with external rivals in the marketplace. Amy Rosen, for example, probably spends as much time trying to find ways for her former peers—now subordinates—to accept her as she spends envisioning strategic road maps for marketplace success. The two are linked, since her business vision can only be executed if her employees sign on to support her ideas. But although she accepts and even embraces marketplace rivalry, she shrinks inwardly when faced with direct competition with other employees. She is like a military pilot who can drop bombs from forty thousand feet but can't stomach hand-to-hand combat. In the workplace, however, it is necessary to play to win in both venues.

Let's examine her situation closely for a moment. If she is truly concerned about how her employees feel, she can extend the most emotional support by helping her team win—and win big. She knows that some of her employees have not yet truly accepted her as their manager. For the most part, she has deliberately ignored the minor sulking bouts, digs, and occasional whispered hallway conversations that stop as she rounds the corner. When she encounters more serious resistance, of course, she privately confronts the offender and states her expectations about appropriate workplace conduct. The main point is that rather than engaging in third-shift hand wringing, as director of customer support Amy can choose to focus her main energy externally, on the competition. If she can explicitly link her concern for deadlines to rivalry with identifiable competitors, she can productively redirect her task dilemma with her team. She can move the team energy away from "Why is she telling us what to do?" or "Why did they make her the boss?" to "How can we crush the competition?"

Her best bet is to lead by modeling a positive winning spirit, motivating and supporting her team to release new customer features and services before the competition gets a toehold. Following this train of reasoning, Amy can forget about sailing into work the next day and apologizing privately to each team member for her loss of control at that last meeting. If she does so, she undercuts her own message that deadlines are crucial for winners. Rather, she needs to hold follow-up one-on-ones to reiterate her directive that (1) the team can win, (2) the upstart firm can beat the big rivals in the marketplace, and therefore (3) the team must hit its milestones. After the pep talk, Amy must get down to serious, tactical probing into why the deadlines were missed, and then use joint problem solving to bring closure with the male teammates. This is where her attention to the interpersonal nuances proves most valuable. If she can keep her employees from becoming defensive, she'll learn the root cause of the delays and help the team systematically attack its problems. This involves an experienced combination of listening, analytical ability, and quickness in framing the key issues.

Apologies have no place in this scenario. As director, she has not transgressed. She raised her voice, pointed out a problem, and left the room so her team could discuss it. Classic guy stuff. But here's the rub: Amy is not making the progress she'd like, because as psychologist Julia Wood has said, "Men and women may be judged differently for enacting the same communication. . . . Because cultural views hold that women should be supportive and friendly, not being so may be regarded as a violation of gender role and may result in negative evaluations of women."[6]

The truth is that Amy Rosen may be viewed negatively no matter what she does. Better, therefore, to get off the bench, into the game, and produce wins—so long as she holds to her own standards of decency and integrity in her behavior with employees. "Country club management," a leadership approach associated with overly lavish concern for people at the expense of production,[7] yields Amy neither respect nor results.

Control Your Thoughts

Some women are far more vulnerable to the self-destructive and exhausting side of the third shift than others who gain confidence from their third-shift self-awareness and affirmations. But most women suffer at least a mild case of third-shift self-doubt, if for no other reason than that they feel they are always being watched and therefore must constantly prove their abilities to others. It is an extraordinary self-imposed burden, known to male minorities, and experienced as a double whammy by most women of color.[8]

In these days of disquiet with affirmative action and sensitivity to "diversity" issues, Anita Gupta stands out in my mind. A soft-spoken woman from Bangalore, India, who occasionally wore a gently flowing sari to work, she was a talented test engineer in charge of a flailing manufacturing site. Asked to turn things around, increase productivity, and shake up complacent employees, she began to do exactly that. After an initial month to diagnose the severity of the problems and evaluate her resources, she formulated a plan of action and moved ahead. She required all day-shift supervisors who reported to her to begin each day with a quick operational session, reporting progress toward the week's goals. She requested that a relatively inexperienced, ineffectual supervisor shift sites and take a position elsewhere in the company where the action was less intense. She changed the bonus structure for hourly employees from an individual-based to a team-based plan. She created remarkably quick results for the bottom line.

Anita also got the entire division into a complete uproar. "That woman," the rallying cry went, "is breaking heads over in Plant 3." Upper management stayed completely out of it, content to read reports of improving gross margins but unwilling to be in the middle of a cat fight down on the site. Anita was left alone to do her best in reorganizing the plant. Every day she came into work knowing that all eyes were on her, *that woman.* "The secretaries gossiped about what I wore," she recalled, "while the line guys bitched about what I said. The other managers were always whispering behind my back about what I was doing, and my own manager wouldn't say a word to me. But I knew he was watching. They were all watching." She caught my eye and laughed: "Some days I would wear my sari just to give them something innocuous to talk about and to keep my sanity and remember who I really am and what I was paid to do."

For most women of any color, it takes continuous willpower to live out their daily work lives free from worry about what others think of them—which is the essence of the task challenge. Indeed, some would say that the unique contribution of women in the workplace is that because they *do* worry about what others think, they are sensitive to the relational temperature around them and are correspondingly able to manage the people issues that can arise and threaten performance on any project. The evidence from working professionals in the organizational development, communications, and human resource fields, however, suggests a rather different spin.[9] Women are more likely to be hobbled than advantaged by their worries, because they send mixed signals to others when decisions must be made, don't take sufficient risks to plunge ahead without full cooperation, and mute their voices far too early in the game.

Anita's story is somewhat unusual because she was able to keep negative and self-doubting internal voices from compromising her external actions or her mission to improve plant performance. Yet shutting down the inner dialogue takes constant vigilance, self-confidence, and even denial on occasion. To the extent that women define themselves through others—a clear finding in all of the gender-based research on adult development—they are certainly going to be highly vulnerable to how others perceive them.

The trick, then, is to use our unique identity as women to empower others, rather than to imprison ourselves. A little bit of the third shift, so to speak, goes a long way. Willpower and repetitive personal mantras can be highly practical and efficient tools to control the second-guessing associated with the task challenge. Anita Gupta went home in the evening, refocused by the progress on goals from the day before, and quietly meditated on the day. She confided to me that she felt buttressed by an inner strength that came to her from her Hindu background and beliefs. Taking a slightly different approach, Amy Rosen devoted a brief, finite portion of her evening to writing on a mental chalkboard one hundred times, "Ignore the guys. Get the win. Ignore the guys. Get the win." Another woman might be unable to concentrate long enough to do this, or might even feel idiotic sitting in a chair in a meditative stupor, and instead type up the words on a card in large, boldfaced type and prop it against her mirror, or on her steering wheel where she could see her own advice daily.

Whatever the specific tactic, the key is the discipline, initially through personal willpower, to systematically teach yourself the message you need to learn. The second tool is repetition. If these things were easy and obvious for us to do, we'd be doing them! Once is never enough for a tough lesson, or to move the third-shift self-doubts completely into the self-awareness column. We know that we learn certain tangible behaviors and skills through practice drills, as we did in elementary school, incrementally adjusting goals upward until mastery is achieved.

Our attitudes are indisputably more difficult to change than our behavior, but a motivated learner can teach herself to *think*, not just behave, in new and productive ways. The trick is to focus narrowly upon a single goal or application where discernible thought control can be consistently practiced. For example, many women whip themselves into a middle-of-the-night frenzy over a stressful situation at work. At three in the morning, they replay the scene again and again. By four they are exhausted, trapped in a mental whirlpool without resolution. At five they get up, too exhausted to think clearly when they reach work. Exhaustion leads to bad decision making and poor leadership in the course of the day. The cycle continues when they wake up during the next night, struck anew by doubts because they've made yet another fatigue-induced decision.

Sleep therapists advise patients to get up and read—actually leave the bed if they can't return to sleep in the middle of the night. But first it is necessary to deliberately and consciously cut off the mental flow, recognizing that our fears apparently circulate through our subconscious while we sleep. Many high-achieving women awake suddenly with the "night willies," thinking about work in the bleakest terms, rarely with an optimistic approach. This is the worst possible time to dwell in the third shift, because it makes problems seem worse than they actually are, and you are too tired to be thinking clearly anyway. A mantra for these women insomniacs is simple and direct: "Stop thinking about this now." How ironic that, of all the women role models, it is Scarlett O'Hara who offers the most effective and most pragmatic advice: "I'll think of it all tomorrow, at Tara. I can stand it then. Tomorrow, I'll think of some way to get him back. After all, tomorrow is another day."[10]

Remember that every woman may reach the same goal—controlling her thoughts—by a unique path. For every woman who goes easily back to sleep after reciting a mantra, there's another who reaches over to a post-it on the bedside table, scratches out her worry, and then, reassured that she won't forget her ideas in the morning, rolls over and returns to sleep, confident that she can handle the issue later. Another may create a ritual worry hour, during which time she keeps her hands busy with craftwork, needlepoint, or bill paying, which demand only surface attention and allow an internal dialogue about a work problem she is facing that day. As soon as the needlepoint is finished or the bills are paid, the worry hour is over.

The real key is self-discipline. It's bad enough to be wiggling under others' judging eyes, but it's intolerable to squirm beneath our own worries and conjectures.

Build Respect from Men in Power

Of course, effectively managing the task dilemma as well as mastering its accompanying third-shift psychology involves more complexity than reciting personal mantras. It requires an appropriate balance of working with men in power and looking for their approval. These are qualitatively different behaviors and attitudes. The latter automatically places a woman in the little-girl–daddy conundrum, with predictably negative results. Imagine if Amy followed this scenario with her boss, Hal, as she struggled to overcome team resistance to her promotion:

Amy: I wish I could figure out how to make them respect me.
Hal: You've got some hard cases there for sure, Amy.
Amy: Can you back me up on this new initiative? I don't think they're going to listen to me.
Hal: If you think that's what you need, I'll try to help you out.

Without understanding much about Hal's personality and motivations from this little scrap of conversation, it is safe to assume that he doesn't really object to his role as daddy. He agrees to help her without exploring other options, or *giving* her a chance to prove herself first before bringing his influence to bear on the situation. In parallel, Amy is a coconspirator in her own approval-seeking behavior because she is the one who asks Hal for help before airing any other strategies. This keeps her in the protégée role. Despite his good intentions, Hal is actually reducing her ability to build respect from her team. An ineffective dynamic colors the relationship between them. Amy asks. Hal gives. Hal feels good about himself. Amy doesn't learn how to stand up for herself. But she gets his approval. The jury is out as to whether she earns his respect.

Listen to another type of conversation:

Amy: I'm having the devil of a time with these guys. It's a learning experience, for sure.

Hal: What can I do to help?

Amy: I appreciate the offer. Right now, I'd like to work this out on my own. If I run into a wall, I'll be back, don't worry.

Hal: Are you sure you don't want me to say something? Why go through this on your own?

Amy: Perhaps I'm wrong about this, but I think my best strategy with this group is to detach myself from you and build my own authority with them. I'm sure there will be times when I'll want to bring you in as the big gun, but that time isn't now. But thanks for the offer. Do you want me to go over some ideas I have to turn things around with them? Or, I can just keep you posted on how things are going.

In this rendition, Hal is the same, but Amy is different. She keeps her options open with him, leaving him room to help but gently distancing herself from him—which is a risk, but one necessary for her own development. She also exercises good judgment by promising to update him on progress, thus keeping him involved but without submitting her ideas for approval. Complete independence can be as foolhardy as having her boss do everything for her. In the end, the middle path Amy has chosen yields the best mutual foundation for a true partnership with an influential man in power. Whether managing upward or working to gain respect from her team, Amy needs patience and resilience if she is ever going to assimilate while maintaining her own practices and values.

She can take a lesson from Sun Tzu, the ancient Chinese strategist who advises modern executives that the best competitive strategy is to avoid the battle altogether. He would remind Amy that, ultimately, superior ideas are always more powerful than superior force, as in the child's game of rock, paper, scissors. It's an appealing thought in the abstract, but how can she put it into action? At the risk of stereotyping, we know that a persistent, if not defining characteristic of powerful men is their need to win. Big ideas help them do so. Amy can build respect by articulating and then acting on big ideas. Yet many women in her position are embarrassed and reluctant to openly trumpet their talents and triumphs.

Recently, I began coaching a senior female executive, Gayle Connor. She is highly respected by others and trusted broadly, but her manager, a division president in a large software firm, recommended her for executive coaching at the same time he promoted her to a vice presidential rank. "She's doing a vice president's work, and she deserved the promotion," he said, "but she sure isn't acting like one." He expressed to Gayle his concern that she has difficulty influencing her peers because she never states her point of view with conviction. "She's too worried about whether she'll hurt anyone else's feelings. The irony," he finished, "is that she has such a great reputation for working with people, she'd practically have to pull a gun on them before they'd think she was doing something wrong."

As successful as Gayle appears to be from her position within the company, she still tends to interact with others using inappropriately self-effacing language:

I have an idea that might work.	Level I (tentative, not confident)
I have an idea that could work.	Level II (better; who cares?)
I have an idea that will work.	Level III (direct, effective)
I have an idea I know will work.	Level IV (confident, credible)
My idea is best.	Level V (over the top, arrogant)

Compared to saying nothing, the Level I script can be a starting point for women who have real difficulty asserting themselves, but the modest, self-deprecating tone undermines the message. The pace in modern corporations is too fast, the competition for resources and attention too great, and the noise level of events too high for modesty to prevail. On the other hand, there is considerable fertile territory between the Level I and Level V statements. With rare exceptions, a Level V statement can strike the listener's ear as an example of reckless, self-centered assertion, alienating others rather than creating interested listeners and followers. For crucial situations, aiming at a Level IV pronouncement is desirable. People want to win. They want to follow someone who has a track record and who displays visible confidence in her own ideas yet is willing to listen and evaluate the input of others. We have come full circle to the task challenge and the need for women like Amy to keep an eye on both the task and the people. Too much concern about just one, as in Gayle Connor's concern about others' feelings, is self-defeating.

Act As If

"Imply power," advises Harriet Rubin in *The Princessa*. "That's the secret. That's the fulcrum by which strategy works: the lever of implied power."[11] While we're waiting for that glorious day when full gender equality arrives, we act as if. During the first two years of his presidency, for example, Bill Clinton acted as though he knew exactly what he was doing (he clearly didn't). Harriet Tubman must have acted-as-if a hundred times during the years she conducted her branch of the underground railroad. God only knows how many times Jane Goodall had to act-as-if during her first few lonely years of chimpanzee study in the bush of Tanzania.

Amy Rosen, too, repeatedly acts as if, when she faces new challenges and first-time assignments such as her directorship. Anxious at times that she should never have been promoted over the guys—because she is newer to the company, because she is their junior in age, because she is less savvy about the industry, because, because, because—she has nonetheless learned that she will devour herself if she lets that inner negative voice overwhelm her. Hence she agonizes privately in the evenings, but at work she rarely shows her doubts—a strategy that works. At thirty-one, she *is* the youngest, newest, and only female member of her team, and she's the boss.

She acts as if she knows what she is doing, and on most days others buy it. Several of her employees are even beginning to draw comfort from the sense that their boss knows what she is doing.

This doesn't mean that she pretends to know things she really doesn't. One of her secrets is to ask timely questions, and to collect reasonable data to back a decision. She is also skilled at pulling her team members around her and drawing input from everyone. Then she musters her courage and commits to a course of action. If everyone around her vociferously rejects her plan—which rarely happens—she reconsiders and invites a new decision-making process. If only a few naysayers try to detract from her decision, she continues on her course, bringing in other supporters of her ideas to convert the malcontents; when all else fails, she simply ignores her negative coworkers as much as she deems prudent.

Thus, to gain respect from her team Amy's personal act-as-if behavioral repertoire must include visible decisiveness and personal responsibility ("I'd love to know more about this problem before deciding, but we have to put a stake in the ground now. I'll take responsibility if I'm wrong"). She must also demonstrate her commitment without needless sacrifice of her personal life ("As much as I'd like to work on this until midnight, I know that we're all tired and not really capable of making a good decision now. Let's call it a night and come back an hour early tomorrow morning to finish this up when we're fresh"). Finally, she must also be perceived as willing to get her hands dirty on occasion, standing and fighting for her point of view to show that she's really serious ("I may ruffle a few feathers here, but this is not a popularity contest. I believe we are going in the wrong direction, and I'm not budging from my position until I hear some stronger arguments from all of you").

Throughout this act-as-if scenario, Amy's third shift may be running full volume in the background. She may be questioning whether her idea will even work, or if her approach is going to be the right one after all. But she has learned that the best way for her to manage her inner doubts is to move forward and act. Her third shift allows her the reflection she needs to analyze a situation and decide upon a course of action. The voices of self-awareness allow her to act authentically, in direct alignment with her inner values. She is often uncertain, but she realizes that reflection without visible action won't quiet her third shift. And it sure won't get the job done. So she acts as if.

Decode Your Boss

A final strategy that Amy should append to her act-as-if modus operandi involves the further work and study required in understanding her boss. (Who said this was going to be easy?) She must make certain that she is crystal clear about Hal's expectations, and that she knows where he stands on any of her bigger decisions. Thus she checks in with him regularly, neither making a dependent pest of herself nor operating as a maverick. It's not surprising that so much has been written about handling one's boss.[12]

The reality is unmistakable: most employees experience job satisfaction through an adequate level of challenge, resources, recognition, and the feeling that they can personally make a difference. In contrast, employees experiencing job dissatisfaction typically point to difficulty with their immediate supervisor, their boss. It's likely to be trickier for women, although the starting place remains the same for understanding the true nature of the employee-boss relationship. Bosses can provide resources, air cover, visibility, and stretch assignments. The best offer just-in-time coaching as a bonus. These commodities are not a given. Rather, they arise from tacit exchange with the employee, who in turn offers task completion, strong ideas, information about what the troops are thinking, and loyalty. Like their employees, bosses are unique individuals, but they share several important characteristics that affect the boss-subordinate relationship. Each of these has a distinctive gender twist.

First, developing a *compatible* work style is the most practical way to enhance the relationship. What does this mean to the average woman who reports to a male supervisor? What if your boss, for example, is like Field Marshal Rommel, complete with a brilliant red scarf fluttering behind him, while you lean more toward a Meg March persona—plain of style, quiet, and reserved, yet loyal, competent, and responsible? Must you learn pizzazz or fail? Must you contort yourself to deliver the old razzle-dazzle that might capture Rommel's attention? Must you adopt not just a more energetic style but one built upon a masculine standard of effectiveness?

You are always most likely to succeed if you work from your strengths, rather than trying to emulate a style diametrically opposed to your own. Nonetheless, you can learn a great deal from the flair of a Rommel-type boss, and you can experiment incrementally with how to turn up the volume of your approach—if not with your clothes, then with your actions.

Let's revisit Gayle Connor, whose natural reserve and modesty has more than once kept her from receiving the attention her ideas deserve; she knows this from feedback she has received repeatedly from her boss. In our coaching sessions we talked about some ways she could improve her presence in formal presentations, be more innovative about them, and have a lot more fun. Her boss was a fairly flamboyant type, always egging her on to assert herself further or to jazz up her presentations. This would lower the risk of a flop (defined by boredom from the audience). In Gayle's case, we struck a nerve when we discussed fun, because she was ever on the lookout for ways to help her coworkers benefit.

We began by analyzing the last staff meeting she had led, when she first discussed the worse-than-usual results for her group. It was a tense hour, and no one wanted to venture any new thoughts about how to turn the situation around. Looking back on the meeting, Gayle and I brainstormed a way for her to present these dismal findings formally at a quarterly review meeting that was to occur the week after our session. Her boss would be there along with a number of other senior managers. After thinking for a while, she decided to begin the meeting by placing a lemon on everyone's chair before people arrived. As they came in, she would just smile, perhaps nodding at their curiosity. When it came time to present, she would pop a pitcher of lemonade in front of the overhead projector. The message would be clear, and then she would launch into her recitation. Of course, Gayle must be certain to back up the theatrical props with real substance, and a detailed game plan to improve project performance and ensure that the lemons really became lemonade.

The "lemonade meeting," as it came to be called later, worked surprisingly well. She was able to create a lighthearted atmosphere to discuss the bad news, and she kept people interacting effectively as she presented her group's recommendations on turning the situation around. She received considerable positive feedback, and it helped her come to stunning realizations about herself. At first, she was nearly terrorized that the whole idea was silly, and that she would make a fool of herself. But she was determined to risk something new. She also realized that her first attempt might not succeed, but that she should keep trying anyway. With the early success of the "lemonade meeting," the strangest thing happened, *because Gayle was completely honest with herself.* People did pay her more attention, and she actually liked the positive regard and compliments once she launched herself into the limelight.

We discussed how so many women hide their light under a bushel, not because they want to but because they don't know how to step out into the light without failing. It is not the light they fear, but the chance that their failure will be publicly exposed to others, perhaps even magnified. The learning here is not for Gayle to become more like her boss; it involves observing and then experimenting with new, interesting ways to improve her own effectiveness and challenge her true fears, rather than assuming that her style is perfect as it is, or that it can't be changed because it is what it is.

Of course, there are many ways to improve style complementarity with your boss. For example, if your boss likes facts, figures, and daily e-mails to report on results, by all means provide them, even if you roll your eyes privately. Why not grease the wheels of commerce? Over time, giving the boss what he wants leads to greater freedom—or at least less frequent reporting in.

What about the opposite style conundrum? What if the woman is a flashy, visionary go-getter and the boss is a dull-as-dishwater guy who's easily threatened by someone with more energy? The answer is straightforward. Tone down some but not all of the dramatics when the boss is around, and always focus on tangible results. Wouldn't you rather be known for solid results than mere flash? Then too, consider how much of your behavior, deep down, is really nothing more than raw resentment that your boss's dullness is rewarded with a bigger job than yours. Is rubbing his nose in his dullness going to improve your case at all? Probably not. On the other hand, why become a pale shadow of yourself, locking up your spirit, creativity, and drive so you won't offend someone? Like most of our choices in the workplace, it's a trade-off.

A second, fundamental approach to boss management is making your loyalty visible. When you are in charge, it's exhausting if you always have to arm-wrestle your employees over every little detail. It's one thing to have to take extra steps to influence peers, particularly in a matrix or team-based organization. It's another thing entirely to submit to the political machinations of gaining resources and support from senior executives. But with your own team, it's nice to enjoy reasonable—though not blind—loyalty. Your boss feels the same way. This means going along occasionally, even if you disagree. If you are in *continuous* disagreement about how to do your job, this signals that it's time to move on.

You might position your conflicting viewpoint up front with your boss. I recall such a situation with Alex Borrone, a warm, straightforward female manager with a giant heart, waving hands, and always a story on her lips. She was vivacious, bold, and outspoken; her boss was frequently taciturn and indecisive. If ever there was a case of the odd couple, Alex and her boss, Scott, were it. Others in the department raved about how she was able to work her boss, but without being manipulative or "sucking up." Instead she was herself, though always conscious of the difference in their styles, which made her thoughtful about how to present herself in front of him when he was feeling particularly insecure or testy about an important decision.

She was able to be true to her thoughts and yet attend to the relationship with him by saying outright, "I certainly don't agree with your approach, Scott. The data suggest that our other strategy will be more successful." This got the issue out on the table quickly, which helped to manage his tension. But she would then tag on a visible reminder of her loyalty. "If you're truly satisfied that this is how to proceed, however, I'm on board with you." This approach was highly effective. It opened the door for a true dialogue about *why* she was hesitant, and the conversation helped to influence him to change his stance, without threatening the foundation of loyalty she was trying to build.

The third rule of thumb to follow with one's boss is to use his or her time sparingly but strategically. Most employees—leaving out the lone ranger types—would love to have more private time with their boss. Returning to Amy Rosen's case, Hal is the company's president and founder, and his calendar is always overflowing with people who simply have to talk with him. He promoted her to director because he thought she would be the employee who would least involve him in day-to-day workplace strife, could be counted upon to produce on deadline, could distill the important from the trivial and report to him accordingly, and could figure out a way to overcome most problems. In sum, he needed Amy to be confident enough to do her own thing, but not so independent that she would balk at all his suggestions or report back so infrequently that he wouldn't know what was going on in his own company

Obviously, Hal has real confidence in her judgment and strength—two qualities, alas, that many of us (men and women) can spend a lifetime trying to develop. Most salient here, his confidence in her stems from personal observation. He has seen her in action, making hard decisions when necessary. He has noted how flexible she can be with others without becoming a pushover. From his standpoint, the gamble of promoting the newest (female) kid on the block over the old boys was a good bet. If she spends too much time worrying on her own time about everything that goes on during the day (a bad habit he knows she's careful to hide, but it creeps through on occasion anyway), he figures she'll get over it if the workload becomes heavy enough. The main thing is that *he* is not going to go home at night and ruin what little free time he has, whipping himself into his own third shift and worrying about whether Amy can do the job.

Line Up Your Players

You can be your boss's best friend, but that's still no guarantee of workplace success. You need others, even if they don't work for you. A few years ago, a Silicon Valley newspaper columnist termed the region the world's largest ADD (attention deficit disorder) theme park. Whether in Silicon Valley or elsewhere on the globe, overachievers tend to run the corporate world. Keeping up with their elevated expectations and constantly shifting priorities can be an exhausting struggle. Stamina helps, but a clear strategy to work laterally through one's peers is the real answer. It's not enough to prod your own team into high gear. In the new world of virtual teams, outside contractors, and sister departments anywhere from Singapore to Amsterdam, you must learn the skills to engage your peers on projects that you're responsible for but they are not. It's the E word that you hear all the time *ad nauseam* but still see precious little of: *empowerment*. Untangled, it's little more than politics, the ability to use positive political skills at work.[13]

Far too many women become churlish at the suggestion that they must play politics, their body language suggesting that such activities are the moral equivalent of drag racing through a school zone while children are outside at recess. They hide behind the view that those who succeed through politics are somehow cheating. These women are being less than honest with themselves. Understandably, women locked out of the club have a tough time decoupling politics from genuinely exclusionary practices and discrimination. Moreover, playing politics is often associated with shallow, ingratiating, manipulative, or outright dishonest behavior behind closed doors. Who wants to spend even more time at the office doing *those* things?

A more productive approach is to look in the mirror. When is a knee-jerk dislike of corporate gamesmanship really envy of others who do it well? When is it intolerance for those who abuse the game and the other players? When does dislike of politics mask simple fear? Let's take a closer look at what's involved rather than avoid this difficult but necessary requirement of corporate life.

Few would debate that the most influential leaders develop organizational strategies to work with others and position their ideas through positive political influence. We expect our leaders to possess organizational savvy, but without offending others by being too political. Hence, there are several ways women can get in trouble over politics: by focusing so much on the quality of ideas that the opinions of others are neglected (this constitutes ignoring politics altogether), by overusing political influence skills and losing credibility, or by hanging out with the wrong people and spending too much time with supporters of one's ideas rather than the resisters (preaching to the choir, if you will).

These challenges confront all managers, yet women often face special difficulties. Amy, for instance, feels uncomfortable running around the firm tooting her own horn. Her male colleagues, though, from their earliest years are much less likely to have conscious or subconscious messages ingrained into them about the desirability of modesty. As a practical matter, this gives guys a head start on corporate politicking. Women have to crank up the volume on their networking efforts to compete.

A useful analogy comes from the advertising field. New products require five times the advertising muscle of existing offerings, just to compete with the ordinary noise level in the market. If Amy barely tiptoes into the politicking game, she's unlikely to glean any benefits from her efforts and can easily lose her confidence, and then tell herself it's a waste of time before giving it a full trial. Moreover, women like Amy Rosen are often less well networked, sometimes even locked out of the comfort zone of the elite men in power. Recent studies in the psychology of gender are illuminating. Just as little boys prefer to play with boys on the playground and little girls with girls, adult networks are still gender-segregated for the most part.[14] To the extent that men hold the reins of power at work, women face a long, hard road to line up the support they may need for a given proposal to succeed. Daunted by the perceived difficulty and time challenge of the gamesmanship task, many women simply give up at the starting blocks.

But it doesn't have to be this way. Imagine, for example, that Amy wants to inaugurate an entirely new customer service that she believes will put the company on the map. The problem is that she has insufficient funds in her own department to properly develop the concept, let alone pilot its execution with a key account. She needs the support of other key executives, but nobody else cares about this problem as much as she does. How should she proceed? Consider these supposedly political activities to be beads on a necklace, all tied together, beginning with the bead nearest the clasp:

1. Anticipate objections in advance.
2. Build a coalition of support around your issue.
3. Choose your battles wisely.
4. Spend face-to-face time with critical players.
5. Identify common ground.
6. Understand what motivates others.
7. Analyze your supporters and resisters.
8. Use both formal and informal communication channels.[15]

Amy's first step is to clear time on her calendar to reflect quietly on all the reasons people might object to her project, to come up with sound counterproposals for each objection. Next, she needs to walk her proposal around, actually asking people for their objections directly ("Why won't this work?"). Or she can bring up objections before they do ("You're probably thinking this is going to cost too much"). Her next step is to presell her thinking to key people in informal face-to-face meetings before committing to delivering formal presentations of her request. Finally, she must get these individuals to publicly commit their support ("I would appreciate your public support at our next staff meeting"). This reduces the chance of people who profess support in a private conversation unaccountably clamming up during the real moment of truth in a meeting when their support is most needed.

Flexibility, not just politicking, is critical. Amy has to define the one or two areas that are critical to success and not concede them, while walking away from skirmishes on other aspects of her proposal. She must choose her battles and even resort to surrendering minor areas of opposition for agreement on the larger goals ("I think you're right about that point. . . . I'll give you this one, so we can get started"). Now is no time to be a purist on the details, but it is helpful to always elevate the conversation to a higher plane, agreeing explicitly on common goals first and using face-to-face time to work through the rest. As the necklace of political activities indicates, there are no shortcuts to success. Personal time, informal chats, and formal reports and presentations are all necessary to motivate a large group of people around a new idea and sustain their interest and commitment.

Resistance is inevitable, of course, and Amy must be careful not to take objections personally. Clearly, this is an area where managing her third shift can be particularly fruitful. If she doesn't succumb to self-doubt, she can start to connect with the people whose support is critical and get them to act as emissaries in soliciting support from others ("Rick, you would be so effective in talking with Bill. He's not happy with my approach. Will you help?"). In sum, she should take a snowball approach to building a coalition of supporters, starting small and aiming her efforts to keep it rolling.

For women who feel overwhelmed by this entire process, it may help to view it impersonally as a people road map (an integral part of routine project management). Most employees feel that a written product road map or plan is essential to timely release of a new product or service, but they may be more naïve and thus reluctant to plan how they can line up people as well.

Give Yourself Permission to Fail, and Then Recover

There's no question about it: managing others is complex, rewarding at times, frustrating at others, and always time consuming because it involves working through others rather than doing the job by oneself. You will always make mistakes, learning how to do the job better and how to improve your relationships with others. To the extent that women (relative to men) innately possess highly evolved relational skills and are attuned to their connections to others, they possess extraordinary potential to become effective leaders.[16] But those women who turn their concerns about people into an exhausting third-shift ritual actually face greater difficulties leading in a corporate environment. It simply becomes too tiring.

After all, the first and second shifts are tough enough. Amy Rosen is lucky. As a single female, at least her third shift is only over work issues. She has no inner voices to torment her with feelings of inadequacy, guilt, and anxiety about trying to combine work with motherhood. In fact, you could say that she has no excuse at all for a third shift in her life. Most days, she doesn't. What's her secret to keeping the inner voices in line?

She allows herself to fail.

In her case, it may be easier because she hasn't yet committed to a family, although Trevor remains a central figure in her life. But she knows she enjoys far greater flexibility, with much less angst, than her female coworkers do who have husbands and children. She sees how they run themselves ragged, how hard they push themselves, how frantic they become to conclude afternoon meetings before the whistle blows at child care. And how bad they feel about themselves.

So many women I have talked with in the past few years seem to be nearly drowning in a sense of inadequacy. Their third shifts are biased toward the negative voices. Worse, they seem to have in common the burden of inappropriate expectations for them-selves. These are women whose third shifts are running night and day because they experience the task dilemma not just at work but at home as well. In the daytime, they smooth the ruffled feathers of their colleagues or just plain grind out the work. In the evening, exhausted from their first shifts, the whole problem rears up over how much time to spend on the task (getting dinner cooked) versus others' feelings (oohing and aahing over little Johnny's art project).[17]

Because Amy's life is simpler, this works for her, not just because of her personal flexibility but because she remains open to experiences. She enjoys learning new things, at the risk of doing some of them wrong. When she visits her friends who have chil-dren, husbands, and large and attractive houses, she doesn't worry that something is wrong with her. (Nor does she conclude that their choices are all fouled up.) She tells herself that she has what she wants for the moment, and if she's wrong she'll live with the consequences or make a new choice.

At work, she also takes visible responsibility for her own mis-takes—and she's made a few humdingers—rather than blaming them on the company or her detractors. Amy would never describe herself as foolhardy or adventurous. Indeed, her staff clearly char-acterize her decision-making style as data-driven, with little room for impulse.

But she excels at recovering and moving on quickly if a deci-sion doesn't work out. This has been crucial to her success at the company. Whereas others have hit the wall with a customer prob-lem, Amy is always instrumental in reorganizing the troops to pur-sue Plan B. Moreover, this capacity to admit mistakes and learn from them allows her the mental flexibility to know that she can walk away if she fails to rally her team to the level that is necessary for her personal well-being. She has enough confidence in herself to know that she'll get another job.

Some women lack Amy's quality of openness, and they suffer from it. Feeling overwhelmed by their current existence, they are slow to consider taking on anything new. Or perhaps they are sim-ply too tired and they just give up. Either way, by blocking them-selves from new experiences and being fearful about reaching out and experimenting or simply taking what they want, women lose out. Harriet Rubin concludes that the proclivity toward self-denial is a pivotal difference between the sexes. She writes of a unique workplace disability, "power anorexia"—an actual preference for powerlessness, since fear of failure is so strong.

Oddly enough, decades of leadership research unequivocally demonstrate that successful managers actually make *more* mistakes than their unsuccessful, plateaued counterparts.[18] Alas, we are all quite different—perhaps congenitally—in the degree to which we embrace change and risk. The popular Myers-Briggs personality tests suggest one explanation of this phenomenon, while providing a specialized vocabulary to label the "types" we see around us everyday (introverts versus extroverts and so on). Certain types of people have a *preference* for order and stability, while others are drawn toward change and risk.[19] The very essence of modern corporate leadership today is one's ability to impart direction as a change agent, a role rooted in transformation and risk. Women cannot play the victim and blame the glass ceiling if their own preference for structure and certainty keeps them from taking the risks necessary to rise up the corporate ladder. Those women who run themselves ragged with a first and second shift must forgive their failures, learn what they can, and move on.

Raise the Bar

A close, unbiased reading of Carol Gilligan's classic *In a Different Voice* might lead the reader to believe that women are somehow morally superior to men because they take extra steps to value the intimate, human aspects of any situation, rather than focus solely on achievement of the task. *The Third Shift* does not take that view; I urge working women to draw forcefully upon their heritage, concerns, and commitment to relational elements of the workplace.

Nonetheless, it is downright foolish for women to ignore the obvious point of the modern corporation: efficient resource allocation in delivering goods and services. Marx might not like these mighty cathedrals of our times, but they get the job done. The U.S. economy is aflame with consumer possibilities thanks to the efficiency of our corporate titans on the one hand and the ability of nimble entrepreneurial start-ups to fill in the gaps and create new industries on the other. The point of the modern corporation, alas, is not to redress society's social ills or to redefine gender equality. This means that the best way to beat the task dilemma during our third shift is to be good in the thing your company rewards: producing results.

The good news is that modern workers, especially the gold-collared knowledge workers who drive the contemporary economy, are beginning to value, and on occasion even demand, a leadership style that involves considerable attention to empowerment, facilitation, and collective envisioning rather than commanding, controlling, and dictating. It is no longer acceptable to take the hill if too many bodies are left along the way. The expectations for leaders have risen. Results are good. Results that take the people on the journey are better yet.

If women exhibit natural aptitude for a relational approach to leadership, they can become the front-runners of corporate change, as Sally Helgesen enthusiastically champions in *Everyday Revolutionaries*. Each woman, she says, will do it in her own way, unlike the lockstep, simple portrait of the Organization Man described by William Whyte, a portrait that ultimately became "*the* paradigmatic figure of mid-century American civilization, the prism through which our culture as a whole might be viewed and understood."[20] In contrast to Whyte's portrayal of a unidimensional, conformist working man, it is the very diversity and fluid needs and styles of working women that define the new workplace paradigm. But the difficulty of bringing such a paradigm into sharper focus is what slows down its arrival and scares the incumbents in power today.

Of course, the average woman at work is probably hard-pressed to personally experience this radical metamorphosis. The solution is to keep up the pressure, every day, at every meeting, at every opportunity, with every new project. Women have the ability to improve not just how corporations produce their goods and services. They have the unprecedented opportunity to affect *what* is provided. With special relevance for the task dilemma—getting the job done versus worrying about how everyone feels—by valuing and modeling relational skills women at work can skillfully facilitate discussions, create deep levels of dialogue among workers, solve problems at a high level, and ultimately ship to market a better product. The ability to manage the task dilemma as a woman in our persistently patriarchal workplace is one of the vital keys to the kingdom, and one most frequently used. Women must make on-off choices every day about whether to focus on the result, or on the person, *at that moment*. The good news is that the merry-go-round never stops. The bad news is that the merry-go-round never stops . . . but some days you get the brass ring.

What's Ahead

Chapter Six dips into how the task challenge plays out for women in entrepreneurial settings. Corporate women may find that their third shift is most strident when it comes to worries over how to manage one's boss, peers, or employees. Women who start their own business tend to obsess over the task challenge first and foremost as it relates to clients and customers. After all, isn't the point of entrepreneurial life that there aren't any bosses to decode? The statistics about women entrepreneurs tell us that most female business owners (99 percent,[21] to be exact) don't have any employees. Thus, for these entrepreneurial women the trick is to sell oneself along with one's product or service. This means wrestling with the task challenge once again—getting it done, and getting the new business, versus worrying about how everyone feels so they'll buy from you again.

Notes

1. The original development of this model was published in Paul Hersey and Ken Blanchard's classic 1969 text, *Management of Organizational Behavior*, now in its sixth edition (Upper Saddle River, N.J.: Prentice Hall, 1992). For updated materials, contact Blanchard Training and Development in Escondido, California, or read Blanchard's best-selling management book, *Leadership and the One Minute Manager* (New York: Morrow, 1985).
2. Julia T. Wood, *Gendered Lives: Communication, Gender, and Culture*, 2nd ed. (Belmont, Calif.: Wadsworth, 1997).
3. Marian Burton Nelson, *Embracing Victory: Life Lessons in Competition and Compassion, New Choices for Women* (New York: Morrow, 1998), p. 4.
4. Nelson (1998), p. 7.
5. Nelson (1998).
6. Wood (1997), p. 359.
7. Robert R. Blake and Jane S. Mouton, *The Managerial Grid* (Houston: Gulf, 1964).

8. See Gwendolyn M. Parker, *Trespassing: My Sojourn in the Halls of Privilege* (Boston: Houghton Mifflin, 1997), for a fascinating window on the life of an African American female executive at American Express.

9. See especially Kathleen Kelley Reardon, *They Don't Get It, Do They? Communication in the Workplace—Closing the Gap Between Women and Men* (New York: Little, Brown, 1995).

10. Margaret Mitchell, *Gone With the Wind* (New York: Macmillan, 1936), p. 1024.

11. Harriet Rubin, *The Princessa: Machiavelli for Women* (Dell, 1997).

12. Despite numerous recent offerings, the best and most succinct approach remains John Gabarro and John Kotter's "Managing Your Boss," *Harvard Business Review,* May-June 1993.

13. Among the very best work on positive use of political skills is Peter Block's approach in *The Empowered Manager: Positive Political Skills at Work* (San Francisco: Jossey-Bass, 1987). The book not only is inspiring, thoughtful, and comprehensive but also involves detailed, concrete suggestions and tactics.

14. Even the process of finding jobs is gender-segregated. According to a study by S. Hanson and G. Pratt, in *Gender, Work and Space* (New York: Routledge, 1995), word-of-mouth information networks mean that women find out about job openings from other women, whereas men get their job leads mainly from men. This intensifies gender segregation in the workplace because "both men and women are channeled into jobs usually held by persons of their own sex." For a fuller treatment of gender segregation and its origins, see Eleanor Maccoby, *The Two Sexes: Growing Up Apart, Coming Together* (Cambridge, Mass.: Belknap Press, 1998).

15. Used with permission of John W. Baird and Michele Kremen Bolton, *The Leadership Box,* ©1996 ExecutivEdge of Silicon Valley, Los Gatos, Calif.

16. Admittedly, a great deal of controversy exists over this assertion that women are "naturally" tuned in to others. Moreover, as psychologist Jean Baker Miller points out in her recent book, *The Healing Connection: How Women Form Relationships in Therapy and in Life* (Boston: Beacon Press, 1997), p. 17, "many women may find it impossible to develop mutually empathic relationships in a society that sees qualities such as empathy as deficiencies. . . ."

17. As Terri Lindstrom, a woman in my study admitted, "I know I'm not really doing anything right. Deep inside, I even know it's not my fault. I know I have chosen this life, with good days and bad ones. But it's so hard to make the good days make up for the bad ones."

She looked at me for a moment and asked:

> Am I too negative? Or just being realistic? On my bad days I feel like I'm stuck in that horrible movie where you have to relive the same day again and again. For the rest of eternity I'll be sitting with my boss when he tells me someone else got the job I wanted. Then I'll be going home, creeping through traffic. I'll be coming inside to a freezing cold house. Again and again. Nothing will be defrosted for supper, and I'll be hearing a message on my voice mail that my husband was called out of town for an emergency business meeting. I'm on my own to deal with everything myself. Again. And again.

18. Morgan W. McCall, Jr., Michael M. Lombardo, and Ann M. Morrison, *The Lessons of Experience: How Successful Executives Develop on the Job* (New York: Lexington, 1988).

19. Interestingly enough, there exist no data suggesting that women are more risk-averse than men. The personality types characterizing risk preferences are evenly distributed between men and women in the database. On the other hand, the Myers-Briggs scale that examines whether individuals prefer to make decisions based on logic, data, and objective criteria—known as the "thinking" style (as opposed to basing decisions on the impact they have on people, known as the "feeling" style)—shows a higher proportion of women than men as "feelers" rather than "thinkers."

20. Sally Helgesen, *Everyday Revolutionaries: Working Women and the Transformation of American Life* (New York: Doubleday, 1998), p. 10.

21. "Women-Owned Businesses in the United States," *Fact Sheets*, National Foundation for Women Business Owners, 1997.

CHAPTER SIX

Women Entrepreneurs

Balancing Logic and Emotion

*I had never understood the unspoken rule which required
that one display false modesty and hang back when there
was a task to be done, waiting to be asked to undertake it.*
JILL KERR CONWAY, *The Road to Coorain*

Opening her third office, in Chicago, was a dream come true for
Juliet DeBono. Five years after leaving a dead-end accounting job
to open her own training firm, she was grossing over $15 million
dollars a year and loving it. Best of all, so were her employees, an
extended family of twenty-three, many of whom had been with her
from the beginning and could be counted on to stay with the
organization.

It wasn't always smooth sailing. With little formal education but
a relentlessly active brain and imagination, Juliet still remembers
how it felt to spend her days as a wage slave in an accounting firm,
hunkered over a spreadsheet, looking for ways to save somebody
else's money. Trying to bootstrap herself into a position of greater
challenge, she regularly approached her boss with ideas to provide
new training services to their clients, but he always pooh-poohed
her. One day she stepped out on her own—with only $700 in sav-
ings. Everyone thought she was nuts, but she didn't care. Juliet was
determined to show them—and herself—they were wrong.

Five years later, she had created self-confidence she would
never lose again, a business concept that stimulated regular calls
from venture capitalists, a five-thousand-square-foot home in a tony

section of town, and a unique company culture that reflected her own personality, ideas, and values. It was heaven on earth to build a company that expressed what she thought was important in the workplace. Most of her employees (and most personnel in the training industry) were female. Like her, more than half of the team were mothers with young children at home. She prided herself on finding ways to aggressively build her firm and extract a healthy salary for herself, yet also meet the broader needs of her workers. She continuously experimented with flexible work plans, schedules, and job assignments that made it possible for women to enjoy challenging work with generous compensation as well as elastic work hours. Her efforts set her firm apart from the competitors and helped ensure loyalty and retention of key employees.

On the other hand, she was scarcely a pushover. In fact, she was better at handling employees in the abstract than in person. On her bad days, she admitted that she had the people skills of a charging rhino. Her personal drive to move the business forward often took precedence over how people were feeling. She could be endlessly patient and inspirational with customers, but employees saw her other side: the anxiety, stress, and quick temper that flared up when things didn't go fast enough or according to her plan.

The designated office visionary, Juliet knew she was lacking in several areas. She placed a trusted lieutenant in the number-two role, a woman whose natural empathy and social agility made her a winner with both employees and customers. Together, these two women effectively ran the adolescent organization as a powerful, symbiotic leadership team. Still, it was always clear who was really in charge. Juliet maintained a strong hold on the reins, though on some days she despaired over the people stuff. Flying solo was a natural for her, so why was it so hard to take others on the ride?

Clipped Wings

Juliet moved from corporation to cottage, from living by a paycheck to living by her wits. In the process, she moved into an entirely new world, enriched the overall quality of her life, accelerated her professional growth, improved her finances, and escaped the intellectual tyranny of tedious work and a head-in-the-sand employer who held her back.

What Juliet did not escape was the task challenge, the ever-present creative tension between attending to the task and worrying about the people. In the entrepreneurial world, the task challenge retains some of the same elements as those discussed in Chapter Five, on corporate life. But the task dilemma for the self-employed involves some entirely new ingredients, a shift in focus from handling peers and superiors to managing customers and employees, with correspondingly different issues for third-shift angst.

The Task Challenge for Women Entrepreneurs

The good news is that the task challenge for entrepreneurs stems from success rather than failure. Only business owners with multiple customers or employees face a full-blown task challenge, because the dilemma inherently involves interaction with others, whether employees or customers. But few wannabe entrepreneurs envision, let alone plan for, the time when successful management of the task challenge spells the difference between growth, stagnation, or survival. To understand how the task challenge plays out for entrepreneurial women, it is helpful to recognize that start-ups evolve through multiple and distinct phases. As depicted in Table 6.1, each stage surfaces the new third-shift worries that are inherent to the uncertain task of transforming a vague dream into an effectively managed business.

Table 6.1. Phases of Entrepreneurship.

The Dream	A Business Concept	A Product or Service	A Company
THIRD SHIFT:	THIRD SHIFT:	THIRD SHIFT:	THIRD SHIFT:
Can I really do it?	Can I manage it?	Can I make enough money? Is this a good idea?	Who or what else do I need to take action? Can I get repeat customers or attract new ones?
Will I listen to myself?	Will I convince customers that my concept is a good idea?	Will I be able to get the resources I need to launch?	Can I organize a larger, more complex operation?

During the *dream* stage, it is the identity challenge more than the task challenge that holds a woman back or moves her forward. The questions that characterize the third shift's internal drama revolve around whether a woman can actually see herself in the dream. Can she handle the new entrepreneurial role? Does it fit with her life? And so on. Men face these questions, of course, but in my experience for women the duration is longer and the volume of the inner third shift is distinctly louder. The task challenge, in other words, remains dormant.

Transforming the dream into a bona fide *business concept* involves moving from reflection to action: researching the market, estimating initial financial requirements and commitments, identifying potential customers, and so forth. The internal worry machine of a woman's third shift now turns to external, prosaic business issues, and the task dilemma begins to overtake the identity dilemma, involving creative tension with others around shaping the concept (attention to the task) and winning the customer or investors over to the idea (attention to people). There's no boss per se in this picture, or an easily designated peer group to influence, as in a corporate setting, where a woman has an idea for a project that she must take through channels for approval and buy-in. There are no corporate politics anymore, but the task challenge remains, in a new form.

If the initial external reaction to the concept is promising, aspiring entrepreneurs move to the *product* stage, developing more detailed product or service prototypes. Even with successful transformation of the dream into a physical product or tangible service, women remain far from the ultimate goal of actually running a successful company. In early stages of product development, most of the focus must stay on the task and acquiring resources for delivery on time, in necessary quantity, and with adequate quality and performance. The people issues for most female entrepreneurs remain somewhat limited during this period, because very few women entrepreneurs actually start a new company with employees.[1] During the product-development phase, their biggest challenge is to detach and manage their own emotions while sticking to the job at hand. Winners and losers at this stage are separated by the ability to drive ahead with laserlike focus on a few crucial goals.

In the final phase of entrepreneurship, a woman's dream becomes a *company,* and the task challenge returns to center stage. The pundits warn us that inventing the better mousetrap never guarantees a successful business. Poor customer management with a great product isn't enough anymore. Only repeat customers define and ensure a real company that can be sustained over time with effective management of both the products and services—the task—and the employees and customers—the salient human elements in the entrepreneurial equation.

Thus, to understand Juliet DeBono's meteoric rise from accountant to successful female entrepreneur, we can view her ascent in terms of the task challenge and how she manages her third shift. Her natural personality focuses instantly on ideas and possibilities. New programs, new services, new customers are veritable aphrodisiacs for self-confident, natural entrepreneurs like Juliet. But even an ebullient entrepreneur, faced day after day with more rejections than invitations from conservative clients, can succumb to her third shift. In general, Juliet manages hers nicely. In our earliest conversations, when she didn't know if she'd be able to survive with one office, let alone open multiple locations around the country, I saw she was insightful about herself as well as the challenges of entrepreneurship:

Self-Awareness	*Self-Doubt*
If this doesn't work out, I have to be prepared to find another job. It will be embarrassing, but I suppose I can live through it. It can't be any worse than my last job.	Maybe I should listen to everyone else. Am I crazy? Or are they crazy not to believe in me?
This self-employment stuff is much harder than I thought it would be. People are rude and don't call back. There are so many stupid taxes. There's a whole new set of problems I didn't even know about.	I just can't get through to these people. Why can't I sell my idea to them? Am I missing something? Am I doing something wrong in the meetings?
I'm at my best when I can start something new. Of course, there's more involved in starting a business than thinking up good ideas.	It's driving me crazy to deal with all these hassles and negative people. They drag me down.

Over time and as customer acceptance improved, Juliet's third shift turned inward to personnel issues as her organization grew into the company stage. She relied upon the successful sales skills that had attracted her earliest clients to recruit her initial employees. But the additional people didn't always turn out to be the resource she hoped for. She quickly learned that there was a lot more to personnel management than good recruitment, and her third shift turned to completely new territory:

Self-Awareness	Self-Doubt
I have always been too impatient. I hate it when other people don't get it and I have to keep explaining things. It doesn't bring out the best in me.	Why can't I hire someone who understands what I need? Am I coming on too strong and scaring people away?
I'm not very good at the people stuff. There must be some other way to do this.	Why are these employees so needy? Didn't I hire the right people?

Ultimately, Juliet realized that she didn't have to do everything herself, or possess all of the leadership qualities necessary for a growing business. The ah-ha came when she hired Wendy Petersen as her chief operating officer—"at the lowly salary," laughed Juliet, "of a washerwoman." Wendy was a godsend, a natural supervisor who was efficient and organized, yet personable and trustworthy. The rest of the staff loved her. For the first year and a half, Juliet tried to emulate her superb interpersonal style, but she never got the same results. In fact, she inadvertently increased the tension in the office for her employees, who saw her as a Jekyll-and-Hyde figure, patient and concerned about them one day, curt and strictly business the next, yo-yoing back and forth along the continuum of the task dilemma. In addition, Juliet experienced immense difficulty integrating her employees' emerging ideas into her own plans. It was ironic. She had left her last employer because he didn't listen to her, and now she was developing a reputation for clipping the wings of her own people.

Her husband was the one who tipped her off. "You're never going to win the Manager of the Year Award. Get over it! Do what you do best. Hire someone to complement you, and get on with your life." It was solid advice that we can all learn from. But what else should we know if we're going to effectively manage the entrepreneurial task dilemma but we can't afford to hire our own Wendy Petersen?

Making Your Third Shift Work for You: Managing the Task Challenge

For every female entrepreneur who, like Juliet, errs too much on the task side, there are a dozen women swinging too far toward the people side. Either way, the suggestions listed here help both budding and existing entrepreneurs:

- You are in charge.
- Show your conviction.
- Manage your time and energy.
- Focus. Focus. Focus.
- Be your own role model. Build a company you can be proud of.
- Your real customers *are* your customers.
- Say no—the customer isn't always right.
- Worry about the right stuff.
- It *is* lonely at the top.

Note that the list begins with the inescapable: you, and only you, are in charge. It's liberating, but for most it's also scary.

You Are in Charge

To succeed as a woman entrepreneur, you need a clear, new professional identity and solid leadership skills. Numerous women told me of their uncertainties when they first started out. "You've decided to start your own business," one woman told me, discussing herself in the second person as though she were addressing herself in her own case study. "You might even have quit your last job. Or if you've been at home, you've tunneled through the laundry and marked a corner of the bedroom as yours, and packed the kids off to school or day care. You sit down at your new desk, your new computer humming quietly, and your phone deathly silent. There are no calls to return, no boss asking you to whip up a report, no guys from marketing hassling you for a release date for your product." She leaned forward in her chair toward me with her punch line. "What now, Coach? How do you make something happen? You're completely free, so why do you suddenly feel trapped and uncertain?"

The entrepreneurial role is new for most women, although American women have been wage earners since the colonial economy (albeit as lowly, stingily paid domestic servants).[2] Naturally, wealthier women from the upper classes with more education have made greater strides, but the point is that women are no strangers to small business, the core of most entrepreneurship. But with the possible exception of the most recent generation, most women have not been raised to lead others at work. For most of us, Margaret Thatcher, Indira Gandhi, Anita Roddick, or Debbie Fields are notable, visible exceptions, women we are proud of, though we may not personally relate to them. As a child, how many of us thought we would actually become like our role models?

I was completely captivated by the anthropological exploits of Margaret Mead, my childhood heroine, but even in the privacy of my own reflections I never seriously pictured myself venturing into the unknown as she had done. During the interviews I conducted for this book, I consistently queried women about their youthful career expectations. For women in their mid-thirties or older, having a career was a no-brainer. The question always reduced to what kind of career. But starting a business? Being in charge? The women I talked with summoned up a collective "Maybe," and no more.

A generation raised on *maybe* faces quite an adjustment to grab the entrepreneurial reins firmly. It is a surprisingly difficult transition from being told what to do, and it requires an especially high level of personal initiative, a quality that women may have always possessed but have suppressed to keep the peace. On the other hand, women have always had to be excellent at handling lonely, even harsh, adjustments. A broader perspective on how women face the unknown can help us remember that we are stronger as women than we often realize. Our history has required tremendous fortitude and ingenuity, which served us on the prairie schooners of the Kansas frontier and will serve us again in our contemporary entrepreneurial efforts.

In a contemporary parallel, a woman in my study discussed the fragility and uncertainty she felt four months after launching her start-up: "Mondays were a blank hole for me. Always. The fear would start building on Sunday morning. What would I do on Monday? Who should I call? What should I do next? Mondays were so open. So empty. The entire day stretched out endlessly with nothing I felt certain about on the horizon. But as soon as I got going, the day would get so full it was Monday again before I knew what hit me."

The essence of today's entrepreneurial experience is that women are in charge, rather than along for the ride, and they must hold the reins themselves. For some women, visible and assertive leadership comes naturally. For others, it's a true struggle, but the must-haves in your entrepreneurial toolkit are two things that any woman can do: (1) visibly show your conviction and excitement through positive personal energy, and (2) discipline your approach to time management.

Show Your Conviction

Even for the most reserved woman, enlisting passion and positive energy is among the most important assets in holding the entrepreneurial reins. Best of all, it's renewable. Unlike millions in venture capital that you can burn through in months, passion comes from within, and you never have to ask permission for more. Better yet, it's contagious. Others follow your lead when they see and feel your conviction.

To elicit the greatest return from your personal energy, begin by focusing it on the business concept that excites you in the first place. With regard to the task dilemma, focus first on the task and defer your worries about people. Build up your idea, concentrating especially on articulating a personal vision that readily describes the advantages you are promising (we discussed how to do this in Chapter Five). Develop a brief business plan that specifies your competitive advantage, your target market, your strategies to reach that market, and your anticipated costs in doing so.[3] Only after your concept is well established in your own mind should you turn your attention to worrying about what others think.

Juliet DeBono exemplifies this point. Stymied by her boss, she convinced herself it was now or never and left her day job. She deliberately transformed herself from an accountant to a salesperson by developing a pitch—a compelling version of her business concept that highlighted client benefits through a simple pricing formula and an initial package of services. Each time she delivered this presentation, she noted what prospective clients responded to and what puzzled or dismayed them, and she refined it further. Even on days when she felt far from energetic, she says, "I plastered a smile on my face and got out there. I believed in myself, and it was just a matter of time until someone else did, too." Because no one else in her industry was offering her approach, her personal energy was the single factor that built up client acceptance. She was very honest about the novelty aspect, admitting that her idea was unproven, so she positioned her services as leading-edge. She also listened very carefully and intently to their concerns, leaving clients with the clear impression that she understood them.

It took months, but eventually she landed her first client, guaranteeing survival cash flow that took her through the first difficult year. It's easy to understand the keys to her success. She is persistent, organized, and hopelessly in love with her idea. With clients she's like a windup doll, her eyes aglow as she regales them with benefits they'll realize from her services. For those of you without Juliet's natural passion and self-confidence to get up every morning and beat your drum, more pedestrian time-management techniques can help you hold on to those entrepreneurial reins.

Manage Your Time and Energy

The second entrepreneurial must-have is using a practical, disciplined system to keep you going and keep you organized. In addition to a formal business plan, an operational *work plan* imposes structure and purpose on your days and activities. I have seen countless women forge ahead successfully once they know exactly what they are supposed to be doing every day; those same individuals floundering if they have no clear picture of their activities. One woman I interviewed articulated this clearly: "As a mom you're just running around all day reacting to your kids—'I'm thirsty,' 'I'm hungry'—and at work you have a zillion emails to reply to and a boss who never runs out of stuff for you to do. I thought it would be great to manage my own schedule. I never knew it would be so hard to figure this out on my own."

Mundane as it sounds, every successful new business owner I interviewed kept some type of weekly schedule, complete with goals to be accomplished and a list of the activities necessary to meet those goals. Some women preferred expensive day-timer notebooks or a handheld electronic gadget; others did perfectly well with three-by-five cards (Table 6.2).

Note that tough activities such as cold calls are dispensed with early in the week, rather than left to hang over your head. However, each day contains a deliberate blend of hard and easy work. "Hard work" can only be defined individually, since it involves those things with which you have least experience or confidence. For many women, this translates into any activity requiring accounting or financial expertise, an area female entrepreneurs routinely identify in formal self-appraisal surveys as weak (while perceiving their ability to deal with people as strong).[4] In the work plan of Table 6.2, you'll see that this woman treats herself to a facial on the day she works on her budget!

You can also see that this schedule deliberately builds in variety and discipline, giving you a solid reason to leave the house on most days, at least for a little while. For home-based business owners, these time-outs are crucial—so long as the trips are really necessary

Table 6.2. Sample Weekly Workplan.

Monday	Tuesday	Wednesday	Thursday	Friday
4 cold calls	Lunch with ABY (supplier) get 3 recommendations for their competitors	New pricing model based on ABY's quote	Follow-up Monday's calls	Make next week's goal sheet
Fix modem			Go to printer with quotes	
Visit customer site to finalize proposal		Meet new bank manager; establish credit line	Facial	Fold 500 brochures
	Shop for new desk chair		Compute budget for next month	Design ad

to create business. It's not uncommon for women to sabotage themselves by going out to shop to relax and distract themselves from slow business. At the end of the month, there are no new customers, only a raft of unpaid bills.

Also note that all of the activities listed in the sample work plan of Table 6.2 are easy to check off when done, to give you a clear sense of accomplishment. In fact, this is the *real* benefit: the work plan offers emotional as well as task support. In this vein, note that the week involves fewer, rather than more, activities than you are likely to complete in a week's time. Achieving your stated goals is crucial to building confidence and personal energy. Contrast this approach with the sense of failure you may feel if you don't make it all the way through your list; how much energy will you have to wind it all up and start again next week? Finally, notice that I've included some downtime and fun things in the sample schedule. Crazy as it sounds, these days many women have to schedule this in if it's really going to happen.

As you grow your business and confidence, your time horizon undoubtedly shifts to a monthly or quarterly focus, with less-detailed daily planning. But for those who are raw beginners at the entrepreneurial game, looking ahead too far at the daily activity level becomes a depressing and meaningless exercise in charting the unknown. This type of tactical work plan is clearly not a substitute for a good product, an exciting vision, or strong sales skills. Nor is it leadership. But like the pioneer women on the Kansas plains who had never held the reins before, taking small steps day after day helps thousands of women safely traverse lonely, dangerous territory toward their destination.

Focus; Focus; Focus

You've heard these colorful phrases again and again: "Take that hill!" "Keep your eye on the ball!" "Lock and load!" "Take no prisoners!" It's all guyspeak, of course, but guess what? Men who pay attention to this language know how to focus. That's why they say these things, to remind themselves not to slow down, not to get sidetracked until they get that result. There's no reason women can't do the same, and millions of successful women do exactly that. Unfortunately, many entrepreneurial women, even after they've powered up their sales pitch to the point where customers are salivating, have difficulty staying the course and following through. They're all potential, never performance. In fairness, women with families and a second shift are drawn in multiple directions, and focusing *is* more of a challenge.

Arielle Gold is one of these women. She's a hummingbird, endlessly flitting from flower to bright flower, taking a few drops of nectar and then moving on. All her clients agree that she is a talented commercial artist. She's bright, personable, and unusually gifted. After you meet her, you are convinced you'll have the best product brochure or sales material you've ever seen. Her ideas are glorious, her presentation dazzling. She whips out her little notebook and jots down the next meeting time with you. Right then and there, you should be tipped off. A wad of loose paper falls out of her engagement calendar when she opens it up. She stuffs it back and races out the door to her next meeting—late again, cramming in a meeting at her daughter's middle school (she volunteered for yet another assignment even though she contributed dozens of hours earlier in the semester) before meeting with her next client.

Arielle is not only over her head and out of control but also a veritable Calamity Jane as a woman entrepreneur. Her clients refuse to contract with her for more than one project. Because she can't focus her considerable energies, she has a tendency to overpromise and underdeliver. Her projects are always behind, and although she talks a good game about planning, there is always something that goes wrong with each and every project. At the root of this problem is her inability to overlook any opportunity. She'll start on one thing and halfway through chase down something else. Nor is this a simple multitasking deficiency. Deep down inside, she is afraid another opportunity won't come and she'll have lost her chance at expanding.

She fails to see that expansion isn't her problem; inability to focus is the real culprit. By overloading her plate, Arielle never really devotes enough effort to any one job she has agreed to take on. She can't build momentum—the ultimate acid test for new entrepreneurs, or for soldiers charging a hill, or for runners sprinting the quarter mile lap, you name it. When small obstacles creep up, she doesn't notice them until it's too late. When obstacles loom larger, she often becomes physically ill from stress, placing herself even further behind in an endlessly negative cycle. Because old clients don't hire her again, she is constantly seeking new ones, a costly and time-consuming process.

Ultimately, Arielle joined a women entrepreneur's group at my suggestion and was assigned a personal mentor, a seasoned business pro with a no-nonsense style. Her mentor gave it to her straight: "Cut down your obligations. You obviously can't fulfill all of them. Have you noticed that as soon as one project starts getting complicated you immediately take on another one? What are you running from?"

No one likes to be psychoanalyzed, but in Arielle's situation a stronger intervention was needed than even a business mentor could carry out. She admitted that she often agreed to take on work—with paying clients, or as volunteer community assignments—because she was worried what people would think if she turned them down. (She didn't even understand that people were already thinking negatively about her for saying yes!) Apparently, she measured her worth only in terms of pleasing others—family, community, customers. She had completely succumbed to the task challenge.

In the end, Arielle withdrew from business, realizing that less-frenetic family time and regular, personal community involvement were actually more important to her than her commercial art business. She speculates that she'll try again when her children finish school. She acknowledges that other women may be able to effectively handle all of these things simultaneously—albeit with moderate success at each. But she sees now that with her personal vulnerability to distraction and overwillingness to help others, she is not a good candidate for self-employment. It hurt her deeply to realize this personal limitation, but at least she now has a better chance of focusing on what actually matters to her most.

Be Your Own Role Model

Some women's personalities allow them to focus more easily than others, particularly if their energies are channeled toward the tangible goal of building a company they can be proud of. As a woman entrepreneur, you have a tremendous opportunity to use effective management of the task dilemma—balancing your concerns for people with the task—to carve out a distinctive company persona and culture that reflect *you*. Your basic personality may have a built-in bias toward one pole or another of the task dilemma; you can express this preference through every act and decision associated with your new company.

Like the concentric rings of a woman's individual identity, your company—even if it's a sole proprietorship—is a unique entity with its own layers of identity. The core inner values of the inner rings are visibly reflected by the policies and workplace practices you and your employees implement. The visible look of your business forms the outer kernel; it includes how you design your company logo and materials, as well as the way you furnish your personal business habitat, and whether you're squeezed into a basement or have just leased a ten thousand square foot storefront (Figure 6.1).

Figure 6.1. Your Company's Identity.

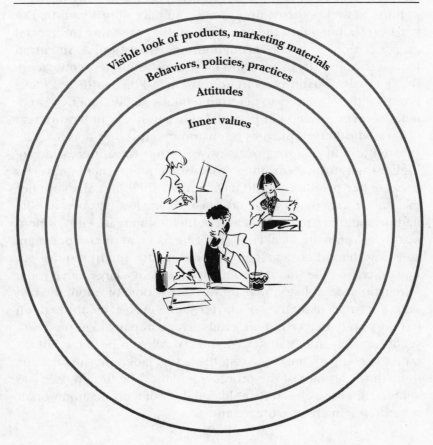

When I reflect upon company identity, I think first of Sheryl Rodriguez Fuller, a brash young Latina I met through this study. Always clad in well-worn jeans, a plain T-shirt, and sandals, she looked as if she'd stepped from the pages of *Mother Earth,* not *Vogue,* but her casual dress belied an astute business mind. Her questions about starting a specialty food company were prosaic and perfunctory. "Would I be better off with a partner, or adding employees?" "How long should I try to run things from home?" "Is it legal to have a commercial kitchen in a residential area?"

From this beginning, Sheryl took a family salsa recipe that drew rave reviews at every appearance and built it into a multimillion dollar product empire. Within five years she was producing spin-off sauces and dressings, all faithful in some way to the initial family recipe, with the help of sixty-four employees. She consistently paid close attention to the task, intuitively understanding the competition as well as the complicated economics of production. But her heart belonged to the people, and this core value influenced every decision she made throughout her expansion. As she hired food technologists, production managers, and salespeople; contracted with distributors and delivery firms; or conducted focus groups with consumers to determine their reaction to a new product, she incorporated her personal convictions about how to treat others, whether employees or customers, into her actions. She refused to add certain preservatives to her food, necessitating higher-than-normal shipping costs for frequent, small deliveries because her products would have limited shelf life. She kept her main plant in a somewhat remote geographic location because she had personal ties to the area and wanted to increase employment possibilities for the local residents. She used an open floor plan, agreeing that other managers in the company might require private offices but she would keep her own desk in a large, open room to remain accessible to the plant workers—some of whom she had known from elementary school. Her values even came through on her corporate marketing materials. The company logo was bold, yet deceptively simple in design, the two colors repeated endlessly on every company surface, from the actual labels on the salsa jars to the interior walls of the processing plant. The design itself was adopted after the eleven-year-old daughter of a production worker submitted it in an employee contest.

In sum, Sheryl Fuller helps us remember that everything you do or say when you start up a business—beginning with your product—expresses you and nobody else. As one CEO I know is fond of repeating, "The fish always stinks from the head!"

To really understand how even the little things make a statement, contrast Sheryl with Juliet DeBono. Take, for example, the gorgeous Klimt area rugs in the lobby of Juliet's spacious new office suite in a custom-built executive tower, the end of a five-year migration from a dingy basement office. The sizzling colors of the designer rugs match the lively Mardi Gras–style posters on the walls, which at closer inspection are recognizable as blown-up ads for the company's burgeoning portfolio of training services.

Neither the rugs nor the slightly zany posters would be found in the typical Silicon Valley world of gray cubicles and functional office furniture. That's just the point. Juliet's identity and persona are completely unlike Sheryl Fuller's; Juliet likes to draw attention, stand out, and offer something completely different. She has broken new ground in job sharing and instituting flextime for her employees. She is always sending employees off to far corners of the globe to attend professional development workshops. She tirelessly scours the Web for new ideas she can bring to her customers. Most of all, she prides herself on being out there on the edge. With regard to the task dilemma, her heart is clearly in the work itself, in the concept, in building something new. With this inner bias—this is, after all, who Juliet DeBono really is—she sometimes gets herself out there on the bleeding edge. More than once, she has moved too quickly with her employees, eager to execute a new idea that captures her attention, and forgotten to take into full consideration how others feel the impact.

In contrast, Sheryl Fuller moves at a much slower pace with both product development and employee satisfaction. She is at her best when she goes with what she knows personally. She has chosen to locate in her hometown, and to grow her product line only by remaining with existing food-processing techniques or basic ingredients she is already using. If Juliet's excellence is rooted in the new, Sheryl's progress stems from understanding the old. They are both right, both successful. They are both happy because they know who they are, and their employees and customers know it also.

Your Real Customers *Are* Your Customers

The ultimate task dilemma for women entrepreneurs is understanding how best to manage customers. In corporate life, cynics tell you that managing the politics is the road to success, and after a decade of experience as an executive coach I'm the first to agree. But the acid test of entrepreneurial politics is vetting the customer. Remember that only your customers bring you revenue. Without revenue there is no need to worry about competitors or your employees. Therefore it is only after understanding who your target customers are; what exactly they need (and consequently what they don't need); and how to package, position, and price those needs that it's worthwhile to worry about anyone else, such as the competition. Only after scoping out the competition is it time to fret about satisfying your employees so they can produce the best possible result in the competitive battle. In my experience, there's a definite hierarchy for the task dilemma in entrepreneurial life, and it begins with the customer.

This reality gives a new twist to your middle-of-the-night third-shift dialogue. In theory, with more appreciation for the relational realm in business, women business owners may possess a formidable competitive advantage if they can act on a special sensitivity to, or awareness of, what customers are thinking. But it's far from automatic because customers are rarely a homogeneous group. Some care most about the result or the price and have little apparent concern for service, while others want their hands held every minute and cast a forgiving eye at the cost of this privilege. We can use the framework of the task dilemma to understand that focusing first upon the task may be most fruitful with the former group of customers. With the latter group, worrying about the relationship may be paramount. In theory, it all sounds fine, but how do you translate this into action?

Imagine this scenario, based upon a woman entrepreneur I know. Lily Carlisle is a talented and experienced event planner. Beginning with catering for her friends' weddings and bar mitzvahs when her children were small, she progressed to managing all aspects of corporate social occasions for well-heeled Silicon Valley companies accustomed to lavish spreads for signature events. Her attention to the details of the task is legendary; she loves to create special touches like custom-dyed handkerchiefs for the bridesmaids and female guests. Her undoing, though, is that she internalizes every small mistake that invariably creeps into the best-laid plans. She never can predict whether her clients will even notice the small things. According to her husband, she spends way too much time needlessly torturing herself with indecision about how much "service" to offer for her standard fees. In terms of her third shift:

Self-Awareness	*Self-Doubt*
No one takes more time to get it right than I do. I suppose I can overdo it, but I know that the smallest detail can sometimes be the showstopper for clients.	I'm too slow. I'm never going to get ahead if I can't trust somebody else to help me with the grunt work. There's too much for me to do by myself. When will I learn to delegate effectively?
If I build a solid relationship with a client, she'll be much more forgiving if something goes wrong. On the other hand, if it's a wedding or bar mitzvah, forget it! Nothing pleases these clients. They're too stressed out. It's better to explain in advance that I aim for the highest quality service, but perfection isn't reasonable.	Maybe I should forget working with private clients. Corporations are so much easier. They don't take everything so personally and it's much less stressful for me. But they're so cyclical. If the economy goes to pot, what will I fall back on?
Maybe I should develop a two-tiered pricing scheme: one for "standard" service and one for "deluxe."	But how do I know what to offer as standard? Won't I be undercut if I don't give more than my competition? Will clients stick with me?

Lily works hard, but without making changes in how she works she's unlikely to grow her business—an important goal to her because she'd like to increase her income by at least 20 percent in the next year without working more hours and without developing a reputation with her clients of being greedy. In conversations with her, it became clear that she literally overserves her clients—thus undervaluing her own time. She admitted that she is a poor negotiator and is often uncomfortable determining a fair market price for her skills. I assigned her two types of homework: (1) to discover what a full range of competitors charge for comparable services, and (2) to brainstorm ways to use tiered pricing and piece-meal services so that she can directly tie pricing to actual services delivered and the time it takes her to plan each event.

Not surprisingly, Lily came back to me with a rueful grin and an armload of calculations. She estimated that she charges approximately 40 percent of what her competitors do, if all her extra services are factored into the calculation. We arrived at a plan for her to restructure her services. Next, we drafted a service evaluation survey to mail to her clients. Subsequent analysis of the data from the questionnaire allowed her to see herself through her clients' eyes, prune unnecessary services, and selectively increase prices for other work. For the first time, she felt completely confident as she undertook negotiations with new clients, armed with data and written testimonials from satisfied clients.

The lesson from Lily Carlisle is that we can easily delude ourselves by focusing so much on the task itself (and dyeing those darling little hankies), or by pleasing the customer so much that we don't charge a realistic price for our time. Either way, we think that we are giving top-notch client service, when in fact we are quite imbalanced in how we manage the task challenge with customers. Like most things in our lives, *we* are the real losers as our self-confidence erodes along with our checkbook balance.

We can similarly lose sight of what is important in our management of employees. Sheryl Fuller is an extreme case but an instructive one for many women entrepreneurs who are not fully comfortable with their own success, or who are still too worried about how others will judge them—a hallmark of both the task and the identity dilemmas. At first, Sheryl's guilt that "I escaped from the *barrio*" made her easy prey for the task challenge. She erred always on the side of her employees. She would spend virtually any sum if she was convinced it would benefit them, but she was extremely reluctant to push any perks her own way. She was also exceedingly generous with funding community needs; her company name was always at the top of the list of sponsors for local educational or cultural events.

She felt particularly uncomfortable with visible differences between her own lifestyle and that of her current employees, whose lifestyle was very reminiscent of her childhood. She continued to wear a modest wardrobe and was reticent about buying a decent corporate car to use in calling on customers and suppliers. It was apparent from our discussions that she was also unwilling to draw a salary commensurate with her responsibilities, or one comparable to founders of other companies with similar revenue and profit streams.

The breakthrough came when Sheryl was faced with building a second processing plant to meet expanding demand. Ironically, the plant would pioneer a new family of sauces based upon a recent consumer trend indicating that tastes were changing radically in her business. Because of limitations in her current plant, she was unable to switch over her line to the new products without closing for three months—an unacceptable position for corporate cash flow and for employees. But if she were unable to bottle new products, her company would have to shut down. For the first time since she left the little shed behind her mother-in-law's house that was her first "salsa factory," she felt stuck.

At about this time, a consultant's study she had authorized as part of civic responsibilities for the local industry council surfaced information that she was paying her workers 15 percent above scale for similar work in the area. Sheryl was in a real quandary *of her own making*. If she opened the second plant, she could employ more people in the area, fulfilling her need to return something to the community she had grown up in. But she couldn't open the plant because she was overpaying her current workers and was short of cash! The industry trend was to reduce prices to wholesalers, so no help would be forthcoming in that direction either. What had gone wrong?

For understandable personal reasons, she had placed her employees too far ahead of her customers. But in the long run her imbalanced choices regarding the task dilemma actually jeopardized the very people she was most concerned about. Ultimately, she broke ground with her second plant by working out a reasonable financial deal with a new bank and the cooperative growers association that was her chief supplier, and a restructured hourly compensation package for newer employees. She continued to serve her community. She tried to be generous with her employees but she was careful to ground her generosity on industry data. She also doubled her market research budget, determined never to be caught flat-footed again by an industry trend she did not predict. In sum, she refocused on her *real* customers.

Say No—The Customer Isn't Always Right

It's one of the smallest words in the English vocabulary, but *no* is one of the hardest things you'll ever say to customers. It implies conflict management, the Achilles heel of millions of women.[5] As women entrepreneurs, our third shift can swing into blazing action when it collides with the most famous of all business advice: "The customer is always right." Saying no is hardest if you're a woman plagued by moderate self-doubt. Your habitual tendency may be to serve and please others, valuing what they say more than your own thoughts. Like Sheryl Fuller or Lily Carlisle, you may be giving away far too much, whether to employees or customers. Or if your industry is characterized by rapid change, you may be offering the wrong products and services altogether, because suppliers or new competitors are often more proactive than customers in developing new industry directions. You may be too reluctant to listen to those little voices in your head that are whispering change is in the air because your customers are dragging their heels. Thus, in your eagerness to maintain harmonious relationships with customers or to minimize other business risks associated with change, you can easily find your business heading down a dead-end road thanks to the self-doubt of your third shift.

Alternatively, overly confident women face an entirely different risk: alienating their customers by taking the attitude that "I know better." Clients and customers are only human, after all, and like any of us they are frequently inconsistent. Clients may come to you prepared to pay top dollar for your expert services but then raise a fuss if they disagree with your advice. In addition, most clients are turned off by arrogance, even though they look to you for conviction in your beliefs. In my experience, there can be a thin line between exuding confidence and self-assurance on the one hand and condescension on the other.

Clearly, there is always a relational element in handling customers, as any effective salesperson will tell you. In the entrepreneurial world, the task challenge with customers is really a personal selling dilemma known to all entrepreneurs, not just women: you are always selling *yourself* first, the product or service second. The gender twist here is the propensity of so many women new to entrepreneurship to hold themselves back, applying false modesty to a situation that requires blunt assurance. Either they aren't selling boldly and openly enough, or they're unable to take low-level differences of opinion in stride, confusing disagreement with rancor and being unable to influence male customers effectively. These women are denying that all sales situations are *conflict-management* opportunities: you want to sell, but the customer doesn't necessarily want to buy, hence the conflict. Newer models of relational selling emphasize partnering and softly greasing the skids, but the underlying potential for conflict is never rubbed away entirely, even when both sides are looking for a de facto partnership.

Women with strong interpersonal skills or solid corporate experience with customers arrive in the entrepreneurial world ahead of the game, armed with great experience as well as strong self-confidence. In particular, they may have developed personal strategies to manage conflict and disagreement, the area of salesmanship in which most women entrepreneurs I have counseled feel most vulnerable to the doubts of their third shift. I have also seen that women who left corporate settings hoping for a less-conflicted work environment may be surprised to find that they have changed the source of their income, but little else. Conflict is ingrained in our culture, its healthy management an essential aspect of adult development.

The difficulty stems from variations in how men and women handle conflict management, disagreement, and push-back; the result is quite different tolerance for what is "acceptable." The difference is not anecdotal but has been confirmed in numerous studies of children as well as adults.[6] To summarize the documented findings briefly here, boys tend to engage in physical roughhousing in a dispute over toys, while girls are more likely to use words, attempting to negotiate and get their way but avoiding an outright fight and being willing to spend much lengthier periods on verbal jockeying than boys. Boys are also more willing to initiate conflict directly when they do choose words, insulting others openly—in many cases as part of a routine exchange. In contrast, girls are more covert and much more likely to offer unpleasant words in private; the intended target must find out through third parties what the first girl said.

These differences continue into the adult world of work, with each sex genuinely puzzled by how the other negotiates, stages, and manages conflict. Women are more likely than men to avoid comment even if they disagree, taking the role of behind-the-scenes peacemaker when conflict arises, and stating that "the worst thing" about their job is having to manage conflicts.[7] Of course, cultural and class differences color all of these studies,[8] but the bottom line is beyond dispute, according to psychologist Deborah Tannen. In a recent publication, she writes convincingly that Western culture in general, and the United States in particular, encourages us to approach the world "in an adversarial frame of mind," where opposition is an acceptable and often highly effective way to get things done. This can obviously be taken to absurd extremes, particularly with regard to customers. Nonetheless, Tannen's thesis suggests that women may be overly sensitive to customers who are more tolerant of disagreement than they realize. When engaged in direct selling or influencing, therefore, women back off too quickly.

Clearly, creative tension is involved in applying conflict-management principles to effective customer management. Women with limited corporate experience should start by rethinking the expectations of customers. What do the customers want from a particular meeting? What do they expect from the product or service? What do they think gives the sales pitch credibility?

As executive coaches, my partner and I have developed an influencing model known as "CPR"—for "credibility, push-back, and relationship"—that women can use to keep their own pulse rates low while managing the task dilemma with customers[9]:

Credibility

Focus on the task first.

Visibly demonstrate expertise.

Use outside knowledge, resources, and materials to back up your ideas.

Provide evidence of experience and background.

Offer testimonials or references from other customers.

Highlight proprietary new products or services you've developed.

Act as *the expert,* but listen intently and frequently.

Ask a lot of questions, and ask intelligent ones.

Use data to anchor your pitch.

Credibility scripts

"I've developed a customized assessment for your industry."

"I've seen this issue before, at _____ and _____."

"The study in the *New York Times* concludes that. . . ."

"I'm very interested in your ideas also. What do you think
   about . . .?

"I was hired by ____ to do a similar project."

In general, establishing credibility is the most important goal
when seeking to launch or expand your business as a female entrepreneur, although many women prefer to begin by developing the
relationship. This is a difficult call to make, but by their own evaluation women say the most frequent challenge they face as business owners is being taken seriously, with four in ten reporting this
difficulty.[10] In situations where you have doubts about your credibility, the suggestions I've listed here may help.

If you've established credibility (or, for that matter, your relationship with the client), you are in a stronger position to handle
resistance and push-back:

Push-back

State areas of disagreement openly, but with sensitivity.

Identify and leverage areas of common ground.

Deal with data and issues, never personalities.

Ask questions to clarify and increase your understanding; don't just
   seek to influence.

State what you are feeling to defuse awkward situations.

Push-back scripts

"I understand your reasoning, but I have a completely different perspective on this issue."

"The customer survey data don't agree with your analysis; why do you think there is a difference?"

"I'm uncomfortable contradicting you, but I believe. . . ."

"You're paying me to be completely honest with you. . . ."

In general, women I've worked with need more practice at this skill than men do. Happily, I can report that women who stretch slightly outside their comfort zone find the effort to experiment with new approaches and scripts for push-back worthwhile. Of course, it's helpful to read the body language of your customer. Some clients do not tolerate any resistance to their ideas, and you have to decide if it is worth it to you to have their business.

Finally, there is the area that many women gravitate to:

Relationship

Observe and respond to the other's body language.

Try to hook your client emotionally as well as logically.

Try to quickly analyze the other party's style preferences (if they seem all business, forge ahead; if they're chatty, take time for pleasantries; etc.).

Ask about the other individual and what is important to him or her.

Observe objects in the other's surroundings and inquire about them.

Don't go overboard with chitchat; lead up to your point quickly.

Send personal notes in between visits, but sparingly.

Listen actively and genuinely; repeat what you've heard to clarify understanding.

Relationship scripts

"I can see from this picture you know something about. . . ."

"What is really most important to you about this whole issue?"

"How can I meet your expectations? My understanding of what you
   said is. . . ."

"You seem like someone who isn't very comfortable with chitchat;
   would you like me to jump right in?"

Used appropriately, the CPR approach can be a valuable influencing model in a variety of customer situations. You need to determine whether a given exchange requires more of one CPR element
than the other two. However, note the interrelationship between
all three elements, and realize that you may be naturally more
skilled at one element of the three. Juliet DeBono knows that she
has a tendency to take credibility and push-back too far on occasion; she starts believing her own pitch and stops paying enough
attention to the customer's response. Occasionally she brings her
COO, Wendy, with her because Wendy is more naturally attuned
to the client's needs for a relationship.

Lily Carlisle, of course, faces the opposite problem. She knows
that she is a pushover, and her CPR strategy is to attend personal-
development courses available through a women entrepreneur's
forum as well as research competitor pricing to work on her credibility. As she makes gains here, the push-back begins to fall into
place, and she manages to greatly improve the balance of "just say
no" versus the "the customer is always right."

Worry About the Right Stuff

Women entrepreneurs should look at the bright side. It can be a
lot better to worry about how to influence disgruntled customers
than how to manage the boss from hell. Self-determination certainly changes the scope of our third-shift worries but can also simply increase it. There may be even *more* to worry about as an
entrepreneur than as a corporate citizen, beginning with the problem that you have no regular paycheck. It is therefore incumbent
upon you not to worry more, but to worry about the right stuff.

Throughout this book, I've offered various suggestions to
women to manage, rather than ignore, their third shift. Our competitive edge as women emerges from our willingness to continuously question our abilities and needs, but without second-guessing

ourselves. We certainly overdo a good thing when our worries get stuck in the right-hand column of self-doubt. How do we convince ourselves that worry is good? At a practical level, how can we become better worriers?

Psychologists and physiologists alike agree that an optimum level of anxiety stimulates performance.[11] The trick is to overcome the fear that worry is always unpleasant and must be avoided, and to find a way to harness this activity—which is probably going to happen anyway—by listening to the right worries as a prod to action. "It is how you *use* that powerful emotion that distinguishes the winners from the losers," whether you are a race-car driver edging around corners, a financial planner trying to attract new customers, or an aspiring entrepreneur trying to summon the courage to leave your day job.[12] In a fascinating study of race-car drivers, psychologists found that successful drivers stepped on the gas, while the losers downshifted to cut their speed and ease their fears. Both types of driver had fears, but their strategies led to different outcomes.

Leaving the racetrack in favor of our entrepreneurial endeavors, we can conclude that for women the trick is to *create growth out of worry*. Most important, growth must be defined personally. For one woman, it is customer growth; for others, new product acceptance, a novel intellectual challenge, or more harmony and satisfaction in developing one's personal life. If you've just moved into the entrepreneurial world, be careful not to trade one source of worry for another. I have talked with too many women who found themselves even more anxious, stressed out, and tired, and working longer hours than they did previously. Now they even worry about their daily personal *survival*—a wretched, nearly choking fear. Where is the gain here?

With closer probing of these women, it became apparent that entrepreneurship had become a *should* in their lives, the feeling that they should go out and start their own business because someone else said they could do it. So they took the bait, researched their entrepreneurial situation, and made the leap. But once they began living the role, they realized there was an astounding price to pay for the opportunity for self-expression and self-determination. In short, they found an inescapable "worry hell," with an endless list of new issues and sources that could bring on a completely toxic third shift. At this point, I would gently inquire whether such a high-stressed woman should stay the course or let herself off the hook, realizing that a secure and structured work situation is better suited to her personality and tolerance for worry.

For women with "normal" worry thresholds—defined as third shifts that contain elements of both self-awareness and self-doubt—entrepreneurial life can transform work from a miserable uphill peddling exercise to a glorious carriage ride on a sunny day. First, we must realize that everyone at work worries about something, whether downsizing, a tough boss, stubborn coworkers, or poorly functioning technology. No one can escape worry. You can only control it. A personal worry chart is one tool that may help. The cells in Table 6.3 help separate "good" worrying from "bad."

The point of a personal worry chart is that good worry is productive; it leads to action and is likely to be about an issue over which you have at least some control. A chart like Table 6.3 may, of course, oversimplify many issues, yet it can still be a starting point to examine patterns in your worrying. For example, it is often tempting to spend an inordinate amount of time stressed out over someone else's behavior, yet because of that person's personality, motivation, or relationship to you there is absolutely nothing you can do about it. On the other hand, there are numerous task and business issues we face as entrepreneurs that can be solved only by productive worrying and ruminating, until we identify what

Table 6.3. Personal Worry Chart.

	Worries I Can Control	*Worries I Cannot Control*
"People" worries		
"Task" worries		

to do—when to expand locations, whether to buy or lease equipment, whether to launch a new product, whether an employee is ready for a promotion, or whether a new customer should be wined and dined or just given plain-vanilla treatment.

A worry chart such as this one—whether it's actually on paper or only used conceptually in our minds—helps us identify whether we're spending too much time with worries from the right side of the diagram, worries I'd indisputably term "the wrong stuff." In contrast, your worries about the right stuff can make all the difference to your business. Using the discipline of a worry chart can help you list the concrete actions needed to solve the worry and get closure. For example, Maxi White, a financial planner I knew with a San Francisco office and a small support staff, was worried about whether she should open a second location in Los Angeles, just a one-hour airplane ride but psychologically a galaxy away in her mind as well as her clients'. At the time we spoke, fully one-third of her clients were located in Southern California, and none objected to reimbursing her for travel expenses. The question was, should she expose herself to a lengthy lease commitment, not to mention figuring out how to perform remote management of new support staff?

It felt as if she'd been thinking about it forever. Indeed, the night I ran into Maxi at a professional businesswomen's dinner, she looked frayed, her third shift pulsing away. One part of Maxi knew it was risky and premature to engage in this nonmandatory expense, but the other part of her felt emboldened and confident, her ego loving the idea of this tangible expression of success with a second office. This was big time!

Idly thumbing through her old American Express bills one day, she discovered that she had made sixteen trips to Southern California in six months. When I found this out, I told her that it was fine for her to worry over this decision, but she needed more data. She agreed to collect leasing rates, get information about business permits, and verify prevailing Los Angeles–area wages. Then she gave herself a self-imposed time limit of thirty days to transform her worrying into an actionable decision.

She called me a month later. Coupling data gathering with research was like a magic tonic. She had decided she would wait another six months to move, by which time she felt certain—from prior experience—that she would have that much additional work from her Los Angeles clients to merit the move. She felt comfortable with her decision—a task worry she could control, and one well worth worrying over until she prompted herself to action. Moreover, she was able to plan ahead for the move, rather than let the entire preparation stack up at the last moment. It was a textbook case of worrying about the right stuff. Next time, Maxi hoped, she said, to be able to "worry a little faster!"

It's Lonely at the Top

Women like Maxi White might not worry so much if they have a partner with whom to bounce around ideas. Connecting with others can be a powerful antidote to destructive or nonproductive worrying. Spouses and friends can be helpful, but only to a point. They are better at rendering emotional support than offering specific business feedback and advice. But many women entrepreneurs are not in business situations that support a partner, and other women don't want one. What else can be done to fight the loneliness at the top? It's not an easy problem to solve.

Numerous working women, particularly those with young families, find that close relationships have become optional in their lives, even though they have never been more necessary. Friendships with other women often come at the expense of time with children. Nurturing acquaintances at work can steal time from spouses, other adult family members, or friends. For entrepreneurial women on their own, the problem is multiplied because it may take time just to identify another woman who can offer a meaningful relationship, let alone find time to meet with her. If you work at home, the isolation can help you focus on your tasks, but the psychological cost can be high, with your third shift running on a kind of autopilot.

Given your time-constrained life, it can be helpful to begin by identifying your largest needs for connection with others, realizing that you will never be able to fulfill them all and have sufficient time to run your business. The first step is to determine if you're the kind of woman who likes to integrate work needs with personal needs, or if you prefer to keep them separate. I fall in the latter camp. As a consultant, I have the opportunity to work closely on many projects with corporate and entrepreneurial women I respect and enjoy, who in other circumstances I would like to have as personal friends. But my individual choice is to separate the spheres in my life, even though this limits the available time I have even further.

I have become a great fan of the leverage principle—what we used to call killing two birds with one stone. I satisfy my need to meet professional women with whom I can let it all hang out by combining the need with the time I devote to working out and staying fit. By choosing to work with a personal trainer after work, I am much more likely to meet women like myself: career women at work all day who have enough self-confidence and economic self-sufficiency to employ the services of a trainer. With regular visits each week, I get enough air time with a small group of women to become satisfyingly close and connected. Perhaps like you, I have worked out many a vexing business or personal issue while sweating to country music on a treadmill alongside another woman who understands *exactly* what I'm going through.

In addition to personal needs for connection, I find it helpful as a business owner to maintain a network of experts. These are a group ranging from tax experts to executive development specialists and computer geeks. Hiring external consultants can be costly, but the right accountant or other type of specialized advisor is invaluable if he or she brings a new perspective and a solid execution plan. As an entrepreneur, keep in mind that many others have trod the road you are journeying, others who may know the potholes and side trips better than you do. In this I have learned from my son, Evan. As a little boy he would ingenuously query me, after I routinely got lost driving home from his friend's house in a suburban maze of indistinguishable streets, "Mommy, why are we taking the longcut?" The trick is to distill what the experts are telling you, weighing their suggestions against your own ideas and inner voices. The research is clear: the very best leaders, entrepreneurial or otherwise, are those who learn from experience.[13] The way to accelerate learning, of course, is to learn through others' experience as well as your own.

In closing, it's clear that our needs for connection as women involve the intellect as well as the heart. Psychologists such as Jean Baker Miller express this distinctive feminine requirement more strongly, asserting that "an inner sense of connection is *the* central organizing feature of women's development."[14] By choosing to test our entrepreneurial mettle, we often place our other needs in jeopardy because we must make choices rather than attempt to do it all and have it all.

Self-awareness is always the key for women entrepreneurs, as with our sisters at home and in corporate life. But I must add that the more active your third shift, and the more it tends to err on the right-hand column of self-doubt, the more useful you'll find the time you can arrange to connect with others.

Separate but Equal

Women who successfully master the task dilemma through their entrepreneurial efforts make up a new generation with far greater economic literacy than their sisters before them. As a group, they are building an inspiring legacy as economic heroines and role models for today's young girls. This generation can look around every day and see with its own eyes a woman "making a job" versus merely taking a job.[15] This is not the landscape that many of us grew up with. Through a combination of environment and biology, we remain vulnerable to the task challenge even as the number of women entrepreneurs across the country explodes.

Statistics argue that women entrepreneurs are managing the task dilemma effectively. The failure rate for women-owned businesses is actually better than that of U.S. firms on average.[16] This is heartwarming news indeed, because statistical studies also indicate that women business owners approach their mission quite differently than men. A landmark study of 127 male and female entrepreneurs employed a unique quantitative methodology to examine cognitive styles used in entrepreneurial decision making, revealing these gender-related differences most salient to the task dilemma:[17]

- Women business owners spend more time than their male counterparts thinking things through, reflecting, and weighing options before making decisions.
- Women entrepreneurs tend to balance logic with feeling in making a decision; male entrepreneurs rely much more on logic alone.

- Male and female entrepreneurs define and describe success differently. Women define success as having control over their destiny, building ongoing relationships with clients, and doing something worthwhile from which they can derive fulfillment. Men define success in terms of achieving goals, almost as if they are completing tasks on a to-do list.

The first result gives independent confirmation about the existence of a female-specific third shift for women entrepreneurs, while the second and third results speak to apparently innate biases toward the people aspects of the task challenge women entrepreneurs possess, versus a male preference for focusing on the task. To the extent that women effectively balance logic with emotion and internal third-shift ruminations with an external action orientation, their potential for entrepreneurial greatness is unlimited. The secret, as entrepreneurial expert Karin Abarbanel advises, is to keep "your feelings and your actions . . . separate but equal when it comes to running your business."[18] A careful rhythm must be maintained between the two, rather than a perfect balance. Clearly, it's more complicated than just saying no—terse advice we've used to admonish teenagers about sex and drugs, but advice that won't work any better for women entrepreneurs.

What's Next

The final chapter in Part Two addresses the task dilemma for women at home and in the community. Earlier, we discussed the mixed signals that our society sends to these women, with the accompanying third shift of guilt, self-doubt, and uncertainty. Chapter Seven identifies points of vulnerability for women at home coping with the task challenge; it then suggests strategies women can use to parent with greater impact, develop their intellectual life, follow their passions, and reduce tedious busywork. In sum, focus on what is important to you, and set limits on your obligations by managing your own third shift as well as others' expectations. It can be quite a dance at times to accomplish this.

Notes
1. "Women-Owned Businesses in the United States," *Fact Sheet*, National Foundation of Women Business Owners, 1997. Fewer than

1 percent of female business owners, regardless of the age of their firm, employ more than one hundred workers. This suggests that on average the people of greatest concern to the task dilemma for female entrepreneurs are likely to be customers, or providers of financial resources such as bankers or venture capitalists.

2.   For a thoroughly readable and comprehensive investigation of working women in this country, see Alice Kessler-Harris, *Out to Work: A History of Wage-Earning Women in the United States* (Oxford, U.K.: Oxford University Press, 1982).

3.   This is not the place for a lengthy discussion about what to include in a business plan. Numerous self-help books and software packages are available to guide women on the specifics of the business-planning process. A particularly useful, straightforward resource is Laurie B. Zuckerman's *On Your Own: A Woman's Guide to Building a Business,* 2nd ed. (Dover, N.H.: Upstart, 1990); a generic manual explicitly focused on the plan itself is David H. Bangs, Jr., *The Business Planning Guide: Creating a Plan for Success in Your Own Business,* 6th ed. (Dover, N.H.: Upstart, 1992).

4.   The seminal study of this type is Robert D. Hisrich, "Women Entrepreneurs: Problems and Prescriptions for Success in the Future," in Oliver Hagan, Carol Rivchun, and Donald Sexton, *Women-Owned Businesses* (New York: Praeger, 1989).

5.   The different social structures of girls and boys, men and women result in gender-specific approaches to conflict management. See the detailed studies of male-female conflict in Deborah Tannen, *You Just Don't Understand: Women and Men in Conversation* (New York: Ballantine, 1990).

6.   See Deborah Tannen, *The Argument Culture: Stopping America's War of Words* (New York: Ballantine, 1998), especially Chapter Six, "Boys Will be Boys: Gender and Opposition."

7.   Tannen (1998), p. 197.

8.   To cite a few examples, working-class girls are more likely to engage in physical fights than middle-class or upper-class girls. Another study found that Latina girls were more likely than girls from other ethnic groups to engage in open disputes. See Tannen (1998).

9.   Note that the sample CPR suggestions and scripts relate most directly to entrepreneurs who are offering services rather than products, in line with the data that most women business owners have an enterprise in a service sector. The CPR model is used with the express permission of its authors, John W. Baird and Michele Kremen Bolton, ExecutivEdge of Silicon Valley, Los Gatos, California.

10. A full description of the study that uncovered this result can be found in the National Foundation for Women Business Owners' *Credibility, Creativity, and Independence: The Greatest Challenges and Rewards of Business Ownership Among Women*, 1994.

11. In his *Worry, Hope and Help for a Common Condition* (New York: Ballantine, 1997), Elward M. Hallowell, M.D., quips that "worry is really a very advanced form of brain activity" (p. 38) and cites numerous visible business leaders, in particular Intel's Andy Grove, who has made a successful corporation as well as a runaway best-seller out of the thinking that "only the paranoid survive."

12. Hallowell (1997), p. 40.

13. Morgan W. McCall, Jr., Michael M. Lombardo, and Ann M. Morrison, *The Lessons of Experience: How Successful Executives Develop on the Job* (New York: Lexington, 1988). This research was conducted to understand what type of experience helped corporate executives be more effective as leaders. I suspect that experience can act similarly for women entrepreneurs, although the precise leadership competencies associated with female entrepreneurial success may differ.

14. Jean Baker Miller, *The Healing Connection: How Women Form Relationships in Therapy and in Life* (Boston: Beacon Press), p. 16.

15. See the introduction by Gloria Steinem to Joline Godfrey's *No More Frogs to Kill: 99 Ways to Give Economic Power to Girls* (New York: HarperBusiness, 1995).

16. A study conducted by the National Foundation of Women Business Owners, *Women-Owned Businesses: Breaking the Boundaries, The Progress and Achievement of Women-Owned Enterprises* (1995), reports that women-owned businesses are more likely than the average U.S. firm to remain in business and that the average age of women-owned businesses is approaching that of all U.S. firms. In addition, "women-owned businesses are as financially sound and creditworthy as the typical U.S. business," using three Dun & Bradstreet measures of financial performance and risk: promptness in paying bills, credit risk, and the risk of going out of business.

17. National Foundation for Women Business Owners, *Styles of Success: The Thinking and Management Styles of Women and Men Entrepreneurs* (Washington, D.C., 1994). The study also notes similarities; for example, with regard to conceptual thinking, women entrepreneurs are more like male entrepreneurs than corporate women.

18. Karin Abarbanel, *How to Succeed on Your Own: Overcoming the Emotional Roadblocks on the Way from Corporation to Cottage, from Employee to Entrepreneur* (New York: Henry Holt, 1994), p. 107.

CHAPTER SEVEN

Women at Home

Understanding the Job Description

> . . . *that hole of kitchen work was one I didn't care to fall*
> *into, because it was easy to see how those women would*
> *pull up the ladder, and there you'd be, hauling wood*
> *and water, making fires and tea, for the rest of your life.*
> JANE SMILEY, *The All-True Travels and Adventures of*
> *Lidie Newton*

It started out like any other day for Elena Dixon, a forty-two-year-old stay-at-home mom, whose teenage son, Marty, had just started driving. Her daughter, Hillary, was in middle school, poised to enter the "developmental Bermuda Triangle" where many girls flounder. When Elena returned home from an afternoon expedition to the supermarket and car dealer, two messages greeted her. The first was from Marty: "Don't worry, Mom. I'm fine. But there's a problem with the car. It's no big deal. Just a little fender bender at Kinko's. I just wanted you to know I'm gonna take care of it and be home a little late." Still slightly dazed from this message, Elena listened to the unknown feminine voice that followed. "Mrs. Dixon? You don't know me, I'm Zoe Clark's mother—our kids are in the same homeroom. Anyway, I'm calling because I wanted to know whether you realized that our daughters had their tongues pierced today. I'm kind of upset, and I didn't mean to leave this on a message machine, but please call me when you get home. . . ."

When Elena first decided that she wanted to be home raising her children, she was thinking about diapers and little red wagons, soccer games and birthday parties with streamers and party hats. In fact, she assumed that by the time her kids were ten or eleven she'd be going back into the workforce full-time, beginning to build up a college fund for them and experiencing new daily challenges. Now she wasn't so sure anymore that she should even be worrying about being anywhere but at home. If today's phone calls were any indication, cutting the apron strings would be very premature. Besides, to be honest with herself, she was ambivalent at best about resuming her own career, dropped like a hot rock seventeen years ago when she became pregnant with Marty: working as an entry-level saleswoman for an office supply chain. Did that even qualify as a career job?

On the other hand, with phone messages like the ones she heard today, she wondered how much impact she was actually having on her kids as a stay-at-home mom. Did it make a difference to anyone but herself that she arranged her life with the care and feeding of her family as job number one? A number of her friends had recently transitioned from homemaker status back to the workforce when their kids entered middle school. More than one woman seemed to be trying to convince her that it would be a great move. But Elena was troubled. She felt that her family needed her more than ever now, although in a different way. And she genuinely enjoyed filling the stay-at-home role. But financially, the Dixons were hanging on by their fingernails. Her husband's fourteen-year-old car was running on optimism and (quite literally) panty hose after a fan belt broke over the weekend. The kids' so-called college fund held less than five hundred dollars, hardly worth handing over to a stockbroker to invest aggressively.

In her mind, Elena had been over the question of the best role for her again and again. She just couldn't decide once and for all. Why was she so reluctant to give up her stay-at-home life?

Our Homes Are Our Castles, Right?

Elena Dixon is facing the task dilemma at home head on. Departing from third-shift concerns about bosses or customers, the task dilemma on the home front forces us to confront fundamental issues: the ambiguity of the true task, and the difficulty of measuring our success in the role meaningfully. The central task can be defined as improving the emotional, physical, and psychological quality of life for family members (including the mother, by the way). Hence, the work product of a stay-at-home woman can't realistically be measured in the GNP and is rarely afforded the status of real work, although our country perennially gives lip service to the importance of children and the family. In addition, millions of American women are raising happy, successful children even though they work full-time. Indeed, 67 percent of American mothers work.[1] Clearly, it isn't necessary to remain home, but for many women it is extremely desirable. Perceptions of the stay-at-home role are influenced by the fact that more than one lifestyle strategy exists to effectively raise children.

The phrase "just a housewife" reminds us that women who make the financial choice to stay at home to meet the emotional and physical needs of others incur substantial psychological peril even though they also face enormous rewards. Some women I talked with enthusiastically announced that "I feel so lucky; I'm having such a good time at home," while others remained uncertain that it was right for them. The latter were grieving loss of status and were considerably vulnerable to the mixed societal messages about the legitimacy of the central task, raising children. As with women who made choices about corporate and entrepreneurial careers, I found among my interviewees that the attitudes of partners was central to a women's inner satisfaction. In my study, some spouses were extremely supportive, proud of their wives' decision to manage the home front full-time. But I also spoke with women whose husbands' words or actions undermined the wives' self-confidence. In these households, the men enjoyed the advantages of the second shift, but the women suffered clear loss of power and status. Moreover, stay-at-home women can also suffer from slights and misunderstanding from their working counterparts. Many working women are genuinely ignorant of the daily realities of the stay-at-home role

"What do they do all day?" the working women and husbands ask, unlikely bedfellows in placing stay-at-home moms on the defensive, as if they have to demonstrate physical proof that they are gainfully occupied throughout the day.[2] In response, the at-home moms may be wondering what the working women are doing at the office all day that is so important that they leave their kids in day care with strangers. I interpret this feminine sniping as a transitional response to the array of choices middle-class American women face today. Recent publications on the topic may unwittingly bring more confusion than enlightenment. *The Nurture Assumption,* for example, published to much acclaim, concludes that peers, not parents, are the most important influence on children. The unspoken corollary for stay-at-home women may be *"Why bother, if this is the case?"*[3] Another author argues that the work environment, with its disparate tasks and challenges, actually provides *relief* from the rigors of home life. Arlie Russell Hochschild, the same sociologist who found evidence of an exhausting second shift awaiting working mothers when they come home at night, champions this view. But Danielle Crittenden reminds us that "happiness eludes the modern woman" because most women actually want to stay at home with their children if they possibly can. In fact, she cites evidence that this figure is growing rather than shrinking, even as women's career opportunities broaden.[4]

In this cacophony of well-meaning but inconsistent advice for women, what are we to do and think? This chapter lends further clarity to the stay-at-home role within the framework of the third shift and the task dilemma, helping us know that each woman must make her own choices and address her own inner concerns. Our homes are our castles, yes, but we feel very vulnerable if we perceive them as under attack. No wonder that as women at home, our third shift can ring with grave self-doubt about the validity of the role, or worse, how we perform it:

Self-Awareness	*Self-Doubt*
It's common for new drivers to have lapses. I did myself when I was seventeen. Marty is old enough to be responsible for his own actions even though I'll probably have to write the check.	I can't believe I let Marty drive before he was ready. Now I've put others in danger, and I'll ruin his self-confidence about his driving if I take his license away.
Tongue piercing today is just another phase. It doesn't mean I'm a failure as a parent. It's natural for me to feel angry and upset about something like this.	Why didn't I notice that something like this was going to happen? Isn't that the point of staying at home with my kids?

Self-Awareness	*Self-Doubt*
It is so difficult to figure out how closely to monitor the kids and how much freedom they should have. I can't always guess correctly when they're ready for more responsibility. It's a moving target.	I should have laid down some strict rules with Hillary about what is acceptable. She can't read my mind. I wasn't clear enough, and now I'm going to ruin my relationship with her by being the bad guy.
This is one of those days when I can see that I might be better off working. I might feel less responsible and emotionally involved in the kids' actions if I had more on my own plate to worry about.	What is everyone going to think? The point of being at home is to be more hands-on and have happier, better kids. What am I doing wrong?

Like all women, those I addressed about the stay-at-home life were a somewhat varied group,[5] yet each concurred that the decision to stay at home involved significant personal vulnerability, even if she was completely satisfied with the role. They mentioned three reasons for their third-shift anxieties. First, the central task at home—raising children—is so hugely important to the women that fulfilling the role properly can be stressful and produce moderate self-questioning. Nurturing those whom we love is a very high-stakes task, not just for the children but also for our own well-being. To the extent that a woman's full development as a healthy, successful adult involves building effective relationships with others, raising one's own children or thriving in one's marriage is a defining task of female adulthood. It may not be sufficient by itself for many women, but in no way does that negate its centrality for the women I interviewed.

Another source of third-shift anxiety was the fact that our society remains ambivalent about the role; hence the rewards and recognitions for homemakers, though different from those for working women, are more difficult to publicize and make tangible. Some of these women felt "sidelined" and invisible, even though they stood by their choice to remain home. A third contributor to anxiety for stay-at-home moms that was mentioned to me was lack of clarity about the central task. This problem arose because of the alternate model posed by working mothers. If children could be successfully raised in homes with two working parents, then stay-at-home moms with limited self-assurance questioned their decision to stay at home. One wondered, "Am I staying at home because I'm afraid to go out and compete in the workplace with other women?"

The Task Dilemma: Getting the Job Done Versus Worrying About How Everyone Feels

My sample was small, but I felt that the nineteen women raised the major themes and uncertainties associated with the stay-at-home choice. Integrating the disparate voices, I remained convinced that the essential task of staying at home—improving the emotional, physical, and psychological quality of life for ourselves, our partners, and our children—fuses the separate poles of the task challenge, defined as "getting the job done versus worrying about how everyone feels." After all, the task itself *is* worrying about others, a relational rather than a task-based focus, but one that involves specific, time-consuming activities over the many years between the infancy and adulthood of our children.

Few of these activities track neatly into objective metrics of success to determine if we're fulfilling our role properly, unless we look at long-term indicators much removed from the day-to-day acts of mothering. Should we use concrete measurements such as divorce rates or child abuse? Or the percentage of children who attend college? Or how many stay out of jail and off drugs? Some feminists conclude that the decision to raise one's children at home is far more than a private lifestyle choice. They see motherhood itself as a political institution, replete with substantial cultural baggage about what is expected in the role.[6] It may feel ironic to some women that a "job" that receives fluctuating legitimacy is also one with an unrealistically high level of responsibility for how children in our society fare. No wonder our maternal third shifts yo-yo back and forth between self-confidence and self-doubt.

Before addressing specific strategies to effectively manage our third shifts regarding staying home, I'd like to mention that our cultural picture of the stay-at-home task continues to be influenced by outdated models. Millions of viewers continue to watch forty-year-old TV sitcoms such as "I Dream of Jeannie," "Bewitched," and "I Love Lucy," where the women seem to have little to do at home other than make mischief or embarrass the men in their lives. These images are wildly inaccurate today—the traditional nuclear family with two parents and a working father comprises the minority of American homes—yet they persistently occupy a backroom shelf in our collective societal consciousness, fueling our third shifts.[7]

In fact, I regularly find myself reminding my daughter—when she is captivated by Lucy's inane comic plights—that the Ricardos are passé, that women today are different, that whether they stay home or not they are not childish creatures who have to be monitored and sheltered by men. "I know, Mom. Lucy's not real," she says, returning her gaze to the TV screen. Still, like many of you, I wonder if my daughter *in fact* knows the difference. Will she have a third shift when she grows up that helps her or holds her back? What can I do now as a parent to help her make the best choices, even though I can't actually envision what she'll face in our society as an adult woman? Am I being the right kind of role model for her? These are the questions that can burn in a woman's third shift. When our children make choices that frighten us, as has occurred in Elena Dixon's family, we wonder if we should we doing something differently. It's only natural.

A Fragile Peace

The uncertainty can be magnified for those stay-at-home women who feel psychologically and physically distanced from the workplace. One study participant said she felt shelved, "on the bench." Regrettably, this woman turned her considerable energies to worry about how others perceived her decision to stay at home with her family. Over time, she found many of the tasks of the home-front role to be tedious and inherently limited in meaning. She was unhappy and losing confidence in her decision, but she was quick to point out that she had not been particularly happy working either. Perhaps we fantasize that making another choice will eliminate all of our doubts and bring us complete harmony, but this rarely happens. On the other hand, many other women I interviewed were thrilled to be home. Indeed, some were unable to imagine any other life: "I have never been sorry about my decision," said one woman firmly, holding my eyes. "Not even for one moment. I can chase my career anytime, but my children will never be this age again. I would completely miss the opportunity to be part of their lives, up close and every day. I'd have to be crazy to do it any other way."

Another theme emerged for about half of the women who experienced a taste of a professional career. "I'm at peace with this role," said one woman who'd been home for seven years after a whirlwind corporate career, "but it's a fragile peace. It takes exactly one comment by a know-it-all working mom who thinks she's got it hard, to blow it up." Another woman, a former high-powered attorney adds, "I don't miss it one bit. With my personality, I would never be able to go to court in the morning and be sane at night for my kid. I wouldn't even try it. Sure, it's a comedown, and not just the money. Moving from plotting litigation strategies to room mother has been a major psychological shift. One was all about *me*. This one is all about somebody else. My kid. My husband. My kids' friends and their homeroom teacher." She chuckled, "You know, it's not all that easy, either. I don't think I've worked any harder with clients than I've done navigating through all the lunchroom politics at my daughter's school. These women are so touchy about everything."

Making Your Third Shift Work for You: Managing the Task Dilemma at Home

To draw a conclusion, let me say that fulfilling the central task of the at-home life (taking care of others) is a difficult job for some but enjoyable for others; it remains unevenly valued in our culture. For all types of stay-at-home women, several strategies exist to make their decision work better for them:

- Parent consciously.
- Define your relationship to work.
- Structure your days; be sure to set limits.
- Develop an intellectual life.
- Be alert to burnout.

Parent Consciously

I have never intended for this book to become a parenting manual on how to raise successful children. But parenting is clearly at the heart of the nurturing task in the stay-at-home role. Hence, the point of this subsection is to help you consciously examine your parenting practices, noting how they affect you and your third shift, as well as your children. It is helpful to begin by reflecting on what you are actually trying to achieve by staying at home. Many of the women I talked with made considerable financial and career compromises to be with their children in a frontline role. The women who felt happiest appeared to have undergone the most self-reflection. Indeed, by staying at home, they felt they could find more opportunities for this important mental activity than their working counterparts managed. Their third shifts wrestled with questions such as these:

- What is most important to you in the stay-at-home role?
- Are you spending your time in a way that reflects those values?
- By your words and actions, do you repeatedly make your values visible to your children?
- What kind of relationship do you want to have with each of your children?
- What causes you the greatest anxiety and frustration in the stay-at-home role? Do you feel that you have any control over it?
- What gives you the greatest joy and strength in the role? Can you control how much you get this?

Arlie Quinn, a self-described "career-gal-turned-mother" of kids fourteen and nine, voiced her thinking with gentle humor and insight:

> I've read a million parenting books, but I was just blowing my money because they all sent the same message to me. Your children are *gifts*. Treat them with care, and you will enjoy them. The books talk about gifts you can give to them, but I think it's the other way around. I'm learning from them. They're teaching me. I had never figured out as much about patience—despite therapy and management-development programs at work—until I had to wait for our

two-year-old to wiggle into his car seat in the backseat of my two-door car. Naturally, the more I tried to manage the process and hurry him, the longer it took. One day I realized that nothing was more important than letting him do it by himself.

Arlie had never envisioned herself as a stay-at-home parent. In fact, her older son was four before she undertook the transition. "I wasn't getting anything from my decision to be at work. I was falling further behind there, and I was never spending as much time with my kids as I wanted. I *enjoyed* being at work, but I *loved* being with my boys." For Arlie, the third shift really began humming after her younger son was born. "I wanted to do this thing right, but, of course, I had no clue what 'right' was. At first, I was always wondering about every little thing. Should I let Ryan play video games, or will he turn into a psycho? Should I let him buy the toys he wants, but then limit how many hours he can play with them?"

As her sons grew older, the same theme kept reappearing. For Arlie, a central third-shift dilemma about parenting involved whether she should affirmatively guide her sons' choices, or sit back and let them experience and experiment with freedom. "After Tonka toys it became the Internet," she continued. "Did I really want him surfing through all that stuff without any limits? Did I only want him to go online when I could see what he was doing? I eventually realized that it wasn't enough to say yes or no to something. I needed to have time to explain *why*. I wanted them to get it. I wanted them to be able to see what I'm doing and what I'm thinking as their mother. In a few years, they'll be tuning me out. I need them to get it *now*."

Other women I spoke with were equally worried about the messages they sent through their own actions. One of the study participants voiced her fears that her eleven-year-old daughter wouldn't seek an ambitious career because she (the mother) had chosen an at-home role. "I'm always telling my daughter that she can do anything, but what message am I sending by not working? Or is choosing to stay at home part of the 'anything'? Plus, I'm afraid to keep talking about it all the time, like I'm trying to sell her on something when I'm really only trying to convince myself."

Looked at objectively, it's clear that this woman may lack confidence in herself. The issue isn't only whether she's working or staying at home. The subtext involves fears that she can't adequately influence her daughter's development. I discovered that mothers of daughters can be particularly vulnerable to unresolved issues with their own mothers, and the stay-at-home moms in my sample were slightly more anxious about their decision to be at home if they had girls rather than boys. They found it immensely validating to learn that other stay-at-home moms also wondered whether they were sending the right messages to their daughters.

If gender has found its way into the third shift of stay-at-home moms, it's crucial to understand exactly how to address this phenomenon—noting, however, that a mother's age influences her concerns. I observed a clear tendency for the baby-boomer mothers to be more explicit about their needs to instill initiative and assertiveness in their girls. But these mothers also expressed greater doubts about how to help their boys be comfortable with their emotions, and sensitive to others; this is a theme documented by William Pollack in *Real Boys,* a two-decade study of hundreds of young and adolescent boys he directed with research colleagues at the Harvard Medical School.[8] Speaking to the issue of affirmative, "conscious" parenting, Pollack notes:

> Fortunately, many of today's mothers are no mindless enforcers of gender stereotypes. After all, this generation of mothers was raised in the bracing atmosphere of feminism. Many have embraced the idea of equality between the sexes, struggled to rediscover their own voices and to find qualities of toughness, assertiveness, and competitiveness within themselves. Today's mothers have successfully battled for the right to work, think, and compete as men do. . . . And at home, these women have struggled with their male companions to rework their most intimate relationships on a more equal basis. . . . Yet, I find that these women, who are so confident about so many gender issues, are frequently still unsure of themselves when it comes to raising their own sons.

Elena Dixon is one who experiences more uncertainty around raising her daughter. She confided to me that she had "come down harder on her daughter for the tongue piercing than her son's fender-bender." After determining that her son wasn't hurt, that no one else was involved, and that their insurance would handle the matter, Elena found herself emotionally detached from her son's accident. "I wasn't happy about it, but it didn't push any buttons for me. He's paying for the portion the insurance doesn't cover and that's the end of it, although I am going to rethink if we should do anything else."

At the same time, Elena recognized that her reaction to her daughter's faux pas was entirely different—and far greater even than her husband's, who was amused and annoyed rather than deeply censorious, angry, or concerned. "But I was furious. What kind of message is she trying to send? She's no slut. She gets A's and A minuses. Why would she want to send everybody a message that she's the kind of girl that puts a ring in her tongue? What must her self-image be?" For Elena, the tongue piercing rang a little bell in her third shift that she, as the mother, hadn't done enough to shore up her daughter's self-esteem. With a dog-eared copy of *Reviving Ophelia* on her bedside nightstand, she was genuinely fearful about what lay ahead for thirteen-year-old Hillary. "After all, I've been down that road myself, and it wasn't easy. I want to support her, but I have to be clear about what is important to me and what I think should be important to a young woman. I don't know if this is just some dumb thing she's doing that doesn't mean anything, or if she's sending up a flare that I should look out ahead."

As parents, it is difficult to accurately predict how your children will overcome the challenges of childhood and adolescence. With regard to managing their third shift as a stay-at-home mom, the women in my study concluded that you can't control everything your children do or think, but they hoped to move closer to the action by staying at home. They believed that the role offered the most promise to increase their opportunities to parent consciously and actively, and that this parenting formed the core of their task as stay-at-home moms. In their view, this was a meaningful counterpoint to the tedious, less-enriching parts of the role: chauffeuring, diaper changing, and housekeeping.

Define Your Relationship to Work

Every woman, as is true of every man, has a unique set of personal requirements for the work she must perform for financial survival or psychological satisfaction. These requirements typically change over the phases and decades of her life and are likely to be tied to early parental expectations and role models she observed as a child. True generational differences exist, with gen-Xers, baby boomers, and older women sharing a common present but possessing distinct attitudes about work and staying home.

As a stay-at-home woman, your first important task is to define your current relationship to work. I found that, in general, your career probably takes center stage if you are younger, seeking advancement, attempting to make your mark, and amassing the financial resources necessary for a comfortable lifestyle. If you are working at a job rather than a career, work may be less important to you, with *job* denoting a current situation and *career* involving a lifetime sequence of development, learning, and personal mastery of new challenges. It is also important to realize that if you choose to stay home to raise young children, you are likely to face considerable stress. *This is natural.* It is not just that you belong to a group that, statistically speaking, possesses limited resources for paid housecleaners, nannies, restaurant meals, and other purchases that can make your home life easier. You have also not yet tested yourself and demonstrated your "value" to others in the marketplace. As a young woman, early in your career, you may not be able to negotiate strongly with employers around your work-life needs. Suitable, meaningful, and equitably compensated part-time employment may be difficult to obtain for women early in their careers.

On the other hand, surveys of working women document that younger women typically attempt to give each domain—work and home—equal attention.[9] But this can mask the elusive balancing act required to successfully perform the constant juggling. Many young mothers have concluded that staying at home can be a better option, finances permitting, because younger women are less likely to have the negotiating power with employers to keep work demands from overwhelming their personal lives. In addition, in my study I also found that younger stay-at-home moms were slightly less conflicted about their choice to stay at home because they weren't as concerned that they would be held back in the workplace. They had risen to maturity with the belief that women's opportunities were equal to men's, and it freed them to exercise choices.

For midcareer women, the psychological or literal route that women may take to a stay-at-home role may differ somewhat. Many individuals I spoke with were simply and purely burned out. They desperately wanted to do it all, but the load had finally become unmanageable. Midcareer women were more likely to have increased financial and psychological resources, their wallets as well as their self-confidence enhanced through years in the workplace. But they also voiced fears that they had more to lose, from a career standpoint, if they transitioned to stay-at-home status. Stepping off the track is forgivable and permissible in some corporate environments, but it receives only lip service elsewhere.

On the other hand, many women in midlife are revising their definition of success to focus on personal and societal accomplishments. They have paid their dues. Though they continue needing to be perceived as valuable to their organizations, many women I interviewed expressed the desire to reassess their priorities and question conventional definitions of success. For some, who became mothers in their late thirties or even early forties, the entry of children into their lives stimulated new perspectives and personal needs. But I also observed the process in empty-nest women whose children were grown, and even in women who had never been mothers. Perhaps I am particularly sensitive to these midlife transitions because in my own life I implemented major changes in my relationship to work—leaving a lifetime, tenured university position that a mere five or six years earlier I would never have imagined I could excise from my life.

Examining the stay-at-home option with an eye on the broader statistics, we note that if we combine the needs of women of all childbearing ages, only 52 percent of women actually prefer to be at home with their children rather than working.[10] Our career opportunities as women today make it difficult for us to settle on a single, right choice. Our inner third shifts clearly reflect broad, external ambivalence about staying at home:

Self-Awareness	*Self-Doubt*
My children are happy and well-adjusted. What else is important? The number of hours I work, as long as it's reasonable, doesn't matter.	We could easily make it on one salary. Am I trading my kids' childhood for a bigger house and the right car?

Self-Awareness	*Self-Doubt*
We live in a transitional era. We should feel lucky to have so many choices. No one finds it easy in practice.	I never feel like I'm making the right choice. If I were the only one affected it wouldn't be so bad, but this can't be good for my kids.
My daughter asks me every morning what time I'll be home after work. She's just curious. It's a habit, like when I ask my husband his plans for the day.	My daughter wishes I could be home when school was over. I'm letting her down and she's such a good sport about it. Am I selfish?

Take the case of Jill Hendricks, twenty-eight-year-old mother of Tony, a healthy, mischievous toddler. She was a sociology major in college. She married the year after graduation and held a series of marginal jobs, none of which offered promising career opportunities, and none of which was interesting enough for her to "become a slave to my job instead of my life." She quit her last job in the eighth month of her pregnancy, determined she wouldn't shortchange her child by holding a job. After reading an article in her obstetrician's office about the mother-child bond, she found that she agreed with Penelope Leach, the controversial expert on childrearing who recommends home care rather than "surrogate" care in preschools.[11] "I took a child-development psych course in college," Jill said, "and we learned about the guy who worked with monkeys to find out how infants learn to attach to their mothers. They did an experiment where some monkeys had real mothers but the others had wire figures in their cages to look like mothers. Which monkeys do you think did better? Whenever I think of Tony in day care, I see those monkeys trying to hug the wire mothers. I know it's irrational, but I want Tony to be home with me."

Jill, her husband, and her young son have cheerfully accepted the trade-offs. They rent a house that's smaller than many of their Silicon Valley contemporaries' and have no plans to purchase their own home. Their single car is fourteen years old. They don't worry about fancy private schooling or expensive day care for young Tony. And she doesn't fret about her career, because in another six months she and Larry plan to start working on a second child.

"As long as I'm staying home, I might as well just do it!" she says. She does not foresee a return to the work world for many years and feels constantly pressured about her decision:

> I'm always fielding calls from my mother, of all people. You'd think she'd be really excited about Tony. After all, he's her first grandchild. But she keeps asking me when I'm going to do something for myself. I try to tell her, "Mom, I *am* doing something for myself. I'm staying home for me, not just for Tony and Larry. I like my life." But she doesn't buy it. She's convinced I'm missing out on something. Ironic, isn't it? Here my mom is worried that I'm spending too much time doing stuff for others, worrying about what they need, putting myself last, when the reality is that, if I go back to work now, I'd only be doing it for *her*! Why doesn't she get it?

Her mom is a boomer who came of age with the feminist movement. She found herself a divorced, single mother at the very age Jill is now. Without a college degree, she had to fight for every promotion she ever earned. Naturally, in her mind, she is wondering why *Jill* doesn't get it! At best, she envisions her daughter's life as one of pleasing others, her home stay a vehicle for improved quality of life for the family, but not for Jill. At worst, she can't help but worry that the decision to stay at home makes her daughter economically vulnerable. After all, half of California marriages end in divorce.

Jill, on the other hand, is content to let the future take care of itself. Her present reality is all she feels she can handle. Moreover, she sees no sensible reason to be continuously harried and stretched too thin, like many of her college friends who simultaneously work and parent. She feels that she is a realist, admitting she feels only a weak tie to the workplace. "It's not like I'd be solving world hunger if I went back to work now. I'm not going to be a Nobel Prize winner. Besides, I don't always seem to have a lot of energy for anything else. Tony is so demanding, it's hard to get anything done. Why should I stay home with him if I'm just going to be doing my own thing?"

In the end, Jill and her mother agreed to disagree. Their perspectives are rooted in opposite personalities and different generations, with the result that each has formed her own relationship to work. Ironically, Jill's mother labored hard so that her daughter would have more choices. As women, we must be especially careful not to judge each other for making choices that we would reject for ourselves.

Rather, it is crucial that we each continue to seek the right choice for us after acknowledging our individual needs, as did Jill. In this vein, many women have found that part-time work can be a useful hybrid strategy. Indeed, the fact that many more women than men make up this country's part-time workforce indicates the possibility that numerous women want to have some kind of paid employment. Of course, it also signifies that many women cannot afford to be at home even part-time without the additional income. Like other options women can consider, part-time work ranges in its satisfactions from meaningful yet stress reducing to "overqualified and underpaid."[12]

In a particularly creative twist on part-time employment, an academic colleague of mine with two young boys successfully negotiated a revision of her full-time, tenure-track position to give her a longer time to reach tenure (ten years, as opposed to the norm of seven) and accrue a satisfactory record of publications. This allowed her time with her family, reduced feelings of stress that she would be denied tenure because she was underperforming relative to other colleagues, and let her immerse herself meaningfully in both spheres of her life, family and work. Although this strategy might not work for other women, it was a psychological lifeboat for my colleague, rescuing her from the tyranny of absolute choices as well as the darker voices in her third shift.

In the end, you must be honest with yourself and others. If you are a woman whose relationship to work is vital to your identity, the stay-at-home task is likely to seem insufficient for you. You will find the role more psychologically challenging than do other women, and you will need more time for a comfortable adjustment. Part-time paid employment—or, as I discuss later in this chapter, fulfilling volunteer work in the community—can help. If, however, you are like Jill, the challenge of combining anything else with mothering may be unacceptable to you. The personal risks of losing connection and intimacy with others may be too great a loss for the rewards you can attain by workforce participation.

Structure Your Days

Careful consideration of how you expend your time and energy can help you attain your central purpose at home. It is all too easy to eat through the "extra" time that working mothers may assume you possess. They may be unaware that they expect more of you, and your own third shift may bring additional or inflated expectations to the role. What is a woman to do?

We can learn from Patty Montgomery, a do-it-all mom who has chosen to do everything a little bit less. She is a stay-at-home mom with a single child, Tomas, an eighth grader who's actually quite indifferent to whether his mom works or not. When he was younger, Patty returned to school at night, somehow managing to earn an M.B.A. in a few years. Four years later, she was still struggling with the best way to use her degree, as though it were an expensive dress that must be worn before it slipped out of fashion. She is unwilling to turn her life upside down by taking a full-time job in which she is at the beck and call of an employer. She is also hesitant to launch her own accounting practice, which her early job history and recent M.B.A. might allow her to do successfully. Most important, she doesn't want to leave Tomas high and dry, even though it has become simultaneously less time consuming but more challenging to understand and meet his needs. Patty's scorecard as a stay-at-home mom involves how she meets his needs without sacrificing her own.

Despite her fierce maternal love for her son, she realizes she is the kind of woman who likes to be involved in a lot of activities. After completing her M.B.A., she knew that work per se wasn't what was missing in her life. Rather, her sense of unease stemmed from her very strong need to connect with others in the community and to improve the quality of life for all through that connection. Patty is African American, her great-great-grandmother born on a South Carolina plantation shortly after President Lincoln signed the Emancipation Proclamation. Her mother and grandmother worked tirelessly in the community, her mother as a social worker, her grandmother without the benefit of a formal education or paid position. With this heritage as a woman of color, Patty finds central meaning in her life through community work, most recently on behalf of battered women. But the importance of economic self-reliance for women of color has been drummed into her all her life, and she is reticent to forgo paid employment completely.

So she has always worked, even if it involved fewer than fifteen hours per week. Not wanting employment to take primacy in her life, nevertheless she would like sustained involvement in the workplace; she has always assumed a visible role in her community. She was recently appointed to an unpaid, part-time community commissioner position. Her charter is to analyze the effectiveness of the city's diversity programs and then recommend creative improvements and develop constituent buy-in. Patty could easily let this mission take over her life, but it has to fit her three-mornings-a-week accounting job and Tomas's endless round of after-school activities.

Given her schedule, Patty seemed fairly relaxed during our interview. "I could probably teach time-management seminars, but I don't want to. If my time is so squeezed that I have to practice disciplined time-management techniques to enjoy my life, I'm overplaying the game." She has learned to set limits on obligations to others and to consciously choose what is important to her, not just to others. This is the only way she feels she can experience the benefits of variety and stimulation without suffering from overload. Juggling has become a bad word for many women, but for her it brings zest to her life and new opportunities. She takes Tomas to some of the meetings she attends as a commissioner, not only because she enjoys spending more time with him but also because she wants him to see firsthand what community work can accomplish.

Although not for every woman, Patty's experience is consistent with an extensive study of working women conducted in 1991. Women who combined several roles were found to have less depression, greater self-esteem, and increased life satisfaction compared to women who combined fewer roles.[13] However, effective jugglers must be good managers of their lives. They must keep their various demands from colliding, and also create some sense of focus out of the variety. Patty's trick is to create a flexible yet reasonably predictable schedule for herself. She knows that she is at her best when a minimal level of structure guides her day and helps her maintain focus. Thus she likes knowing that her commissioner duties involve six prescheduled monthly meetings, with networking and socializing activities generated randomly around her son's and husband's schedules as well as her own level of energy and commitment, which varies. With only a single child, she finds it easy to accommodate last-minute demands and recognizes that her friends with more children have trouble doing this. It's all about trade-offs.

Patty particularly likes the routine of knowing that she works only on Monday, Wednesday, and Friday mornings. Her flexibility does not extend to her employer; she has made it clear that even a client crisis isn't enough for her to increase her hours. Naturally, this limits her career path, but she is looking only to "keep my hand in"; she can focus completely on what she's doing at that moment, because it isn't in direct conflict with anything else. This allows her to feel successful at what she's doing—an important building block of her self-esteem. By controlling the conflicts and trade-offs in her life, Patty manages her third shift very effectively, allowing her to enjoy the life she has structured for herself and her family. She lunches occasionally with other women from the accounting firm, and several are genuinely envious of her situation. By not trying to have it all, she appears to have enough. So far, it feels pretty good.

On the days when the occasional doubts creep in, she tries to remain objective. Her third shift pipes in that the reason her son doesn't ask for more time is that he has felt squeezed into her life too often in the past, and he's just given up asking. But she doesn't give in to these third-shift doubts because the reality is that she devotes sustained attention to her son and always has. She makes time for frequent talks and outings with Tomas, knows his friends, and has made a point of meeting one or two of his key teachers. She checks with other parents about his behavior at his friends' houses. As an eighth grader, his world is different from hers, but she has learned how to glimpse it accurately. By all reports, Tomas is a normal, well-adjusted teenager.

Another part of Patty can be vulnerable to third-shift concerns because there remain so many unfulfilled needs in her community. The commissioner's role is just a drop in the bucket compared to the work that really needs to be done for battered women, and she wonders if she's really doing enough for others. This is when it's most important to be realistic, sharpen her focus, and maintain the limits she has set for her time. It is so easy to overreach and end up exhausted, like many of her friends. Shaking her head, she says, "They are women rushing from place to place . . . never satisfied" that they are effectively fulfilling any of the roles they have chosen.

Patty's recipe for success may not work for others, although the basic ingredients hold. Jill Hendricks, the young stay-at-home mom with less interest in a career, faces entirely different issues of focus and personal limits. As for many young mothers, her life often scales down to the moments she snatches during Tony's morning and afternoon naps. After eighteen months as a mom, she is still learning how to use these "free times" effectively. When questioned on this point, she replies that "I kind of like leaving them open. Some days I scrub like crazy to get the drudge stuff done before he's up and into everything. Other days I take a hot shower, knowing I don't have to be worrying that he's putting a knife in his eye. And then sometimes I just get on the phone and have an adult, uninterrupted conversation. I don't plan it too much, and I don't try to get too efficient, either."

The point for Jill is that she focuses these times on her, thereby maintaining for herself a daily, self-regulating system of limits. It makes all the difference because Jill is clearly a relaxed, spontaneous stay-at-home mom; it's a function of her particular personality and background. Her path contrasts strikingly with Patty's, whose life is considerably more complicated but by her own choice. Patty has arranged the rhythms of her life with the cultural heritage of slavery in mind and a family heritage of community service. She has the personality of a "quester," a term for the group of people who are never satisfied with the status quo, who are always reaching out to explore and do more with their lives, and whose lives tend to be focused outward.[14] Jill's personality, by contrast, is such that her life is arranged around her need for intimacy; the focus of her life is inward. She has a small circle of very close friends with whom she interacts regularly. She likes to have sufficient free time to be responsive to their needs. She empathizes with the unserved community needs in her area but feels the best use of her time and energy is to focus them on her family, rather than spreading them over several fronts.

Jill is pleased with her slow-paced life, but she admits to a moderate third shift. "I get cabin fever some days, and there's nothing I can do about it. I know it always goes away, but it's still hard to get through those times. I can really get down on myself in a hurry." Her admission isn't uncommon. Studies show that stay-at-home moms can be more prone to depression than mothers who work, and moms who work part-time report significantly less depression than mothers with full-time jobs. Mothers with children under school age demonstrated the highest levels of psychological difficulty of all the women surveyed.[15] Does this mean that we should all go out in search of work? Absolutely not! Rather, we should concentrate even more fiercely on listening to the positive, self-aware voices in our third shifts, downplaying rather than denying the negative whispers:

Self-Awareness	*Self-Doubt*
After three hours sleep last night, I realize that I may be on edge all day. I think I'll take a nap with the baby this afternoon. What a luxury!	I don't have any energy today. I'm sure not making good use of our decision to stay home. I never seem to get anything done I'm supposed to.
We have to stay focused on what is really important to us. It's hard to live in a small apartment when so many of our friends have already bought a house with their second income.	We'll never be able to catch up with this housing market. We just keep getting further behind. Should I go back to work?
I must be the luckiest woman in the world. The whole day is stretching out in front of us and we don't have to do anything but be together and please ourselves.	The whole day is stretching out in front of me with nothing more exciting than grocery shopping. And I'm even too tired to do that.

Keep in mind that we can be vulnerable to the negative voices of our third shift whether we go out to work or stay at home. The problem isn't the choice itself, but whether we can remain focused on what led us to make our choice in the first place.

Develop an Intellectual Life

Elena Dixon wants to raise Hillary as a "smart girl," a young woman with a sense of purpose in her life who feels good about herself and her achievements. In this vein, Elena is constantly currying lists of extracurricular activities and nonschool opportunities for choices that build Hillary's self-esteem, while introducing her to new experiences. In particular, she wants her daughter to have a taste of success at something. This is probably why the tongue-piercing episode is hitting her so hard; it definitely doesn't fit in with her image of Hillary as smart, and Elena wonders whether it's a sign that Hillary is slipping onto a side road of adolescence that will veer further from the positive sense of self she wants for her daughter. She also wonders if Hillary sees her own mom as smart, accomplished, and happy. It's hard for her to feel completely confident that she is sending the right message by staying at home.

At the root of Elena's concern are the studies she has read about gender inequality in the schools, with their accompanying warnings that smart girls continue to take less rigorous coursework than do bright boys.[16] She knows that early choices about schoolwork can make a major difference in later options. For Hillary to pursue a science career, for example, she has to choose which algebra course to take in middle school, so that by high school she can take higher math and start college with an edge. On the other hand, Elena fiercely resists this culture of acceleration, which sends everyone—parents and children alike—into a constant spin of activity, shouting a self-confidence-eroding message that you'll never catch up if you don't make the right choices now.

So she tries to moderate the amount of pushing she's willing to do, as well as downplay her overall preoccupation with academic achievement. It's a tough balance for her, one that frequently calls up a vociferous third-shift debate:

Self-Awareness	Self-Doubt
I want Hillary to succeed. But I have to be very careful about defining what success means. Hillary lives in a different world than I did and she is an entirely different girl.	Hillary is taking the easy way out. I must have been pushing her too hard. I wonder if I should just back off so I don't push her further off the track?
They say that middle school girls go through lots of phases. On Monday she's one girl, on Tuesday she's trying on a totally different identity. I shouldn't panic just because she drills a hole in her tongue.	I'm afraid this is the beginning of more self-destructive behavior. Why don't I trust myself that we've done a good job and Hillary will turn out fine?

Self-Awareness	*Self-Doubt*
I'm still the parent. After all, Hillary is only thirteen years old. I want to be very clear about what the standards and boundaries in this house are. Structure is important at this age.	I don't want her to think I'm too tough. She'll just pull further away from me. But she needs to pay more attention to grades. How will she ever be able to have choices otherwise?

Elena recognizes that a complementary strategy exists to "invite" Hillary into pursuing a track that ensures fuller choices for her downstream. She is a visible and *intentional* role model. She constantly seeks out new experiences that enrich her thinking and knowledge. She continuously articulates that intellectual achievement ranges beyond high test scores, perfect grades, or a line on a resume. Developing an intellectual life, she reminds Hillary, is about challenging one's "cerebral self"—and having at least *some* inner life of the mind. It is not necessary to be a snobbish college professor or to acquire thousands of books. Rather, developing an intellectual life is about learning and extending one's own reach and curiosity beyond the immediate confines of day-to-day life. The purpose of such a pursuit is to satisfy one's own curiosity while also bringing more back to one's surroundings and key relationships. With the reach of the Internet today, millions of Americans can browse a stunning array of topics and hobbies without even removing their bedroom slippers, incurring only a nominal monthly expense to connect to this dynamic source of knowledge and experience.

Of course, we all have varying needs for intellectual stimulation (and varying tolerance for spending hours in front of a computer screen), and our needs vary over the seasons of our lives, as do our strategies. The up-until-midnight freshman dorm conversations that seemed essential to our souls at age nineteen may be irrelevant or tiresome at age thirty-one. Women like Laurel Andersen who transitioned abruptly from a high-powered job to at-home status may need more intellectual stimulation than women who worked at dead-end positions before coming home. The age of your children can also affect your mental energy. If you've been up five times during the night to tend a sick baby, carving out extra minutes the next morning to read Proust won't be high on your agenda.

When I think about the intellectual life of women, I am reminded of my own mother, whose one great goal in life was to complete her college education. As a young woman in the 1930s from the wrong side of Cambridge, Massachusetts, she entered Boston University on a scholarship but then dropped out after a serious car accident necessitated a lengthy absence. Somehow she never made it back to school full-time. But her interest in knowledge never waned. Throughout childhood, my strongest memory of my mother was her inexhaustible appetite for books and classes. She was always either attending a class or starting a new college program. She was a true artist in ferreting out inexpensive but challenging and informative courses that piqued her particular interests.

My mother was never sufficiently organized to muster all of this course work into the structured, disciplined set of requirements that would result in an actual baccalaureate degree. She agonized over her shortcomings as a role model because she never attained a formal degree or held a prestigious job. Ironically, I received quite a different, and possibly stronger, message from observing my mother follow her interests informally. I saw that learning itself is important, and that stretching one's mind has little to do with a sheepskin, but everything to do with desire. My mother died of breast cancer shortly before I completed the oral examinations for my doctorate. Without her early example of love of learning, I would not have undertaken or enjoyed this challenging journey. I hope I can be as powerful a role model for her grandchildren.

I caution you, however, to personalize your own search for intellectual fulfillment and to recognize that I may be injecting my own bias into this discussion. As women, we vary in our requirements for nourishment as healthy, complete adults. Our wheel of life is composed of many spokes, spiritual, emotional, physical, and intellectual; the size of each spoke is uniquely determined for each of us, and the definition of intellectual stimulation is entirely personal. Some stay-at-home moms snatch the odd moments of their day for reading—fiction, nonfiction, childrearing manuals, or cereal boxes, anything that uses the gray matter or offers armchair transport to imaginary worlds and people. They find the time and money to attend the occasional concert, play, or movie in accordance with their individual tastes and pocketbooks. They form book clubs with aggressive reading lists and rich discussion of topics of their own selection.

Other stay-at-home moms use craft making and hobbies to indulge their outside interests, carefully budgeting both time and finances to accommodate them. In my study, stay-at-home women pursued everything from orchid collections and bonsai gardening to chocolate making and carpentry. A final portion of the interview sample found that their preference for intellectual stimulation involved maintaining a respectable resumé and keeping their business skills and edge intact. As an example, I have known more than one academic woman who took a multiyear, unpaid leave from the university to be a full-time mother to young children. But these women continue to act as "scholars." They gave themselves unpaid part-time "work," continuing to conduct research and publish their results—albeit at a much reduced pace relative to their full-time colleagues—while attending biannual professional conferences to maintain a presence in their discipline and to keep up with new studies and ideas. In the meantime, they were able to devote themselves to the task of greatest importance in their lives: developing happy, self-confident children. Admittedly, these women had the advantage of financial affluence. Single mothers, and many of the married women in my study, have learned to live with far fewer choices and opportunities. But satisfaction does not equate perfectly with income. The women experiencing most harmony with their choices simply used whatever resources and support they possessed to find something of interest to them and get involved.

Consider whether you are waiting for that perfect time to pursue something of interest to you. Is there really a better time than now?

Be Alert to Burnout

Like a motor that has been pushed too hard for too long and stops running when it burns out, many contemporary women suffer sometime during their lives from a debilitating psychological disability: *burnout*. Women at home can be vulnerable. High-achieving women who place excessive demands upon themselves and like to excel are in more danger than others. Individuals in the caring professions are also at high risk, with medical personnel and counselors well up on the list too. Nonprofit workers of any kind can be especially susceptible because there is so much to be done with so few resources. A friend of mine commented on her own experience: "Nonprofit work is like sticking an intravenous needle into your veins. It just keeps sucking and sucking until you pull it out." I was shocked by her words, even as I understood just how burned out this woman was.

At the heart of burnout is limited impact and limited recognition—not just long hours and physical fatigue, which can be overcome with rest. The experts describe burnout as "a state of fatigue or frustration brought about by devotion to a cause, way of life, or relationship that failed to produce the expected reward."[17] Burnout may feel like a sudden loss of energy and interest, coming without warning, but it typically has a long fuse because the most capable, self-reliant individuals who are most at risk of burnout are also those individuals who hide their weaknesses and doubts. They can be kind and giving to others, but not to themselves. They can be women at home who have poorly navigated the waters of self-sacrifice.

With respect to the task dilemma for stay-at-home moms, burnout is most likely to occur if you worry too much about others' feelings and needs, or if you worry too much about what others are expecting from you. The burnout occurs when your inner need to gain approval by meeting others' demands is so great that you ignore your true needs, striving instead to keep up an external image as a mother or community volunteer that may not match who you really are. Patty Montgomery is a perfect example of a stay-at-home woman who has escaped burnout by understanding her own motivations and desires and then organizing her life's choices around them. She has what she wants now, but it wasn't always that way.

From her earliest memories of her mother and grandmother, Patty internalized certain beliefs about women's roles—roles that were emotionally taxing, took long hours, and involved seemingly endless service on others' behalf. "I don't think I ever saw my mother sitting down," she said. "You are put on this earth to help others." As Patty grew to adulthood, she began her career as a CPA.

In her early years, she never felt her workload was quite enough; she always strove to do more than others. In addition, she continuously "tacked on volunteer assignments for . . . evenings and weekends. I was very involved with starting up a halfway house for unmarried, pregnant teenagers. That worked so well that we expanded our efforts to become a women's shelter. I had some initial luck fundraising from one of our best clients, and pretty soon I was taking that on as well. I was doing fine until Tomas was born. Then I became incredibly stretched. That's when we decided one child would have to be enough." It was also when she recognized for the first time that perhaps she should question and modify the pathways her mother and grandmother had followed to better fit her own temperament, needs, and lifestyle.

As we continued talking, it became clear that Patty had always felt the weight of intense expectations from her mother, even if they were unspoken. In a way, the decision to have only one child placed even more pressure on her, because theoretically that meant she would have extra time for her career and her community work with women's shelters. In thinking about how capable her mother seemed, Elena had never really felt free to leave a full-time job with only a single child at home. After all, her mother had raised three kids without a husband, without a college degree, with a quarter the income, and with a much deeper level of societal racism than Patty had ever known.

But eventually it didn't matter anymore that her mother was a supermom, because approximately five years ago Patty began to flounder badly. She didn't know what to give up in her life. She felt that any choice would let someone else down. Deep inside, her third shift was whipping her with guilt because she didn't feel she was actually doing all that much anyway, compared to her mother and grandmother, "who'd had it so much harder." How could she tell anyone that she really just wanted to be at home with Tomas? She was completely burned out, overextended, and she didn't realize it. Something had to go in her life.

When her husband suggested that she switch to a part-time position in her accounting firm, she gratefully acquiesced, reversing her burnout cycle. Gradually, she began to feel rejuvenated and more effective at everything she attempted. The decision was less psychologically difficult than she had expected, because it was right for her. Whereas once she feared the loss of anything less than climbing to the very heights of her profession, now she was relieved to back down the ladder. Whereas once she feared that unless she kept driving herself she would let her mother and grandmother down, now she felt confident that she was a good daughter and a good citizen of the world exactly as she was. The dialogue of her third shift altered completely from self-doubt to self-awareness and self-confidence. She began to enjoy her life again.

In my interviews for this book, I met many other high-achieving women with major contributions to make to their family, their workplace, or the larger society. I could identify, after a short conversation, the women most susceptible to burnout: those ambitious, talented, energetic individuals who give 1,000 percent to anything they take on. Underachievers, and even average achievers, rarely suffer from burnout.[18] In some ways, I worried most about the stay-at-home moms. Echoing society's ambivalence about the stay-at-home role, many of these women placed unusually high demands on themselves. They felt that they should bear more of the load at their children's schools, "or who else would do it?" They felt that they should provide their children with as many activities and experiences as they could afford, or "what's the point of staying home?"

If our lives as women involve too many shoulds, our third shifts crank away with too many scripts from the self-doubt column and not enough from the vantage place of self-awareness. As we run faster, we move even further away from our true selves. The shoulds take over our lives—a disease of others' expectations rather than our own:

Self-Awareness	Self-Doubt
I don't have to prove myself to anybody. I must organize my life around my own values and needs. This is how our kids will learn this important lesson.	I should get more done in the mornings when my daughter is in preschool.
I don't want to focus on five things at once. There will be other times in my life when I will get in the harness again and be a whiz-bang at work or whatever I decide is important to me.	I should at least get a part-time job. I'm going to set back the civil rights movement unless I show others what I can do.

So be alert to your own capacity for burnout. Examine your answers to these questions carefully and objectively:

- Do you find it difficult to portray the image you like to others?
- Do you find yourself frequently disappointed by others?
- Do you often feel completely drained, without believing you've accomplished as much as you wanted?
- Are you so busy that you have no time for the little things you once enjoyed: sending holiday cards, phoning friends, and reading for fun?
- Do you tend to get sick more often than you used to?
- Does it take you a long time to wind down on vacation or whenever you don't have to be doing something?
- Are you forgetful and irritable?

There is no magic test for burnout, and it may take a subtle form for women at home, particularly those with very young children who may be sleep-deprived as well. Some women who answer all of these questions with a yes might nevertheless be able to push their own mental reset button and then take off running again, refreshed and happy. By contrast, women who affirm only one or two of these questions might actually be stuck and require counseling or a major life change to break loose and renew themselves. Either way, the point is to monitor your activities; most important, monitor *how you feel* about your activities. If you're nodding and smiling on the outside and frantic on the inside, you know that your life is devouring and not nourishing you—and that it's time for a change.

Being There

Throughout this chapter, I have assumed that the central task for women at home is improving the emotional, physical, and psychological life of the family. This task can be performed effectively and enjoyably by fathers as well as mothers, and by extended family members or paid but loving caretakers. Through the research I have conducted for this book, I have come to believe that a woman's third shift is especially difficult to manage when it involves worry about a child. In *The Mother Dance*, Harriet Lerner concurs:

"A child is an excellent, almost unavoidable, lightning rod" for worry energy.[19] Women who stay at home can actually be vulnerable to *more* worry about their children because they see them more, and because they have fewer distractions to blunt their focus. Alternatively, women at home have the opportunity to actually *decrease* their third-shift worries, for exactly the same set of reasons: they are at home and can spend more time influencing their children; they can see firsthand what the lives of their children involve. Because they are *not* distracted by workplace demands, they can act readily upon any worries they do have.

In this book I argue that we have control as women and as mothers over the worry energy of our third shift. We can use strategies like those described in this chapter to increase the proportion of our third-shift ruminations that are positive, supportive, and encouraging. But bringing up baby—from the first trip home with a newborn to the mixed emotions you may feel if an adult child decides to return home to live—involves a complex array of emotions, decisions, and experiences that touch women in the most intimate depths of their third shift. For many women, the fiercest tugs on self-concept stem from their personal successes or failures in mothering. "There's only one sure way to see what it's like," they say to other women contemplating motherhood, nodding their heads knowingly. "Your life is going to be so different." Others I interviewed were cavalier, or perhaps only more private, about their experiences, but these women also admitted that bearing and raising children involves an amazingly broad array of talents and activities, from the trivial to the sublime, from wiping snotty noses to ensuring the continuation of the species. Both the working women and the stay-at-home moms, the gen X young women and the older baby boomers, admitted that even the most mundane task of mothering has the potential to color a woman's self-image in a way that a similarly pedestrian chore at work cannot.

For most of us, mothering is deeply affected by our personal family experiences as children, and our need to fulfill whatever dreams and desires we felt were lacking in our own history. On a positive note, we always strive to replicate early experiences that warmed and supported our development. If we had warm memories of fly-fishing with our mothers, or jogging with our fathers, we are likely to try to interest our children in these activities, seeking to replicate the same rich bonds we once enjoyed. The stakes are high as mothers. Hence it is scarcely surprising that in my study stay-at-home women as a group faced greater self-questioning and vulnerability than did the corporate or entrepreneurial women. In some ways, these mothers placed greater psychological burdens on themselves than did working parents who hedged their bets by spreading their self-concept over multiple realms (risking, of course, that they would satisfy demands imperfectly in each).

Those at home may not wish to hear this, but the women in my study were keenly attuned to societal ambivalence about the stay-at-home role. My guess is that educated, middle-class, Silicon Valley stay-at-home moms may suffer more from this ambivalence than is the norm in other areas of the country. Over and over, the local media publicize the rewards for workforce participation in this high-tech mecca. Attention to work-family imbalance is increasing, but even when it captures the headlines attention to the topic is fleeting, as though it's a secondary story. Like traffic gridlock and high real estate costs, balance is an annoyance to the real business of developing new technologies and building new companies. It is stubbornly resistant to the quick fix, so no one in the mainstream seems to want to concentrate on this vexing issue for long.

I have also heard many stay-at-home women admit that they overcompensate in fulfilling their task challenges, completely filling up their calendars with a profusion of enriching experiences for their children. Not surprisingly, this tendency is far more noticeable as family income and the mother's educational attainment rise, not only because such women can afford more after-school activities for their children but because these women tend to expect more of themselves and their children. One mother observed, "I can't tell anymore if I'm overloading the kids. They are the ones that like to get involved in everything. I do think that it would feel selfish if I slowed down the pace because I'd rather just relax. My role is to allow them to do more, within reason. Let's be honest here. I'm at home, sure, because I cut the umbilical cord from my job without a glance back. But I see my role as *being there* for them."

"Being there" may be as much a state of mind as it is a specific place or set of visible, tangible tasks for mothers. Being there is invisible to the GNP, but it's the whole *megillah* when your child needs you. And when you need your child.

What's Next

In the next chapter, we move to a related, yet entirely different dilemma for women: the *balance challenge*. The core of this difficulty involves finding a way to spend time on achievements for yourself versus service to others. Corporate women can be vulnerable to this dilemma, often taking on service and support positions rather than jobs in the heat of the action, or being too quick to bring in food at staff meetings. Entrepreneurial women may choose to help others by developing products or services with less status or financial rewards, as opposed to finding themselves starting companies to deal with high-visibility products. Stay-at-home women, whether involved in community work or not, may be most prone to this dilemma, losing track of themselves in their zeal to develop others who need their attention and focus.

The next chapter addresses the balance challenge as a meta-challenge, tackling simultaneously the three realms of corporate life, entrepreneurial endeavors, and stay-at-home lives. It is my hope that the broader discussion of this dilemma helps women hold a mirror up to their own lives so that they can make the choices promising the best personal result.

Notes

1. Bureau of Labor Statistics, "Current Population Survey" (Washington, D.C.: U.S. Department of Labor, 1996).
2. Most of the discussion in this chapter centers on middle-class stay-at-home moms. The number of women without children who stay at home is exceedingly small, drawn either from a wealthy segment of society or completely disadvantaged women of the "underclass" who have no skills for the workplace.
3. Judith Rich Harris, *The Nurture Assumption: Why Children Turn Out the Way They Do* (New York: Touchstone/Simon & Schuster, 1998). A developmental psychologist, Harris argues somewhat provocatively that children are shaped by peers and their inborn temperaments more deeply than by the influence of their parents.
4. See Arlie Russell Hochschild, *The Time Bind: When Work Becomes Home and Home Becomes Work* (New York: Henry Holt, 1997), for a

study of working parents who are beginning to view their workplace as a kind of "surrogate home." See Danielle Crittenden's book, *What Our Mothers Didn't Tell Us: Why Happiness Eludes the Modern Woman* (New York: Simon & Schuster, 1999). A journalist, Crittenden reports on a 1997 Roper Starch poll and NBC News/*Wall Street Journal* poll of women's attitudes, finding that approximately 40 percent of women—whether they worked or stayed at home—found the trend toward more mothers working outside the home to be a "step in the wrong direction."

5. The total stay-at-home sample in the study was nineteen. Interviews were arranged with local women I knew or who were referred to me by other women in the study because they could participate, given the time commitment. Twelve women were participants in the Center to Develop Women Entrepreneurs. These women were considering self-employment but had made no definite moves; hence their current status was full-time stay-at-home mom. This snowball sample suffers from the liabilities of convenience, but it offers a range of perspectives, including women frustrated with their lives at home, as well as women exceedingly content. In addition, the study involved seven women on the cusp of transitioning between home and work or work and home, adding further insights and robustness to the discussion.

6. For example, see Adrienne Rich, *Of Woman Born: Motherhood as Experience and Institution* (New York: Norton, 1986). In this view, all of our roles as women are colored by the larger expectation of women as mothers. Rich analyzes and questions the legitimacy of these expectations when motherhood is defined by our patriarchal culture.

7. See Susan J. Douglas, *Where the Girls Are: Growing Up Female with the Mass Media* (New York: Random House, 1994), particularly Chapter Four, "Genies and Witches."

8. See William Pollack, *Real Boys: Rescuing Our Sons from the Myths of Boyhood* (New York: Random House, 1998). See especially Chapter Five, "The Power of Mothers."

9. Judith R. Gordon and Karen S. Whelan, "Successful Professional Women in Midlife: How Organizations Can More Effectively Understand and Respond to the Challenges," *Academy of Management Executive*, 1998, *12*(1), pp. 8–27.

10. This statistic refers to the Roper poll reported in Crittenden (1999).

11. Penelope Leach, "Are We Shortchanging Our Kids?" *Parenting*.

12. For more consideration of part-time work, see Chapter Four in Deborah J. Swiss and Judith P. Walker's *Women and the Work/Family*

Dilemma: How Today's Professional Women Are Confronting the Maternal Wall (New York: Wiley, 1993).

13. Faye J. Crosby, *Juggling: The Unexpected Advantages of Balancing Career and Home for Women and Their Families* (New York: Free Press, 1991).

14. The term *quester* comes from Carole Kanchier's study of five thousand adults, described in *Dare to Change Your Job and Your Life* (Indianapolis: JIST Works, 1996).

15. See Chapter Four, "Tempering the Fast Track: Part-Time Careers," in Deborah J. Swiss and Judith P. Walker, *Women and the Work/Family Dilemma: How Today's Professional Women Are Confronting the Maternal Wall* (New York: Wiley, 1993). Terri Apter, in her book *Working Women Don't Have Wives: Professional Success in the 1990s* (New York: St. Martin's Griffin Books, 1993), allotted an entire chapter to depression, "a female ailment." Among her other observations, she discusses the sense of powerlessness involved in depression and its similarity to feelings of one's loss in association with grief. Depression, however, involves mourning for the loss of one's sense of self; hence women isolated through their at-home status can be prone to depression. Apter quotes a 1976 study by Ann Oakley, author of *Housewife* (New York: Pelican), who found that "housework may be the sort of job which prevents those little successes, and triumphs, which light up one's day."

16. An excellent survey of research on gifted girls, barriers to achievement, and how their potential is realized in adult life is Barbara A. Kerr's *Smart Girls: A New Psychology of Girls, Women and Giftedness,* rev. ed. (Scottsdale, Ariz.: Gifted Psychology Press, 1994).

17. Herbert J. Freudenberger, *Burn Out: The High Cost of High Achievement, What It Is—and How to Survive It* (New York: Anchor Press, 1980), p. 13.

18. Freudenberger (1980).

19. Harriet Lerner, *The Mother Dance: How Children Change Your Life, Seldom-Heard Wisdom, Stories, and Healing Advice* (New York: Harper-Collins, 1998), p. 97.

PART THREE

The Balance Challenge:
Who Comes First?

Spending Time on Achievements for Yourself Versus Providing Service to Others

*Many of society's casualties are men and women who
assumed they had chosen a path in life and found that
it disappeared in the underbrush.*
MARY CATHERINE BATESON, *Composing a Life*

Imagine an immense hotel banquet room, filled to bursting with
women talking to each other. Tall, leggy women and short plump
matrons. Curly-haired blondes and Cleopatra-style brunettes.
Expensive, dry-clean-only silk blouses and stonewashed denim over-
alls. The energy in the room is electric, infectious, and distinctly
feminine. Hundreds of hands are gesticulating wildly; voices are
shrill and excited. The women are laughing and hugging, rushing
up to each other to talk or just listen.

The women hail from every corner of the globe, California and
North Carolina to Michoacán, Mexico, and Bangalore, India. They
include highly paid professional women and stay-at-home moms,
recent high school graduates and accomplished physicians, high-
tech executives and carwash attendants. Whenever I think about

the balance challenge—spending time on achievements for yourself versus providing service to others—I see these women. They
form an indelible image—of a Mentoring Faire, held several years
ago in San Jose, California.

Nearly one thousand women who could have slept in or
caught up with their week's second shift came in on a cold, rainy
Saturday in February to learn from other women. The official
topic of the Mentoring Faire was entrepreneurship. Indeed, the
hotel hallways were crammed with hundreds of women who had
already begun their entrepreneurial journeys and were seeking
networking opportunities with bankers, customers, and colleagues. But a great many other women attended simply to look
and listen, driven by their inner aspirations to serve or achieve
something new of their own. These women are the living embod-
iment of the balance challenge.

Hundreds of these women had intentionally placed their professional or entrepreneurial needs on hold in lieu of service to others (usually family), many unconsciously, most willingly. A good
many of them admitted they were out of the habit of acting for
themselves. "My family still needs me" was a common utterance, as
was "This isn't a good time to start a business. But I'm here to learn
how to do it so I'll be ready." Or "We really need to use our savings
for the kids' college tuition. I can't just throw twenty thousand dollars into a business that might not work out."

When I began my formal study of women more than five years
ago, the question I initially most wanted to answer was why some
women push themselves forward, while so many others continue
to hold themselves back. Thousands of transcript pages later, I am
convinced that the only thing separating a woman's desires from
accomplishment of her dreams is how she manages the balance
between spending time on achievements for herself versus providing service to others. It is a question of who—time after time—
comes first.

Unlike many other authors, who view balance narrowly as a
work-family juggling act, I have defined the balance issue broadly,
posing questions about how a woman chooses personal achievement for herself over service for others. This requires deeper
understanding of how a woman's third shift frames her choices
regarding achievement and service, rather than purely pragmatic

discussion of how much time she spends at the office versus at home with her family. In a chicken-and-egg argument, I would say that my definition of *balance* is the egg, while the commonly understood meaning of balance (as work-family conflict) is the chicken.

I have devoted this final chapter to an integrated examination of how these questions of balance form the final chorus of our third shifts, over and above whether a woman elects a corporate career, chooses an entrepreneurial or community role, or makes a decision to stay at home and participate actively in family and community life. In essence, the dilemma of balance is a meta-challenge, a kind of super roll-up of the identity and task challenges discussed earlier in the book.

The identity challenge revolves around a woman's quest to discern her authentic self amid the competing and often contradictory outside influences and values that define how an adult succeeds, finds meaning, and manages herself. The task challenge, which builds on the identity challenge, centers on a woman's need to maintain satisfactory relationships with others at the same time she gets the work done. The third shift for both challenges, as we've discussed at length, has to do with all the second-guessing that women do because they're not sure that they're managing these challenges successfully.

Issues of balance take us even further into the choices that a woman must make between emphasizing her own professional achievements in the workplace over service for others, typically on behalf of family members. Underneath the core issues of identity and task is the residual question for women, *Who comes first: self or others?* This is the essential tension throughout women's life structures and the reason balance is so difficult to attain.[1]

With this in mind, when I delve into the myriad aspects of balance I think of the thousand female faces at the Mentoring Faire. Why do some women grab hold of life and reach for the moon, while others settle and make do for themselves (a phrase from my grandmother's generation that always makes me shudder with frustration)? "Making do" feels like a personal failure to me, while to my grandmother it was a badge of honor, an understandable justification of her decision to make do with what she had, always placing herself at the end of the queue. An immigrant from a *shtetl* in Lithuania where boys were honored and every villager lived in perpetual fear of the next pogrom, it is completely clear to me why this kindly and exceedingly intelligent woman taught herself to be satisfied with serving others, measuring her worth by how smoothly and unobtrusively she did so. In her world, women had few choices. Ignoring their true needs and feelings, they were accustomed to putting themselves last. In a world without choices, making do is the easiest way to survive.

Note

1. You may recall from the discussion of the psychology of development in Chapter One that a life structure is the "underlying pattern or design of a person's life at a given time." According to Daniel Levinson, author of *The Season's of a Woman's Life* (New York: Ballantine, 1996), life structures express how we use our self-knowledge about what kind of person we are.

CHAPTER EIGHT

The Crux of the Matter

Defining Personal Achievement

*. . . I was thinking about us, and I've decided that we're
a completely new type of woman. We must be, surely.*
DORIS LESSING, *The Golden Notebook*

Modern women are so much freer than they once were to choose their own point of personal harmony and equilibrium on the continuum of service and achievement that constitutes the balance challenge. Yet, in my twenty years of experience as a university professor and management consultant, and having carried out more than one hundred formal interviews with the women involved in this study, I am struck again and again by the many women whose lives remain dictated not by the much-publicized external glass ceiling of the workplace but by an *internal glass ceiling* of their own third shift. This ceiling results in self-imposed limits on action, and genuine lack of self-knowledge about their true needs and desires. A woman with an especially strong internal glass ceiling lives in the shadow land of her self-doubts. Unconsciously, she lowers her expectations, the risks she will take, and the ultimate achievements she can attain—leading to an internal, self-sustaining, negative cycle. Her lack of personal achievement causes her to doubt herself even more. It becomes easier to turn away from challenges, just as this type of woman has turned away from herself by denying the importance of her own needs and true feelings. Listen to the contrasting voices of the third shift:

Self-Awareness	*Self-Doubt*
I will feel better about starting a business of my own when I don't have to worry about preschoolers. It makes more sense.	I'm the only one in my M.B.A. class who isn't moving ahead. Did I make a mistake by dropping out to have my kids first? I'll never catch up.
I love being in the midst of something exciting at work. It doesn't mean I love my kids any less; I just need a different kind of stimulation.	I can't figure out how to make everyone happy. It feels so selfish to choose what I want instead of what my kids might like. Why can't I grow up and be less self-centered? If I were really self-confident, I wouldn't need the trappings of a fancy career.
Being a philosophy professor is a very tough choice for a woman. All the "great ones" are men, and my colleagues still think I'm just a dilettante. I'm not going to make myself crazy proving myself to these guys.	What was I trying to prove by choosing a career with so few women? I've given up so much to do this, and I'll still never be able to become one of the guys. So why should I even bother anymore?

The B Word

In my view, issues of balance are the most troublesome of the challenges women face because they pose tremendously vexing dual internal and external issues. Women get it coming and going, especially if they choose to work from desire rather than true financial need. On the outside, they perform the second shift (service to others) after clocking in at their day job (achievement for self) when they are tired and unlikely to be at their best. On the inside, they listen to self-critical voices in their third shift, feeling that they have fallen short of a self-imposed standard to perform well in both worlds.

As is the case for many of the women I have profiled throughout this book, the self-imposed demands of high-achieving women can be the worst because they expect so much from themselves in everything they take on. But even if you're not a classic overachiever, managing balance is difficult and stressful because it speaks to how you measure your own worth as a woman. This process begins early, with young women's educational and vocational choices, long before schedule conflicts and day care pickups enter your life. Ultimately, as you move through your adult life, balance entails an entire constellation of questions: how many (or any) children to have, how aggressively to pursue advancement at work, and to what degree the need for personal achievement and mastery can be met outside of the workplace. Table 8.1 offers a profile typifying the choices along the balance continuum.

In sum, the issue of balance is the flash point for women because how they manage it determines whether they choose a corporate, entrepreneurial, or stay-at-home life, and in what order they pursue these choices. Even more important, how women manage the B word determines whether they invest their life's energy in the activities and accomplishments that offer the most harmonious combination of value and purpose.

To see this phenomenon more clearly, consider Carole Lockwood's story.

Carole is an inspiration to others, and even to herself on occasion. She's a sixty-year-old entrepreneur and a classic late bloomer. Her generation married straight out of college. They didn't work for fun, and the middle-class women of that time didn't usually work for money, either. Her first career choice was to become an opera singer. But before she knew it, she had three children and was expecting a fourth. Besides, in her heart she knew she really wasn't good enough to go the distance, and she didn't want to do anything by halves.

She followed her husband to Washington, where she made a half-life for herself as a government translator, setting the foundation for her lifelong love of international relations and overseas travel. Just about the time her translating business began to seriously take off, her husband, an engineer, needed to move again for his job—this time to Palo Alto, home of Stanford University and, back in the late sixties, a small number of tiny electronics companies.

Stymied at first by the move, but always energetic, Carole took a job as a secretary in a pharmaceutical company as she continued to raise her family. In a few years, she worked her way up to be a human resource manager. Then the company was sold and she was

Table 8.1. Managing Your Choices.

Emphasis on Self	Relative Balance	Emphasis on Others
Children		
No children	One or two children	Two or more children
Full-time day care	Mix of day care, nanny, family members as caretakers	Day care only for kids' socialization
Late start to child rearing after education completed or "dues paid" at work	Part-time day care	More activities for children, as budget permits
Education		
Educational attainments completed relatively early	Slower start on career; graduate school postponed	Flexible approach to "using" or completing education
Job and Career		
Career selection may include "male bastions," where female needs and occupational flexibility are less tolerated but prestige is higher	Part-time work or nonmanagerial track chosen; more flexible, family-friendly careers; less upward workplace mobility; divided focus; less willingness to relocate	Financial sacrifices; focus on jobs versus more demanding careers; interrupted work advancement
If entrepreneurship is chosen, goals for the start-up are ambitious	If entrepreneurship is chosen, firm is a modest service venture	Entrepreneurial goals less likely
Career track may include fast-track promotions and transfers even if family life affected; pattern of		

increasing responsibility at work and continued need to prove oneself at new jobs; family fits around work demands		

Personal Life

Higher divorce rate for women may lead to increased work focus	Financial adjustments; exploration of other interests as time permits	Financial sacrifices; exploration of other interests; mastery associated with hobbies, not just work
Involvement in community through financial donations or at expense of family time; longer hours at work; limited involvement with nonwork interests and hobbies	Limited involvement in schools, community	Active involvement in schools and community

Focus

Family fits around work demands	All demands fit around each other	Nonfamily demands fit around family
Intense inner drive for mastery	Pronounced inner drives for both mastery and intimacy	Pronounced inner need for intimacy
Personal achievement	Relative balance	Service to others

out of a job. Somehow the sixties, seventies, and even eighties flew by. Her children were long gone. Her husband didn't want to move for his job anymore. It was time to win back her life.

She became an independent consultant for start-up companies, helping them create policies and practices, hire people, meet venture capitalists, and work on any of the million and one details that could make the difference between being a star and being DOA. As she became genuinely addicted to her work, her thinking and her confidence blossomed. One day she realized a way to join her old love of things international with her passion for start-ups. Backed by an increasingly broad professional network, she launched the first international business incubator in Silicon Valley—and in the entire nation. Every week, delegations from Beijing, Prague, Kathmandu, or Johannesburg visit her brainchild, a business nest for fledgling start-ups where they can share office space, marketing, and other resources.

It seems clear that Carole achieved balance through a sequential strategy, first raising her family while working at jobs rather than career positions (a midcolumn strategy on the balance continuum of Table 8.1). Born at the tail end of the Depression, her early childhood was during World War II, an historic era that taught young women how to support the men at the front—and how to step aside when they came home from the war. If alive today, her parents would have described their daughter as clearly "type A" and goal-oriented, but it didn't occur to them to raise her for a profession.

She expressed her need for achievement by parenting four girls, unlike the smaller family size that was the norm of the day, and by taking on regular part-time work to give herself mental refreshment and pin money; she was secure in her belief that her husband was the real breadwinner. When asked about her choices and whether she feels that she compromised or sacrificed her own needs on behalf of others, she replies: "I can honestly say that I did what I wanted. But you have to understand how the world around you shapes what you think you want. When I was twenty or thirty or even forty, I never wanted to be an entrepreneur. I just wanted to be busy, to be doing something I liked." As an afterthought, she offered: "The hard part was figuring out what to do. Having the girls didn't take too much thought. But the other . . . starting this incubator . . . it took me a long time to understand what I could do, and what was worth going after in the world of business. The mental part was harder than actually getting the funding, convincing others, and executing the start-up."

Gender and Achievement

Some readers may wonder if women's innate achievement drives differ from those of men. After all, a significant gender gap remains in our contemporary cathedrals of accomplishment (the Fortune 500 boardrooms, venture capitalist firms, and university computer science programs). From neurosurgery to manufacturing, women are absent at the very top, even though they are making strides further down. The Bureau of Labor Statistics predicts that, after comprehensive 1998 figures are compiled, the salary gap between men and women will have closed to full-time women workers earning 77 percent of the median male wage, with much smaller gaps for entry-level women and for working women without children who take less time off from the workplace.[1] It is, of course, debatable that such salary statistics even form a reasonable proxy for achievement in the first place. Women often intentionally choose lower-paying industries or niches in a particular profession (examples are family medicine and psychiatry, which are traditionally lower paying than other medical specialties), seeking a type of achievement that cannot be expressed through salary surveys alone.

Pay differences aside, no empirical evidence exists to support an inner achievement gap between men and women. If more men than women are helicopter pilots, CEOs, and prime ministers, it is experience and opportunity—not aspiration—that is lacking among the women. Gender aside, our inborn personalities, in combination with social and familial expectations and role models, define our inner needs for achievement. Like men, women tend to emerge from the womb as either hard-charging and driven or relatively easygoing.[2] But the combined fields of Jungian psychology and personality theory have found no visible inner difference in the achievement orientations of men versus women. However,

Table 8.2. Women's Share of Occupations.

Occupation	1983 Percentage	1994 Percentage
Secretary	99	99
Private child care worker	97	97
Registered nurse	96	94
Bank teller	91	90
Librarian	87	84
Office clerk	81	80
Psychologist	57	59
Physician's assistant	36	54
Sales clerk	48	49
Postal clerk	37	44
Pharmacist	27	38
Mail carrier	17	34
Lawyer	15	25
Physician	16	22
Architect	13	17
Dentist	7	13
Police officer, detective	6	11
Engineer	6	8
Firefighter	1	2
Auto mechanic	<1	2

Source: Naomi Neft and Ann D. Levine, *Where Women Stand: An International Report on the Status of Women in 140 Countries.* Copyright © 1997 by Naomi Neft and Ann D. Levine. Reprinted by permission of Random House, Inc.

expression of achievement clearly varies across gender, as studies of occupational segregation by gender confirm (Table 8.2).

Stunningly persistent cultural biases continue to influence expression of women's achievement. Only last summer I was traveling with my family in a scenic, mountainous corner of Idaho near Utah and Wyoming. The four of us were attending a local county fair and entered a Quonset hut sheltering the public health exhibition. As we walked toward the first table, a smiling woman volunteer approached our little group, handing a paper nurse's cap to my daughter, Clare, but a paper stethoscope to my son, Evan.

My husband tactfully stepped to the side, grinning as he caught my eye. As cheerfully and nonjudgmentally as possible, I asked for a second stethoscope for my daughter, saying, "She wants the same opportunity her brother gets." The woman was clearly astonished. There was no doubt in my mind that no one else who had attended the fair had even noticed, let alone reacted to this unintentional but clear incident of gender bias—and one performed by a woman. In Silicon Valley, New York, Chicago, or Atlanta, we may take for granted practices and beliefs that our counterparts elsewhere cannot.

With respect to the role of the third shift, I believe another type of gender gap remains: a difference in how women feel about the ways they balance personal achievement and service to others. In my experience, men rarely express the same wistfulness, guilt, frustration, or self-castigation when faced with outright choices requiring them to determine who comes first. Compared to women, they seem little affected by an inner third shift and are far more likely to accept their own imbalance toward personal achievement in their lives.

Still, the term *working father* is redundant in our society, notwithstanding the emergence of attention to men's roles and needs by nonprofit think tanks such as the Families and Work Institute in New York City.[3] We recognize that boys must deal with their own self-esteem issues, arising from sexism and the "mask of masculinity" that depresses male willingness to express a softer side.[4] So it may be that men are increasingly experiencing and expressing work-family conflicts. A 1991 Gallup poll revealed that 59 percent of American men derived "a greater sense of satisfaction from caring for their family than from a job well done at work."[5] A more recent, comprehensive study conducted between 1992 and 1997 showed no significant differences in the level of work-family conflict expressed by mothers versus fathers.[6]

But a gap you can drive a truck through remains between actual and espoused male behavior. Men may check off the "correct," socially desirable boxes on surveys of work-family conflict, but our workplaces are even less tolerant of masculine involvement with family life if it detracts from focusing on work. Fewer than 15 percent of eligible men avail themselves of formal paternity leave when their wives are having a baby.[7] Today's journalists are subject to "paternity leave preoccupation," too readily equating a single statistic—paternity leave usage—with men's commitment to their families. Nonetheless, the balance challenge is clearly experienced differently according to one's gender.

It strikes me that the definitive gender gap in issues of balance has not been addressed at all by these studies. Men and women alike may experience inner uncertainty for their choices, but men seem to sidestep the gnawing third-shift demands that place responsibility on themselves when things go awry. Thus, for example, the Families and Work Institute studies indicate that working parents of either gender with young children in day care spend considerable mental energy worrying about the quality of their children's daily experience. But women are far more likely than men to actually alter their schedules to adapt to day care rules and strictures, particularly when comparing the behavior of the most senior executive women with high-ranking executive men. In addition, women are much more likely to blame themselves for placing their work needs above their children's needs if difficulties ensue with a child's day care. This observation is consistent with gender studies cited earlier in this book that found men blaming external factors in the situation when things go wrong, while women hold themselves responsible.

So when it comes to day care, men are likely to focus their mental energies on changing the situation as quickly as possible, and secondarily changing their own schedules and work requirements. But rarely do men express a feeling that *they* have chosen wrongly, in balancing achievement needs with service to others in the family. Perhaps this is because men hold a forgiving and well-rounded view of the role of work in their lives. Their breadwinning is not only selfish or self-aggrandizing personal achievement but a vital, if indirect, service to the family.

Therefore, a broader examination of balance, as defined in this book, spotlights a woman's inner third shift as the core of the dilemma. It is this sense of personal responsibility for the lives and feelings of others that makes women so much more vulnerable to an internal glass ceiling. It is also why women find balance so very difficult to manage effectively, even on the days when there are no troubling calls from the day care center.

Making Your Third Shift Work for You: Finding Balance

The concluding pages of this book, as in the chapters before this one, offer some final strategies for women struggling with the inner and outer realities of issues of balance.

- Reach out; share your third shift with others.
- Ease up on yourself; treat yourself as well as you treat others.
- Broaden your perspective to identify your life's work.
- Go for the win-win; find service opportunities that everyone values.
- Allow others the joy of developing themselves.

These strategies are independent of where you choose to serve or achieve: in a corporation, through a start-up, in the community, or at home. As with every chapter before this one, actions begin with reflection. The third shift is invisible and psychological, experienced by some as a tyrannical mental devil on one shoulder and a powerful mental angel on the other. You are the only one who can use your twin voices to attain the life you want, in your head, in your heart, and out there in the world.

Reach Out; Share Your Third Shift with Others

One of the best ways to really understand something is to talk it through with someone else you trust to listen, rather than judge or criticize. Our individual needs as women may vary, but to the extent that the adult development of most women includes a desire for sustained connection with others, reaching out is an important psychological activity that can be overlooked in our busy lives. I have met few women who effectively manage their balance dilemmas without finding a way to occasionally yet regularly air their third shifts with others. Like dirty laundry left too long in an airless closet, a surprising amount of psychological mildew can accumulate without fresh light and air.

Specifically, women who find acceptable ways to share their third shifts with others derive tremendous enlightenment, satisfaction, and even concrete survival tips as they swap stories and feelings. They also report a tremendous lightening of their emotional burden. But many women are afraid to let the emotions behind their third shifts leak out to others. Stephan Rechtschaffen, M.D., a pioneer of the wellness movement, suggests why this is the case: "America is a society that treats emotion contemptuously. Men who cry are thought of as sissies; women who cry are considered hysterical. And so we keep busy."[8] We struggle to hide—even from ourselves—our true feelings. And we are extremely cautious about sharing them with others.

Fortunately, a good many women have learned that the risks of letting it all hang out are far less than those associated with bottling it all up. The result is an eclectic array of available strategies and forums for women to learn from each other. Sharing strategies can be formal and include a price tag (networking groups, personal or executive coaches, consultants and advisors) or informal and free (friends, coworkers, new acquaintances). Some women are especially open and divulge their most intimate thoughts to a stranger, while others are private and reserved, unwilling to share until sufficient time has passed to build a genuine bond with another individual. For all types of women, the common requirement is willingness to reach out and open up to others, as appropriate, and to be a good listening partner in return.

With regard to our third shifts as women, an objective listener not only offers encouragement and support through the nonverbal cues of body language but can also identify specific points of confusion and misperception; she may be particularly helpful in identifying our blind spots. By definition, we cannot identify our own blind spots, or they wouldn't be blind spots! The feedback we can cull from others about them is especially crucial for genuine self-awareness, that portion of our third shift that helps us grow and take new chances through our life's choices.

The need for genuine, informal discussions with other women facing similar issues has resulted in a recent groundswell of women's networking groups across the country, particularly in corporate settings where formal women's networks provide open-ended support, access to other women in the company, collective advice to management, and career development opportunities. In some companies, formal women's groups have even been instrumental vehicles for organizational change.[9] Catalyst's recently published guide to women's networks urges women to consider four factors in finding participants:

1. Commitment level to the group
2. Interpersonal skill level and listening ability
3. Diversity of backgrounds, ethnic membership, ages, and interests
4. Collegiality, the intangible chemistry among women that buttresses meaningful exchanges[10]

I might add that these requirements greatly augment any type of women's gathering, from reading groups and baroque quartets to an enclave of female physicists.

My own experience in launching a women's community organization taught me that women can derive tremendous benefits from expending effort to start a networking program and regularly attend its activities. The singular benefit of formal networks is that they force you, as a busy woman with a hair-on-fire-schedule, to take time out to talk with other women (especially if you've paid for the function in advance and don't want to lose your deposit). The women in my study, as those who attended our functions, were quite explicit about the benefits to themselves. Although the purpose of the network was to help them launch their own businesses, they gained perspective and camaraderie, support, and courage as well.

Ease up on Yourself; Treat Yourself as Well as You Treat Others

Most of us were raised with a variation upon the Golden Rule: "Treat others the way you would like to be treated yourself." Ironic, isn't it, that my recommendation for women is the very inverse of this old saw? Far too many women have strayed toward the treating-others end of the continuum, from what I've seen. In many instances, the distraction of serving others keeps women from focusing on themselves and their own self-doubt. Negative thinking can quickly deteriorate into a genuine negative cycle because no one likes to be around someone who exudes negative energy. Therefore, the first step in treating yourself well is to ensure that you listen to a positive inner message, and not just the vicious inner cycle of self-doubt portrayed in Figure 8.1. Otherwise, others may treat you as poorly as you are treating yourself.

This cycle of third-shift self-doubt can occur no matter how you spend your days, at work or at home. As discussed previously, young mothers at home are the most vulnerable to psychological isolation and negative thinking.[11] If you are such a woman, the relationships with your children and your spouse are likely to be affected, further fueling your sense of isolation and negativity. In the entrepreneurial arena, the negative cycle has its most damaging impact on customers. They can literally read your negativity and lack of self-confidence, and they will take their business elsewhere—thus "validating" that you are not an effective entrepreneur. Finally, in the corporate world, classic derailment theory is especially clear about the consequences of negativity. Leaders can attract no followers if

Figure 8.1. Negativity: A Self-Fulfilling Prophecy.

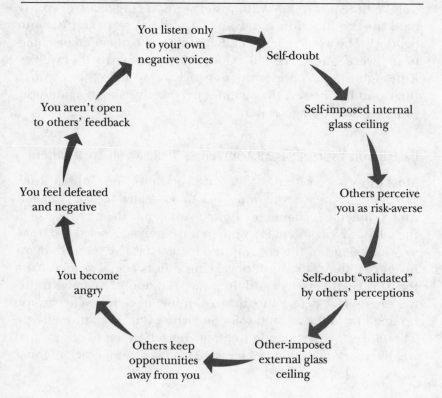

they are perceived as negative. Even if you are described by others as highly intelligent, knowledgeable, and capable, others are likely to see you as abrasive, overly critical, and unable to effectively extend support and encouragement once you are labeled as negative.[12] Over my last decade as an executive coach, my most rewarding work has been with clients who faced their own negativity; internalized the need for change; and sustained visible, behavioral improvements that broke their negative cycles. They began to treat themselves better, leading in turn to better responses from coworkers.

In any case, the best way to break the negative cycle is to reduce the probability of starting it in the first place. This means getting a handle on your self-doubts before they flare up and build into an impenetrable internal glass ceiling that alters your behavior and willingness to take appropriate risks. Here is where a solid listening partner can have great impact. Women who practice chronic self-flagellation may require the services of a licensed professional, but all of us as women suffer from occasional twinges of uncertainty. I believe that these bouts can be painful, but they are useful to us because if we listen to them without succumbing to them we face ourselves openly and set ourselves up for learning and growth. To ensure that we regularly monitor our lives, while balancing our mix of service and achievement, these questions can be a great stimulus for thought and action:

- Are you happy with the way your life is going?
- When were you last happy? What does it take to make you happy and satisfied?
- What does it take to make others happy and satisfied?
- Are you able to get what you want without feeling guilty or believing you've let others down?
- Do you feel in charge of your own choices, or do you defer to others?
- What evidence can you point to that shows you treat yourself as well as others?
- How do you define the personal achievements of your life?
- What are you most proud of in your life?
- Is there anything you would like to change in your life? What stops you?

Broaden Your Perspective to Identify Your Life's Work

Overcoming negativity and your internal glass ceiling (if you have one) are required steps to finding effective balance between serving others or achieving for oneself. But the two steps are insufficient. It is essential to understand your true *calling* in life, the particular activity or career that excites you and offers you genuine pride and satisfaction. Achievements or service related to calling allow you the best chance of excelling.

Your pathway to this calling need not be perfectly linear (Carole Lockwood offers one such example). You may even have more than one avocation (as I use the word here, not your livelihood but your life's "real work") throughout your life. For many women, the material circumstances of their lives, conflicting priorities, or the desire for active involvement in family life may mean that pursuing one's calling must, at times, be woven through the background, rather than the foreground, of life. But this is OK.

In her comparative biography of five women, celebrated author Mary Catherine Bateson helps us gain broad perspective on this issue. She views life as an improvisatory art, beginning with her own "disgruntled reflection on my life as a sort of desperate improvisation in which I was constantly trying to make something coherent from conflicting elements to fit rapidly changing settings."[13] For women in general, as for many creative people, there is no predestined, single path through life, initiated with early commitment to a particular career, followed by acquisition of the relevant educational pedigree and then by achievements on that single path alone—like a jumbo jet nosing down from a dark sky onto a brightly lit, narrow runway.

This linear movement through one's life or career is a useful model for some but is inappropriate, and even painfully confining, for others. Nonetheless, the third shift of thousands of women echoes with the shoulds, that common malady arising from comparing the more linear careers of men or childless women with their own. One way to still this inner turmoil is to take Bateson's approach to heart, understanding that energies need not be narrowly focused on a single ambition but may be refreshed through the improvisation of refocus and redefinition. Consider also that you may be viewing your achievements through too narrow a lens.

I think of Dawn Simmons in this regard, a highly gifted artist in my study who developed unique, eye-catching techniques in collage design with a variety of imaginative media, from metal to marshmallows. Despite efforts at turning her art into a business, she was unable to support herself without a day job at a local university. Much to her surprise, she found herself devoting increasing time and mental energy to her job, greatly enjoying the mental refreshment it offered as well as its modest financial rewards.

She shifted how she practiced her art, never abandoning her active participation in it or relinquishing her identity as an artist, knowing this was her true calling. Rather, she braided it into her life in another way. She surrounded herself with other artisans, steeping herself in their community and participating regularly in local events. Most significant, she continued to actively strive to master her craft even further, always experimenting with new designs and methods, and selling the occasional piece.

From the standpoint of balance, Dawn reminds us that the type and degree of achievement are less important than their centrality to your true avocation. Thus, some women may need to actually publish a book or be promoted to a vice presidency to feel they have achieved something. Others, like Dawn, can experience the most profound sense of achievement in completing a collage involving new methods or materials. Her life is a study of continuous redirection and reconstruction, a pulling together of different elements—not unlike the paper collage art she creates.

Early in her book, Bateson asks: "At what point does desperate improvisation become significant achievement? These are important questions in a world in which we are all increasingly strangers and sojourners. The knight errant, who finds his challenges along the way, may be a better model for our times than the knight who is questing for the Grail."[14]

The purpose of identifying your life's true work, over and above whether you choose corporate, entrepreneurial, community, or stay-at-home status, is threefold. First, it allows you to identify a life worth living. Second, it helps you understand how to find and follow an "authentic" life that expresses your natural calling. Third, as a result you work on a personal legacy you can leave behind to help others while increasing your own sense of fulfillment, self-acceptance, and self-worth.

Notice that these elements of purpose involve a sequence of first *seeing* what your life involves, then *understanding* how it expresses you, and finally *using* that knowledge to leave a tangible legacy behind. To better acquaint you with how to do this, it may be helpful to offer my own life as an illustration. I can say with assurance that it took me many years to actually recognize a central theme in my life's choices and activities and to articulate that theme cogently and comprehensibly. Today, I can say that the central work of my life is development—of self and of others, the milestones along the way more faithfully represented by a mosaic rather than a lifeline.

An outsider could review my resume and genuinely wonder why I "hopped" so much, from mental health administration to start-up marketing, from community service and academia to consulting, with brief "breaks" in between to have children and indulge a childhood passion for horses. In the privacy of my inner third shift, I acknowledge that others may be unable to decode the events and passions of my life as an integrated journey. I alone may be able to recognize the single common thread of my achievements and service to others.

So, step back and connect the dots of your real life to discover the picture that emerges. When I was a graduate student, my advisor, Bill Ouchi (the renowned author of *Theory Z Management*) told me that it was a wonderful idea to "map my field" as I aged. He said that it might take as much as ten or twenty years to really understand its outlines, or even to imagine how my scholarly contributions over time would affect the boundaries of the discipline of strategic management, my specialty. Ouchi was thinking about how I could increasingly broaden my perspective on the scholarly body of knowledge I had chosen for my career as I progressed from doctoral-student status through the academic way stations of my field (assistant, associate, full professor), but I have borrowed his advice as a way of thinking about a woman's life.

Rather than creating a map, however, I have found it meaningful to work with a life mosaic, an interrelated set of pieces that can be formed together in infinite ways, so long as the mortar between the pieces is strong and lasting. Here's one way to do it. Find a blank sheet of paper and cut it into an even number of equally sized squares. On each square, briefly write something that describes a time, an event, an achievement, or a feeling of *persistent* importance to you in your life. When you are finished, put all of the squares together to form a larger whole (accepting that some of your squares may be blank). The idea is to move the pieces around freely until you are satisfied that they yield a compelling, meaningful picture.

The next step is to put your life mosaic away for a few days and let your third shift "incubate" its true meaning and major themes. When you are ready to return to it, play with the pieces again and shift them around some more. Force yourself to find a label for your mosaic as one way of articulating your life's theme and the potential legacy you can leave behind. Rearrange your squares one more time with your central theme in mind, as I have done in Figure 8.2 for the squares in my life, all of which point to different ways of honoring the theme of development that guides my life's work and legacy to others.

Identifying this kind of holistic appreciation and acceptance of your life's work is like finding the picture in the Rorschach inkblots. It requires concentration and mental openness. When you view your life as a mosaic unfolding over time, you are not dependent upon any one piece. Your third shift eases, knowing that your entire life—not just tomorrow or the day after or the week after that—can fluidly build to a pleasing balance of service and achievement that is right for you.

Go for the Win-Win; Find Service Opportunities That Everyone Values

No matter the degree to which we are self-aware, it is a singular feature of human beings that we all yearn for external validation. Our individual personalities require somewhat different amounts of it, which change dramatically over the course of our lives and individual developmental cycles. For example, women in midlife who have attained career achievements consistent with their early expectations may need little or no approbation from others. My sample includes several such women who have radically downshifted to lower-prestige community service work or quieter at-home existences after several decades of fast-lane corporate life. My sample also includes an equal number of women, like Carole,

Figure 8.2. My Personal Life Mosaic: Important Parts of the Puzzle.

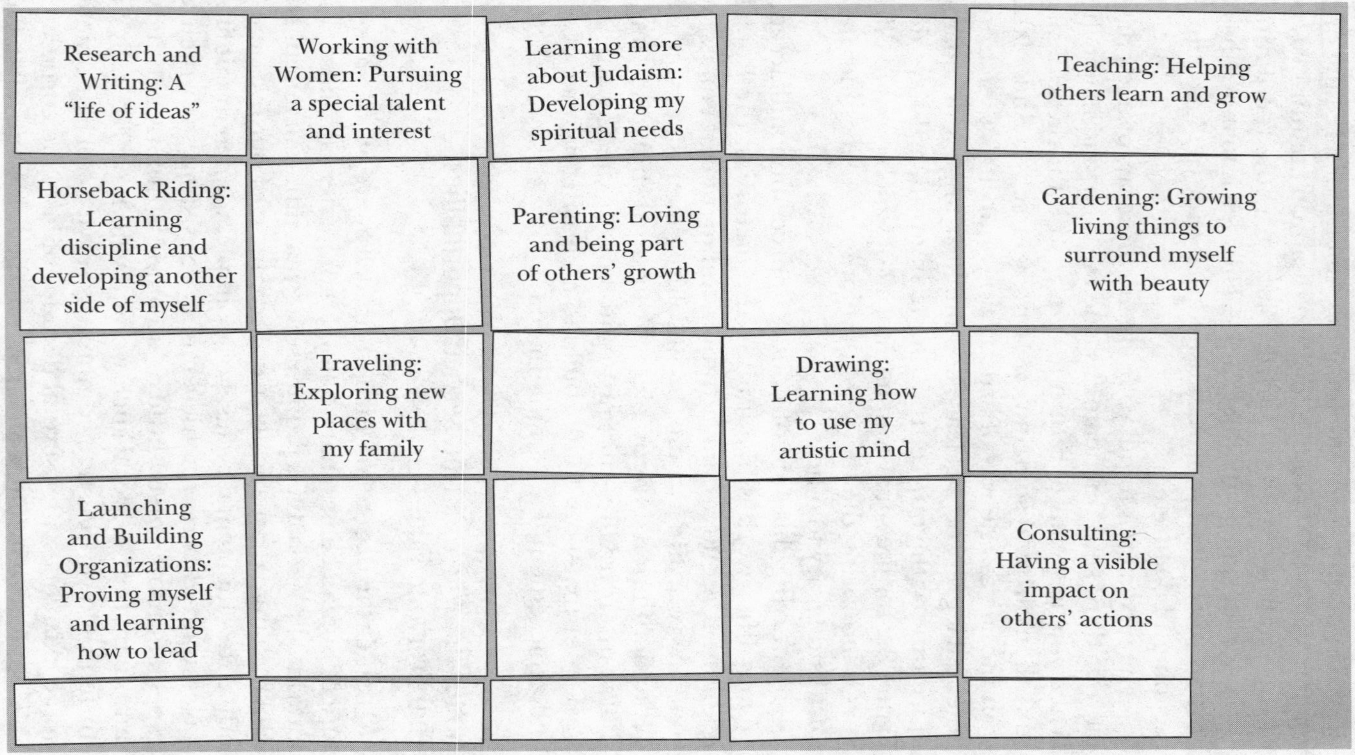

Research and Writing: A "life of ideas"	Working with Women: Pursuing a special talent and interest	Learning more about Judaism: Developing my spiritual needs		Teaching: Helping others learn and grow
Horseback Riding: Learning discipline and developing another side of myself		Parenting: Loving and being part of others' growth		Gardening: Growing living things to surround myself with beauty
	Traveling: Exploring new places with my family		Drawing: Learning how to use my artistic mind	
Launching and Building Organizations: Proving myself and learning how to lead				Consulting: Having a visible impact on others' actions

who never fully tried their achievement wings until midlife. For the Carole Lockwoods of the world, acknowledgment from others was a crucial pillar that supported her new, unfamiliar role and accelerated her transition to it.

Given your current situation and needs, you must always decide for yourself the degree to which your life choices are influenced by others' expectations and judgments. A harmonious third shift around balance is impossible without this unflinching personal honesty. As I write this, I am coaching a woman, Marianne Hobbes, whose demotion during a companywide reorganization delivered a near-fatal blow to her pride and feelings of self-worth. After the dust settled, she found herself in a new job, but without her cherished title of director. She embarked on a vigorous campaign to find another position in the company, a job with sufficiently large scope to reestablish her old rank as a director. At the same time, she devoted considerable thought to how she could keep others from learning about her demotion. Despite her usually high levels of productivity, capability, and keen business acumen, her workload in her new position suffered, hurting her reputation even further. Understandably, her feelings about herself, her career, and even the role of work in her life changed. The negative voices of her third shift pounded her with self-doubt each night, while her boss jumped on her case during the day, telling her to buck up and get over it.

Many women in this study erred too strongly toward the service end of the balance continuum, but Marianne faced exactly the opposite problem: she was too far toward the achievement pole, and it got her into trouble. When her title was first removed, her internal world fell apart and her third shift went on red alert. She experienced prolonged depression, painfully waffling in and out of anger at herself, her boss, or her company amid bouts of self-castigation for what had happened and how she had handled it. Through discussions taking place over several months, she began to see that she could either leave the company or turn what had happened to her into a learning opportunity and a chance to renew herself and rebuild her skills. Marianne knew that other women would have left the company in a huff, or even sued for discrimination. But she genuinely felt that her loyalty would help her career more than a job switch would.

There is no definitive way to know if her decision to stay was the right one. What I do know is that she made a choice that eased the negative voices in her third shift, and this was the key to her rebirth, in others' eyes as well as in her own. Staying and overcoming her situation allowed her to regain self-respect, and over time her self-confidence returned. How did this process unfold?

First of all, Marianne's biggest challenge was to rebuild her credibility. Curiously, she was viewed negatively, rather than tolerantly or even positively, because she was perceived as a do-whatever-it-takes overachiever. The corporate world abounds with such individuals, but the reality too often is that female overachievers—particularly if their leadership style is too energetic, too directive, or too confrontational—find peer acceptance much more difficult to attain than do their male counterparts. In this case, her achievement drive was viewed as personal empire building, and few trusted that she did anything unless it benefited her.

Thus, we reframed the problem Marianne was facing: rebuilding her credibility was not an issue of finding a new job with the title of director. Rather, rebuilding her reputation and credibility became a hunt for opportunities *to serve others,* but on important and visible assignments rather than dead-end "doormat drills" to become a good corporate citizen. We began to identify new challenges that suited her temperament and experience and that others would perceive as positive, important opportunities to serve the company. In our conversations, she disclosed that she loved her director title, and the prestige, salary, and attention it gained her. What she didn't actually like, however, was the job content—public relations, a field she had been in for twenty years and that had long since lost its magic for her.

Without the director title to worry about anymore, Marianne took a new position in the company in product marketing, at a senior management rather than director level. She still wishes the rank were higher, but she genuinely believes she will earn her stripes again. Product marketing is one of the core functions of the organization. By moving into this area, she has actually increased her company visibility, her impact on results, and her lateral network. In this core function, she must collaborate with and support nearly a dozen technology groups. It is really a people job, a marketing role secondarily. But most important, she loves the work and the new challenges. She feels renewed, rapidly learning additional skills, deploying them effectively, and already producing results *for others*. Her peers no longer avoid her in the hallways, reticent to talk with an angry and bitter colleague. Instead, they are coming to her for new ideas and invitations to serve on task forces where marketing talent is needed. Rather than focusing so zealously on activities that only help attain her individual goals, Marianne is growing a reputation for helping others, greatly increasing her credibility while enhancing her own job satisfaction. There has been no mention yet of a promotion with the vaunted title of director, but it's clear that the tide has turned.

Throughout this painful period, Marianne's third shift has been instrumental to her learning. She has deliberately focused on judgment-free self-awareness, recognizing that she can be too quick to jump to destructive self-doubt. Her increasing attention to serving others sustains this positive cycle. You could say that she has mastered the win-win. There are no losers here.

Allow Others the Joy of Developing Themselves

Of course, there are many ways to serve others, but doing everything for them is not necessarily the best approach. This holds true in the workplace and on the home front, each life arena posing its own issues with respect to balance. At work, junior employees must make a few of their own mistakes and learn to handle their own challenges independently without being rescued by a boss. The best managers practice situational leadership, incrementally adjusting the degree of emotional support and straightforward directives for employees over time.[15]

On the home front, many parents face a parallel struggle, and some may experience difficulty letting go and permitting their children sufficient space to learn how to manage their responsibilities on their own. Try to match the level of difficulty of the assignment with the child's maturity, building up capability gradually, in small steps, keeping it positive and fun. I offer a seemingly trivial example, but its application can be broadened indefinitely. Suppose you wish to teach your school-aged kids how to prepare breakfast on their own. Beginning the lessons in the hectic hour before school starts is not the right approach. Instead, shoot for an instruction period on a quiet weekend morning (is this an oxymoron?). Organize the resources and materials first. Personally model and perform the necessary actions, and take them through the steps one at a time. You probably won't be able to have them do all of the steps on their first attempt.

If you have several children, help them operate as a team. Assign initial roles or allow them to choose how they want to work together before you begin. Then watch *them* perform the actual cooking tasks while you offer encouragement and support from the side, exactly like a swimming coach who rarely jumps into the water yet still improves an athlete's speed and stroke.

Focus on one thing at a time. Initially, it's a good idea to offer to clean up so your kids can fully concentrate on and enjoy the task they are learning, which is preparing breakfast and not learning how to clean. (This should be fun, by the way!) As their competence builds over time, add a greater portion of cleanup to the regular responsibilities. Give them small rewards frequently and consistently for their efforts. Don't overlook simple praise as a reinforcer. Then shoot for a visible, grander event so your kids can showcase their new skills for you—perhaps cooking a deluxe diner-style breakfast for the entire family, a joint celebration with you of what they've learned. Children love to show off new skills.

This entire process takes time, the wisdom of Athena, and the patience of Job. But it pays big dividends for everyone because it reframes the concept of service to development of others. The process just described is a proven leadership approach in business as well as a sound parenting strategy to teach independence while building and mastering concrete skills. You can modify this generic approach, whether you're training line workers to assemble aircraft at Boeing or flipping pancakes in your kitchen with your kids. In their outstanding leadership classic *The Leadership Challenge,* James M. Kouzes and Barry Z. Posner describe the five steps of exemplary leadership, three of which are (1) enabling others to act, (2) modeling the way, and (3) encouraging the heart.[16] In my description of the approach to helping children become competent chefs, note that I explicitly applied these three elements of leadership from the Kouzes and Posner model. In a start-up, at a local church, a high-tech firm, or in your own kitchen, it can be very rewarding to recast how you think about serving others.

Wherever the venue, serving others can be thought of as direct or indirect. Direct examples are obvious: everything from chauffeuring children to furnishing treats for office gatherings, adding additional services for customers without charging for them, and volunteering regular hours for your favorite charitable institution. My personal experience may parallel yours. When done in a balanced way, helping others yields as much pleasure and benefit to you as it does to those you serve, if not more. This is why anonymous bequests and offers of help sometimes yield the most inner satisfaction of all.

But there exists another type of service altogether, one that also involves tremendous returns for all parties. Such service is indirect in the sense that it leads to achievement and mastery for others, rather than involving personal services per se: picking up dry cleaning, washing dishes, or writing someone else's speech for an important executive briefing. The underlying difference is in the outcome. Personal services are aimed at convenience rather than developing skills and abilities in others. I urge you as a woman to consider your mix of both types of service, because the opportunities for internal satisfaction and external recognition are far greater with the latter. Viewed in this way, service not only involves development but corresponds closely with empowerment, a buzzword thrown around so cavalierly these days that it may have lost its true meaning: the ability to enable others to succeed by supporting them and sharing power.

Strictly speaking, the first step in empowerment involves mastery, not service to others. Albert Bandura, a Stanford University psychologist, found that the most important thing a manager can do to empower others is to "help them experience personal mastery over some challenge or problem."[17] Other dimensions central to empowerment are shown in Table 8.3.

This table is a treasure trove of ideas for women to rethink how they serve others and balance that desire with their own opportunities to excel and achieve. Pure personal service to others can be uninspiring and even degrading at times. At the other end of the balance continuum, complete, self-centered achievement can be viewed with distrust. If overdone to the extent of other gratifications in your life, it warms neither your bed nor your soul. So aim to apply more empowerment in your work or home-front situation, creating wins for everyone. Isn't that what real balance is all about?

Table 8.3.　Five Core Dimensions of Empowerment.

Dimension	Outcome	Methods
Self-efficacy (a sense of personal competence)	Competence	Create personal mastery experiences; model; provide information
Self-determination	Choice	Provide information; offer resources; organize teams
Personal control	Impact	Personal mastery experiences; offer resources; organize teams
Meaning	Value	Offer support; emotional arousal
Trust	Security	Model; offer support; create confidence

Source: Adapted from David A. Whetten and Kim S. Cameron, *Developing Management Skills*, 3rd ed. (table 8.2, p. 486). © 1995, 1991, 1984, Addison-Wesley Educational Publishers Inc. Reprinted by permission of Addison-Wesley Longman.

An Inner Oasis

When I developed the conceptual framework around which this book is organized—the three dilemmas of identity, task, and balance—I wanted to help women rediscover the harmony that makes life such a wonderful and exciting gift. I was convinced that the title of a study about women and their particular challenges should be "Walking the Tightrope." My agent and editor tactfully reminded me that this metaphor has been overworked. But as I find myself approaching the very end of this volume, I see that the title would have been completely wrong but for another reason entirely. Who among us can experience harmony if we feel that our lives are a tightrope, and that a single misstep can cause a fatal fall—or at the very least, a long climb back up a tall ladder? Even if we cross the tightrope safely, winning is losing if we sacrifice harmony. The outer person can be satisfied with seeing achievement, gaining acclaim, and winning respect from others. But the inner, third shift of women demands something more. If she learns how to manage it, a woman's third shift can be a refreshing oasis from the cacophony of the outer life. The creative tension inherent in finding balance is hollow without inner harmony, a condition stemming from a tolerant and accepting third shift rather than a critical and self-doubting one. For women, the hallmark of our age is *choice*. Whether such choice becomes your nemesis or your path to nirvana, it is the delicate balance of self-awareness and self-doubting in your third shift that makes all the difference.

With this in mind, I ultimately abandoned the working metaphor of the tightrope (an image that also conjures up too much emphasis on external causes for a woman's lack of inner harmony). How many of us look outward when we feel out of harmony? Indeed, there remains much to blame and protest in the outer world. Glass ceilings should probably be called cement ceilings; they can seem so impenetrable at the very highest levels, except in the rarest of instances. Women continue to be vulnerable to outright sexual harassment, particularly in industries and worksites where their numbers are small. Recall the recent public scandal of the first female cadet at the Citadel, who retreated in shame and horror from the hazings, disrespect, and outright hostility she encountered. Also keep in mind that a woman cadet has just graduated, and dozens more are following her.

There is, of course, much to report on the brighter side of women's progress, but that is really beside the point here.[18] The central purpose of this book is to help women understand the role that their third shift can play in life choices and satisfaction. The consultants are howling today that the secret to life is scoring well on "emotional intelligence," a relatively new label coined by Daniel Goleman for self-awareness, self-regulation, motivation, empathy, and social skills.[19] With regard to the third shift, Goleman's definition of self-awareness is especially germane: "knowing what we are feeling in the moment, and using those preferences to guide our decision making; having a realistic assessment of our own abilities and a well-grounded sense of self-confidence."

Indeed, many a woman I know has succeeded thanks to emotional stamina on the inside, as well as personal stamina on the outside. I hope to make an even stronger case for the importance of what I've termed an *inner oasis*. If you make personal choices about your life and career on the outside that do not ultimately bring you harmony on the inside, that is, in your third shift—the occasional flurry of self-doubting notwithstanding—your choices are in need of reexamination, if not dramatic change. Feminine progress that involves financial freedom without psychological liberty is no freedom at all. It is instead a little death for ourselves, and ultimately for those whom we love most.

It is my deepest hope that the concrete techniques discussed in this book for managing both the external dilemmas of identity and task and the meta-challenge of balance—in combination with the corresponding voices of the third shift—lead you to greater harmony with the life you have, as well as offering practical strategies to change your life, should you wish to pursue a new path. Throughout this book, I have sought to blend the hundred-plus female voices in my study with the hundreds of clients and adult students I have coached and mentored in the past two decades. When appropriate, I have shared my personal insights and experiences to bring a point to life. In the writing of this book, my own third shift has flared up many times. My fingers have literally paused over the keyboard when I've started to prescribe advice that I have not listened to myself.

It remains impossible for me to tie a bow at the end of this book about women's lives and choices, and the ever-present creative tension that accompanies those choices. The ribbon would unravel too soon. I fall back instead upon the thesis of Carol Gilligan, a personal role model[20] who raised her own voice to argue that women's development is centered in and discovers its voice through connection to others. It is not that women choose relationships over achievement; it is that they require both to fully realize their potential, thereby creating the dilemmas unique to women that are discussed herein.

So look around you. Listen and observe. In the workplace and elsewhere, you must not permit a male standard of development to become the de facto standard for both sexes. The final lesson of the third shift is that too many women are motivated quite differently from their male counterparts, measuring their success as well as their sorrows through another lens, in another voice, and with a differing result.

I believe that it is the rare man who acts on his third shift (if he has one), while it is the rare woman who does not. It is my genuine hope that, after reading this book, women will act fully and freely on the insights stemming from increased self-awareness, rather than holding themselves back and erecting an internal glass ceiling from the painful shards of self-doubt.

I close with these words from a woman in my study: "Life is short, and you should do some things you want. Damn it, it's time."

Notes

1. These Bureau of Labor Statistics are cited by Joanne Jacobs, "Women Deserve Equity, Not Advantage," *San Jose Mercury News,* Apr. 12, 1999. They are also quoted in Cathy Young's *Ceasefire! Why Women and Men Must Join Forces to Achieve True Equality* (New York: Free Press, 1999).

2. Seminal research on achievement orientations typically used male populations for testing, such as David McLelland's study, published as *The Achieving Society* (Princeton, N.J.: Van Nostrand Reinhold, 1961). Several decades of study based on Jungian psychology; the Myers-Briggs personality model developed by Isabel Briggs Myers and her mother, Catharine Cook Briggs; and the Keirsey-Bates temperaments, developed by David Keirsey and Marilyn Bates In *Please Understand Me: Character and Temperament Types* (Del Mar, Calif.: Premetheus Nemesis Book Co., 1984) indicate that the strength of an individual's achievement orientation and drive differs across congenital personality types.

3. An excellent resource on this topic is James A. Levine and Todd L. Pittinsky, *Working Fathers: New Strategies for Balancing Work and Family,* (Orlando: Harcourt Brace, 1997).

4. See William Pollack, *Real Boys: Rescuing Our Sons from the Myths of Boyhood* (New York: Random House, 1998).

5. Pollack (1998), p. 17.

6. Pollack (1998), p. 17.

7. Pollack (1998), pp. 128–136.

8. Stephen Rechtschaffen, M.D., *Timeshifting: Creating More Time to Enjoy Your Life* (New York: Doubleday, 1996), p. 40.

9. Indeed, this topic is so important for corporate women that in Chapter Two, "Gender at Work," I ended the list of strategies for their facing the identity challenge with this item: "Hang out with women. Don't worry about what the guys think."

10. See the Foreword by Sheila W. Wellington in Catalyst, *Creating Women's Networks, A How-to Guide for Women and Companies* (San Francisco: Jossey-Bass, 1999).

11. As cited in note 12 of Chapter Seven of this book, see Deborah J. Swiss and Judith P. Walker's *Women and the Work/Family Dilemma:*

How Today's Professional Women Are Confronting the Maternal Wall (New York: Wiley, 1993), especially their fourth chapter.

12. Michael M. Lombardo and Robert W. Eichinger, *Preventing Derailment: What to Do Before It's Too Late* (Greensboro, N.C.: Center for Creative Leadership, 1989).

13. Mary Catherine Bateson, *Composing a Life* (New York: Plume Books, 1989), p. 3.

14. Bateson (1989), p. 10.

15. The situational leadership model, developed by John Hersey and Kenneth Blanchard, appears in Chapter Five of this book.

16. James M. Kouzes and Barry Z. Posner, *The Leadership Challenge: How to Keep Getting Extraordinary Things Done in Organizations,* 2nd ed. (San Francisco: Jossey-Bass, 1995). For the sake of completion, the other two steps are to challenge the process and inspire a shared vision.

17. Quoted in David A. Whetten and Kim S. Cameron, *Developing Management Skills,* 3rd ed. (New York: HarperCollins, 1995), p. 492. The study referred to is in Albert Bandura, *A Social Learning Theory* (Upper Saddle River, N.J.: Prentice-Hall, 1977).

18. Still, it is important to assert that women are less likely today to be victims than in any previous historic era, at least within the United States. In *Women's Figures: An Illustrated Guide to the Economic Progress of Women in America* (Washington, D.C.: American Enterprise Institute for Public Policy Research, 1999), Diana Furchtgott-Roth and Christine Stolba cite a record of achievement, rather than victimization, highlighting the role of women's personal choices in recent economic progress for women: "Unfortunately, that ambiguous legacy of choice is often ignored in favor of an image of women as victims of widespread discrimination. Such a portrayal of women overlooks an important factor: *the possibility that many women do not want to reach the top of the corporate ladders* [my emphasis]. The mass media uncritically accept as the standard of equality the requirement that women's achievements be statistically identical to men's achievements in all areas. The standard is insidious: it suggests that something is wrong if women do not earn the highest salaries. That is insulting to all women who choose flexibility, a friendly workplace environment, and other non-monetary factors in the course of their careers" (p. 80).

19. Emotional intelligence is "a different way of being smart," according to Goleman, author of *Working with Emotional Intelligence* (New York: Bantam Books, 1998). He devotes very little of his book to an explicit comparison of emotional intelligence in men and women.

He concludes that "a major review of data on male-female sex differences argues that men have as much latent ability for empathy, but less motivation to be empathic, than do women. To the extent men tend to see themselves in terms of something like machismo, the argument goes, they have less motivation to seem sensitive, because that could be seen as a sign of 'weakness'" (pp. 318–323). In several studies, however, women demonstrated greater capacity for empathy—the ability to detect another person's feeling, "to sense what people are feeling, being able to take their perspective, and cultivating rapport and attunement with a broad diversity of people."

20. You will recall from earlier chapters that she is the psychologist who conducted the seminal study of women titled *In a Different Voice* (Cambridge, Mass.: Harvard University Press, 1982).

Afterword

It is hard to fight an enemy who has outposts in your mind.
ANONYMOUS

In the seven years it has taken to complete this book, from the earliest efforts of data collection to the final details of proofreading endnotes, I have listened to and learned from the voices of thousands of women who face hard choices in their lives. I have been awed and inspired by how they rise to meet their personal or professional challenges. As an afterword to the identity, task, and balance challenges, I must share with you the brief stories of three women I talked with today, each of whom is embarked on quite a different personal journey, and each of whom is stimulated to find something more for herself—something that increases the connection among who she is, what she is doing, and most significant of all, what she is feeling. Each woman is a master at using her third shift to listen to herself. Each understands how to balance the negative voices with the positive ones. So each excels at translating her third shift into action that takes her closer to what she wants—and who she is.

My breakfast meeting was with Crystal Maddison. She is soft-spoken and unassuming; when you walk into her office she smiles warmly and works hard at making you feel comfortable. Crystal can work too hard at that. In the past, we've discussed how she can strengthen her leadership presence, make tough decisions even if the consequences may be hard on others, and still feel good about herself and her leadership style. She is a willing, thoughtful, and extremely determined learner. She is also a very experienced, senior, corporate-level human resource vice president, responsible for the well-being of several thousand employees. Her company is at a crossroads, and the board of directors is considering replacing the president, in whom many have lost confidence. The stock price is ailing and the new-product development pipeline has slowed down to a dangerous trickle. Everyone seems to be in waiting mode, so morale is awful in Crystal's company, and no one knows when (or if) it will turn around.

"Why do you stay?" I ask her, understanding the feeling of futility that can come from waking up before dawn every day, gulping down a muffin and coffee, then rushing into gridlock on the freeway, only to arrive at a workplace where everyone around you wishes they were somewhere else. "It's not time for me to leave," she replies. "I have a job to do. I can help. I didn't like what I was seeing around me, and it forced me to evaluate what's important to me. It's hard here now, sure. There were eight resignations yesterday just in my department. But I have to get things stable. I know that I'm not the same person anymore. My commitment has changed. But for now, I feel good about being here." Her boss says she's different than she used to be; "It's obvious that you've really thought this through, Crystal. You're so clear when you're speaking now. You know exactly where you stand." Crystal is operating differently from how she used to, and it has taken a corporate downturn to bring her inner strength to the outside where others can see it. Her third shift has been instrumental in bringing her to this point. Paradoxically, she grins, knowing it's her internal thinking process that helps her gain a stronger sense of herself and her capabilities. "But I don't obsess over everything anymore. I just get out there and do it. It feels good to be free." She knows how, when, and how much to use her third shift.

My second meeting today was with a former graduate student, Chitra Ramachandra, who wanted reactions to a business plan she has developed with a friend. Their idea is powerful, a Website targeted specifically at the hundreds of thousands of Indian women who have emigrated to the United States. Most of these women live in households with above-average family income and high levels of computer ownership. They form a desirable, even though compact, niche market. The problem, of course, is how to make money on the 'Net. Will the Indian women who browse the Website be willing to pay for this customized privilege?

Chitra is correct to worry about this because she has spent years serving in the nonprofit community without salary, but with tremendous recognition from others. She knows that Indian women, as part of their background and culture, are wont to please others. They can be tentative at asking for what they really want, or spending on themselves. Is it ridiculous to try to make money from a labor of love? Is it sensible, and is it worthy of her efforts? Is it reflective of her values?

Chitra is an outstanding community figure who has won numerous service awards. Her name appears regularly in the local press, but never on a pay stub. For years, she has been the leader of a networking group for Indian women, volunteering to take on any task that helps others connect with the resources they need to succeed with their dreams. She has hooked together private investors with budding entrepreneurs, young Indian engineers with prospective Indian wives in this country who suit them, and corporate recruiters with prospective employees. She seems to know everyone. She is a natural broker and networker, fearless at digging up new information, new sources, and new acquaintances to help someone else. She is a genuinely caring, selfless soul who places little value on the material goods that seem so important to others. But lately, something is changing. She doesn't feel good anymore about herself and her efforts. "I want to make some money," she says, her eyes piercing. "I need to know my own value in the market."

We discuss possibilities and problems with turning their labor of love into a moneymaking venture. As budding entrepreneurs, the two friends are clearly motivated and highly prepared, their initial business plan logical and orderly. Inside her third shift, however, Chitra remains troubled and conflicted—but it is this internal combat that will lead her to victory. She is sorting out her true needs, struggling with answers and strategies to meet those needs. She knows that real validation comes from the inside, but she feels a new need for greater external validation. "I want to empower other women. This is what I love to do. But I also need to make some money for myself. My husband doesn't care. No one else cares. But it is important to me. I cannot just volunteer for others anymore."

Chitra has tried other paid work, part-time efforts to ensure that she can oversee her household, spend time with her son, and

actively lead her Indian networking association. She has not felt
particularly successful at any paid work. As an observer, I can see
that her passion is elsewhere, and this somehow limits her results.
In contrast to the string of successful events and accomplishments
she has attained through her community work, her paid labors
bring her little but further self-doubt about her capabilities. Now
she is turning to finding the conventional financial rewards she
seeks through her real passion: bringing other women together.
The route is uncertain. I have real questions about elements of her
business plan. Yet I have an inner confidence that she will overcome the difficulties. She will persevere, even if the journey is long.
I'm eager to try to help, pleased and flattered that she has always
kept our connection together, long after she left my classroom. She
will ultimately succeed because her third shift will not leave her
alone. It continuously pushes her to new efforts that connect who
she is with what she does and how she feels about herself. Ultimately, it also gives her new perspectives and new successes. On the
Web. In her pocketbook. And in her heart.

I finished my day with a phone call to Donna Reagan, a business associate who left a glitzy day job for the sheer pleasure of
being at home with her children. She had worked through her
older daughter's infancy, and with the birth of a second child she
knew she didn't want to miss her new son's first few years. She is a
capable veteran businesswoman; she quickly lined up several short
but interesting projects to keep her hand in at work in a limited
way and produce additional income. It's not much compared to
her prior, full-time salary, but that doesn't matter to Donna. Her
third shift has helped her gain what she needs to feel good. She is
doing what she wants. Where she wants. And when she wants.

"I feel so lucky," she warbles over the phone. "It's even better
than I thought it would be." Donna finds that she likes the decompression from her fast-paced career-girl life. She is a full-time
mommy, except for two mornings a week when her four-month-
old goes to day care (her daughter is in kindergarten). She likes
the break but doesn't want her son in day care for any more than
two short periods, twice a week. It allows her the time to express
another side of herself and take in some limited consulting work.

Doing outside projects, Donna says, "keeps my brain working,
and it gives me another lens through which to learn and grow out-

side of my mommy thing. But don't get me wrong. It's the mommy thing that got me to leave work in the first place. I don't want another day job, I don't think. At least not for a really long time. I'm having too much fun. We cut out jack-o-lanterns today, when my older one came home from school. Tomorrow the baby is in day care during the morning, and I have this really exciting new consulting job I'm working on. It's so cool. Who said you can't have it all?"

Because Donna used to have a very small part of it all—when she was working sixty hours a week, tired from the seventh month of her pregnancy, and with a preschooler awaiting her anxiously at the nursery school playground every day, worried her mother would be late picking her up—Donna has a clear perspective on what "it all" means. Her third shift nibbles on what she terms "anticipatory worries." "I'm sure it can't last, this feeling that everything is working out so well. I'm so used to being tired all the time, and worse than that for me was questioning myself so much. In retrospect, I think the questioning was worse than all the hours and all the work. It just drained me."

A careful planner, it was six months ago, after thoroughly researching books on the topic and talking with more than a dozen women, that she made the decision to leave her corporate job and stay home. She and her husband discussed what would be different, what the financial implications were, and most important what she was searching for. "A life! I was looking to reclaim my life," she said, when she first made the decision to go home. She also spread the word that she wanted some, but not too much, contract work. She has already turned down two projects, figuring that she'll continue to get the occasional call for follow-up work after the project she is on is completed. "I know I can always get another job if that's what I want. Maybe it won't be as good as the position I left. But I can't worry about that now. It would ruin what I have today." Donna does have it all. She's one of the lucky ones, not because she has it all but because she is happy with what she's chosen.

Thinking about the stories of all of the women in this book, I feel more strongly than ever that we are fortunate to be alive today as women, at least in the United States. Our choices can entrap us. They can defeat us. Or they can ennoble and empower us. In my office I have pictures of women on every wall, and in every corner: Jamaican women dancing; a Depression-era woman frowning, a young child in her arms; a perky carhop on roller skates leaning saucily onto the running board of a pink Caddie; a clever sepia sketch of my aunt in the posture of "The Thinker," drawn by an artist-boyfriend more than thirty years ago.

Sharing an antique, oak table with a well-thumbed thesaurus is a Hopi figurine and a small deck of cards, each revealing a picture of a historical figure on one side—Josephine Baker, Elizabeth Cady Stanton, Mourning Dove, Bessie Coleman, Nellie Bly—and a thumbnail sketch of her exploits and achievements on the other. As I write, I am surrounded by these pictures and visions of women, reminding me that each of us is unique and that no universal truth holds equally well for all of us. Yet I believe we have in common as women today a powerful inner need—reflected in the dialogues of our third shift—to better align our outer lives with our inner needs and beliefs. Our separate destinies depend upon it.

In closing, I ask your tolerance in sharing a set of guiding principles and assumptions as you take the suggestions in this book and try to enact them in your lives. First, when I talk about women in general, and their developmental path in particular, I am talking about the central tendency toward an average. Most, but not all, women identify with the assertions I have made. There are many exceptions, but their existence does not negate the importance of the initial rule.

Second, I have focused upon women in this book, omitting in-depth discussions of men. My study was never meant to be a comparative research project per se, or else I would have interviewed an equal number of males for direct contrast and counterpoint. To understand ourselves well and make informed choices, we must better understand the men we live with—at home, in our community, and in our offices. But we must first understand ourselves.

Third, this book is not about male bashing or asserting that women are superior in any way to men. The existence of the third shift suggests that we are in general *different,* and we must therefore develop toward our adult identities and destinies somewhat differently. We may face contrasting psychological and practical dilemmas. We may seek to solve them in a dissimilar way. But we are no better than others.

We are often, however, more uncertain. In many ways, women today live in a surreal world, floating back and forth between an outdated cultural mirror that prescribes certain genderized roles, and then careening suddenly toward the possibility of an entirely new image, with as-yet-unknown life scripts and patterns for its many actors and actresses. Throughout this book, I have not sought to predict or manipulate the future that women face. Instead, I have chosen to ground my inquiry in the present. Let the wheel of destiny turn as it will; the only moment that really counts is the one we are living in now. It is my hope that this book goes no small distance toward making that moment, for women, not a self-inflicted curse of discontent, fear, and self-doubt, but instead an instant of joy, enlightenment, and self-acceptance.

Appendix
The Women of the Study

The research for this study was conducted between 1993 and 1996. It involved a core sample of 117 women, classified into four groups:

Group	Number	Percentage
Entrepreneurs	39	33
Corporate or professional	43	37
Stay-at-home	19	16
Community	16	14

Each woman was classified into only one group, according to self-assessment of her current *primary* status. Women classified in the community category could be working as unpaid volunteers or holding paying jobs.

Interview Questions

The *entrepreneurial* women in the study were asked:

- What led you to start your own business?
- What do you believe to be the critical moments in your life, preparatory to starting your own business?
- When did you first think about running your own business?
- When did you make your first active move toward starting your own business?
- What would it take for you to define yourself as an entrepreneur?
- How will you define your success as an entrepreneur?

- What have been your greatest obstacles or fears?
- Is there anything else you'd like to share?

The *corporate* women in the study were asked:

- What led you to your current position? Do you consider this a job or a career?
- What do you believe to be the critical moments in your life relative to your work?
- When did you first think about working?
- What type of preparation did you take to improve your experience in the workplace?
- What would it take for you to define yourself as successful in the workplace?
- What have been your greatest obstacles or fears?
- Is there anything else you'd like to share?

The *stay-at-home* women in the study were asked:

- What led you to stay at home?
- What do you believe to be the critical moments in your life, relative to your being at home?
- When did you first think about staying at home (if you previously worked)?
- When did you make your first active move toward staying at home?
- What will it take for you to define yourself as successful at home?
- What have been your greatest obstacles or fears?
- Is there anything else you'd like to share?

Women in the *community* were asked:

- What led you to work in the community?
- What do you believe to be the critical moments in your life, relative to working in the community?
- When did you first think about working in the community?
- When did you make your first active move toward working in the community?
- What would it take for you to define yourself as successful in the community?

- What have been your greatest obstacles or fears?
- Is there anything else you'd like to share?

Here is a complete breakdown of demographics, to better understand the makeup of the women of the study. However, I have included a brief interpretation as well.

Age

Most women in the study were between ages thirty-one and forty, with the youngest woman twenty-two and the oldest seventy-one. More than 65 percent of the study participants were baby boomers, which counts those women born between 1946 and 1960.

Household Income

Most women in the study had household incomes between $41,000 and $70,000. Two were on welfare, and three had household assets of more than $1 million (not including their homes).

Highest Educational Level Attained

Most women in the study held baccalaureate degrees, although a small percentage had earned M.D.s or Ph.D.s. The modal category was a B.A. or B.S., with nearly 77 percent of the sample college-educated, biasing the sample upward.

Family Status

The most common family status in the study was married with two children, but participants were also interviewed who were single, or married but without children. Children living at home as well as adult children qualified to be included in the categories with children.

Racial or Ethnic Group

The most common racial or ethnic group of the study's participants is Caucasian (91 percent), with lesser representation in the African American, Latino, Filipino and Asian American, and Indian (that is, from India) communities.

	Age					Household Income					Highest Educational Level Attained					Family Status						Racial or Ethnic Group						
	21–30	31–40	41–50	51–60	61+	<$25,000	$26–40,000	$41–55,000	$56–70,000	$71,000+	High School	Assoc. Degree	B.A., B.S.	Master's	M.D., Ph.D., Postdoc	M/No Children	M/1–2 Children	M/3+ Children	S/No Children	S/1–2 Children	S/3+ Children	Caucasian	Native American	African American	Latino	Filipino, Asian Am.	Indian	Other
Entrepreneur N=39 %=33	1	18	11	7	2	4	6	9	9	11	7	5	17	6	4	4	18	4	5	6	2	26	0	4	3	5	1	0
Homebased	1	10	7	4	2	2	4	8	7	3	5	4	9	3	3	0	12	3	2	5	2	17	0	2	3	1	1	0
Product	0	1	7	3	0	2	2	1	2	3	2	3	8	3	2	1	4	2	2	2	1	8	0	1	1	1	1	0
Service	1	17	4	4	2	2	4	8	7	8	5	2	9	3	2	3	14	2	3	4	1	18	0	3	2	4	0	0
Corporate or Professional N=43 %=37	8	12	14	7	2	3	9	16	9	6	4	5	21	9	4	6	16	5	7	6	3	25	1	5	2	6	3	1
Stay-at-Home N=19 %=16																												
No paid work	4	5	7	2	1	0	4	8	2	5	0	3	12	3	1	0	14	4	0	1	0	12	0	3	0	4	0	0
Part-time work (15+ hrs wk)	1	2	2	1	0	0	1	3	1	1	0	0	5	1	0	0	4	1	0	1	0	3	0	2	0	3	0	0

Community

N=16 %=14

Paid full-time	0	1	3	2	1	0	1	4	1	1	1	1	4	1	0	1	3	1	1	0	11	1	1	2	0	0
Paid part-time (15+ hrs wk)	2	3	3	1	0	0	2	4	1	2	1	1	5	2	0	2	4	1	1	1	4	0	1	0	0	0

Total in Sample: 117

If you are interested in learning more about your own third shift, understanding how to help your organization develop its women more effectively, share any research you have conducted on contemporary women, or learn about executive coaching, keynote presentations or other executive and women's development programs and opportunities, please contact the author directly at

ExecutivEdge of Silicon Valley
18 Park Avenue
Los Gatos, CA 95033
(408) 354-6023
Mbolton@ExecutivEdge.com

Index

A

Abarbanel, K., 111, 127, 240
Accommodation, in corporate workplace, 72–74
Achievement, gender and, 289–292
Acknowledgment, 42
Acquinas, Thomas, 94
Adams, Gloria (case history), 99–131
Adolescence, American, 39
Adult development: and inner harmony, 14; two standards of, 36
Adversarial frame of mind, 230
African Americans, 72, 73
Alamo, 51
Albrecht, K., 119–120
Alcott, L. M., 1
All-girl academies, 39
All-True Travels and Adventures of Lidie Newton (Smiley), 243
Allen, Gwen (case history), 29–60, 63, 70–72, 94–95, 149
Allstate, 78
Alwether, Rita (case history), 124–126
Ambition, 39
America's Competitive Secret: Utilizing Women as a Management Strategy (Rosener), 75
Analysis of results, 165
Anderson, Laurel (case history), 135, 266
Androgyny: and definition of true androgyny, 29–60; myth of, 29–60
Anxiety, age of, 3
Apple Computers, 122
Aroused Heart, The: Poetry and the Preservation of the Soul in Corporate America (Whyte), 47

Asian Americans, 72, 73
Assertiveness, 69–70
Assimilation drama, 72–74
Attachment, separation *versus,* 36
Auden, W. H., 3
Authenticity, compatibility of, with subordination, 31
Automation, or liberation, in corporate workplace, 94–97
Autonomy, 79
Awareness, gender, 74–79

B

Baker, J., 320
Balance, issue of, 284–289
Balance challenge: and identification of life's work, 298–301; and indirect service to others, 305–308; and opportunities to serve others, 301–305; overview of, 279–282; and positive inner message, 295–297; and sharing third shift with others, 293–295
Bandura, A., 307
Bangalore, India, 184
Bateson, M. C., 33, 272–273, 279, 298, 299
Beck, M., 32
Becoming Gentlemen (Guinier), 93
Beloved (Morrison), 166
Berman, Evelyn, 171
Berman, Florence, 170, 171
"Bewitched" (television sitcom), 248–249
Beyond Ambition (Kaplan), 55
Bly, N., 320
Boeing, 306

Borrone, Alex (case history), 195

Boston, 170

Boston University, 267

Breakaways: questions for reflection during, 45; strategies for, 43–46; virtual, 43

Breaking Point: Why Women Fall Apart and How They Can Re-Create Their Lives (Beck), 32

Burnout, questions to determine capacity for, 272

Business concept phase, 210

Business readiness, 110

C

Caldwell, Jennifer (case history), 62–97

California, 114

Calvinism, 54, 96, 146

Cambridge, Massachusetts, 170, 267

Cameron, K. S., 308

Cannon, Lucy (case history), 116

Career balance sheet, 77–78

Carlisle, Lily (case history), 224–226, 228, 233

Casey, Marlene (case history), 162–163

Cather, W., 135

Catalyst, 77, 82, 92, 294–295

Center for Creative Leadership (Greensboro, North Carolina), 33, 55

Center to Develop Women Entrepreneurs, 160

Cerebral self, 266

Change, sustained, 55

Child development, maternal influence on, 156

Children, decision to have, 71–72

Chinese philosophy, 169

Chira, S., 10, 140

Choices, management of, 286–287

Cisneros, S., 62

Citadel, 309

Cleaver, June (television character), 140

Clinton, W. J., 190

Clothes, sexual content of, 66

CNBC, 81

Cohabitation, *versus* subjugation, 85–90

Coleman, B., 320

College reunions, 145

Columbia University, 146, 171

Columbia University Dental School, 171

Company, identity of, 221–222

Company stage, of entrepreneurship, 211

Compatible work style, developing, 192

Competition: conquering *versus*, 181; women's ambivalence about, 181–182

Composing a Life (Bateson), 279

Compromise, *versus* sacrifice, 159–162

Conflict: aversion to, 70; management of, 229

Confucius, 59, 173

Conley, F. K., 71

Connectedness, 12–13, 34

Conner, Gayle, 189–190, 193

Conquering, *versus* competing, 181

Control, 57

Conversational traps, 86–87

Conway, J. K., 207

Corporate workplace: guilt about leaving, 103–104; identification with, 102, 104; task dilemma in, 103–104, 176–178

Country club management, 183

CPR (credibility, push-back, and relationships) influencing model, 230–233

Creative tension, 230

Credibility, 230–231, 304

Crittenden, D., 246

Cultural equilibrium, 31

Cultural schizophrenia, 32

Culture, dominant workplace. *See* Workplace culture, dominant

Culture, subordinate. *See* Subordinate culture

D

Daddy stress, 3
Daly, Yvonne (case history), 17
Davis, Sheila (case history), 179–180
Day care, 156
DeBono, Juliet (case history), 207–240
Decision making, in corporate workplace, 68–72
Developing Management Skills (Whetten and Cameron), 308
Dilbert, 104, 123
Discipline, 186
Distinctive legacy, 34
Diversity issues, sensitivity to, 184
Dixon, Elena, 243–275
Domestic identity: and being positive role model, 145–148; and being yourself, 148–152; and clarity about expectations, 152–155; compromise *versus* sacrifice in, 159–162; loss of balance in, 158–159; and nurturing issue, 156–158; parity with spouse in, 162–164
Dowling, J., 150–152, 159, 160, 165
Dr. Seuss, 149
Dream stage (of entrepreneurship), 210

E

Edison, T., 117
Emotional intelligence, 36, 309
Emotional readiness, 109–110
Empowerment, 197, 307; five core dimensions of, 308
Engagement, rules of, 76
Enlightenment, 52
Entrepreneurial character. *See* Entrepreneurship
Entrepreneurial identity, 101–104. *See* Entrepreneurship
Entrepreneurial readiness: and business readiness, 110; and emotional readiness, 109–110; and financial readiness, 111–115
Entrepreneurial success: assessing readiness for, 108–110; and delay in leaving day job, 123–126; and expression of personal uniqueness, 120–123; financial readiness for, 111–115; ingredients for, 107–129; and need for strong personal vision, 115–120; and risk, 126–129
Entrepreneurship: and hallmarks of entrepreneurial character, 117; and metamorphosis to entrepreneurial identity, 129–131; phases of, 209; and transition to entrepreneurial identity, 101–104
Erikson, E., 36, 50
Everyday Revolutionaries (Helgesen), 203
Exclusion, language of, 86
Executive Female magazine, 111
Exemplary leadership, 306
Expectations, clarity about, 152–155
Experimentation, 165; with new behaviors, 52

F

Failure, fear of, 118
Faludi, S., 143
Families and Work Institute (New York), 3, 291, 292
Farrell, M., 80–81
Fields, D., 104, 214
Finances, 111–115
Financial readiness, 111–115
Flexibility, 85, 199
Forbes, 53
Fortune magazine, 17, 82, 102, 145, 289
Fox, M., 95
Franklin, Elyssa (case history), 47–49, 53
Freud, S., 47, 150
Friedan, B., 144
Friedlander, Elsa (case history), 59
Fulfillment, 141–142

Fuller, Sheryl Rodriguez (case history), 222–223, 226–228

G

Gallup poll, 291
Gandhi, I., 214
Gender, 284; and achievement drives, 289–292; and analysis of company's gender awareness, 74–79; as assimilation drama, 72; and career momentum, 74–79; and cohabitation *versus* subjugation, 85–90; in corporate workplace, 62–97; and development of style and persona, 81–84; and leadership style, 68; and leaving personal legacy, 84–85; and networking with other women, 92–94; and physical appearance, 66–68; and solicitation of feedback, 90–92; and woman's identity, 64–65
Gender awareness, analysis of corporation's, 74–79; corporate stages of, and action, 74
Gender card, 18, 65
Gender denial, 32, 66, 94
Gender equality, 5, 284
Gender inequality, in schools, 265
Gilchrest, E., 169
Gilligan, C., 36, 202, 309
GO Corporation, 105
Godfrey, J., 104, 123
Gold, Arielle (case history), 219–220
Golden Notebook, The (Lessing), 283
Goleman, D., 309
Goodall, J., 190
Gordon, Nina (case history), 13–14, 17
Green, Nicky (case history), 84–85
Greensboro, North Carolina, 33
Guinier, L., 93
Gupta, Anita (case history), 184–185

H

Hallowell, E. M., 11
Harmony, 14–16, 57–59

Harris, J. R., 246
Harvard Business School, 79, 144–146
Harvard Medical School, 253
Hawthorne, Carole (case history), 14–16
Healing, 44
Heat Wave (Lively), 173
Helgesen, S., 203
Hendricks, Jill (case history), 257, 263–264
Herera, S., 81
Hill, L. A., 79
Hindu, 185
Hobbes, Marianne (case history), 303–305
Hochschild, A. R., 246
Honesty, 59
House of Mirth, The (Wharton), 29
House on Mango Street, The (Cisneros), 62
How to Succeed on Your Own (Abarbanel), 127
Human development, field of, 33
Human needs, pyramid of, 141

I

"I Dream of Jeannie" (television sitcom), 248–249
"I Love Lucy" (television sitcom), 248–249
IBM, 77
Identity challenge: description of, 30–33; effective breakaway strategy for, 43–46; enlisting support for, 53–56; and going against the grain, 47–50; and harmony, 57–59; and lessening activity level, 52–53; management of, 40–59; risk-taking and, 50–52; and self-investing, 56–57; and self-reflection, 41–43; and shift to entrepreneurial identity, 101–104; universality of, 32
Identity challenge, at home. *See* Domestic identity
Identity challenge, in corporate workplace: and analysis of company's

stage of gender awareness, 74–79; assimilation and accommodation in, 72–74; automation or liberation of women in, 94–97; and career momentum, 79–81; cohabitation, versus subjugation, as goal in, 85–90; and decision making, 68–72; and development of persona, 81–84; and leaving personal legacy, 84–85; and networking with women, 92–94; and physical appearance, 66–68; and solicitation of feedback, 90–92

Implied power, 190–192

In a Different Voice (Gilligan), 36, 202

Inc. magazine, 104

Individual breakthroughs, steps involved in, 52

Individuation, *versus* relationships, 36

Inner message, positive, 295–297. *See also* Balance challenge

Inner oasis, 308–311

Intellectual stimulation, 267

Internal glass ceiling, 6, 283, 298

Internalization, of new behaviors and attitudes, 52

Intimacy, *versus* mastery approach, 34

Introspective personality, 70

J

Jews, 72

Journals, use of, 49, 53

Jung, C. J., 289

K

Kaplan, J., 105

Kaplan, R., 55

Kee, Joan (case history), 128–129

Killer instinct, 181

Killinger, D., 53

Kingston, M. H., 99

Klimt, G., 223

Kofodimos, J., 33, 35

Kouzes, J. M., 306

Kremen, Meyer, 171–172

L

Leach, P., 257

Leader, self-image as, 101–104

Leadership: experience, amassing of, 110; and feminist leadership style, 82; by modeling, 183

Leadership Challenge, The (Kouzes and Posner), 306

Leadership experience, amassing of, 110

Lee, Anita (fictional), 73–74

Lerner, H., 272–273

Lessing, D., 283

Leverage principle, 238

Levine, A. D., 290

Liberation, automation or, 94–97

Life mosaic, 302

Life structures, 33

Life's work, identification of, 298–301. *See also* Balance challenge

Lithuania, 170

Little Women, 1, 88

Lively, P., 173

Lockwood, Carole (case history), 285–311, 298

M

Maddison, Crystal (case history), 315–316

Male bonding, 35

Mantras, personal, 186–187

March, Jo *(Little Women)*, 88

Marx, K., 202

Masculine behavior, 69

Maslow, A., 141–142, *153*

Massachusetts Institute of Technology (MIT), 100, 146

Mastery, 33–34

Maternal identity: and being positive role model, 145–148; and being yourself, 148–152; and clarity about expectations, 152–155; compromise *versus* sacrifice in, 159–162; and fulfillment, 141–142; loss of balance in, 158–159; and nurturing issue, 156–158; parity with

Maternal identity *(continued)*
  spouse in, 162–164; self-awareness
  versus self-doubt in, 142–143; and
  working women, 137–140
McKenna, E. P., 154
Mead, M., 214
Meaning, 96, 105
Miller, J. B., 31, 238
Mismeasure of Woman, The (Tavris), 4
Mistakes, permitting, 202
MIT. *See* Massachusetts Institute of
  Technology
Money, facing one's true emotions
  about, 111
Moneyphobia, 111
Montgomery, Alabama, 59
Montgomery, Patty (case history),
  171, 260–262, 269–270
Morrison, T., 166
Moses, 43–44
Mother Dance, The (Lerner), 272–
  273
Mother Earth magazine, 222–223
Mother's Place, A (Chira), 10, 140
Mourning Dove, 320
Multiple roles, 39
My Antonia (Cather), 135
Myers-Briggs personality tests, 202
Myths of Motherhood, The (Thurer),
  140

N

Native American religions, 45
Native Americans, 72
Neft, N., 290
Negativity, 296
Nelson, M. B., 181, 182
Networking, 293–295; four factors in
  finding participants for, 294–295;
  with other women, 92–94
New York, 3, 77, 291
*Nurture Assumption, The: Why Children
  Turn Out the Way They Do* (Harris),
  246
Nurturing, devaluing of, 156–158156

O

Occupations, women's share of, 290
Oral histories, 18
Organization woman, 95–96
Organizational development (OD)
  specialists, 54–55
Ouchi, W., 300
Outcomes, *versus* distinctive legacy, 34
Outsider, role of, 31, 106

P

PaineWebber, 80
Palo Alto, California, 285
Parks, R. M., 59
Paternity leave preoccupation, 292
Paycheck anxiety, 113
Persona, development of, 81–84
Personal achievement, defining,
  283–311
Personal legacy, 84–85
Personal worry chart, 235
Personality, introspective, 70
Peters, T., 51
Physical appearance, 66–68
Pink ghetto environment, 30
Pipher, M., 39, 254
Political activities, list of, for corpo-
  rate workplace, 198
Pollack, W., 253
Posner, B. Z., 306
Power anorexia, 202
Princessa, The: Machiavelli for Women
  (Rubin), 190
Product stage (entrepreneurship), 210
Professional archetype, lack of, 95–96
Proust, M., 267
Psychological disengagement, 44
Psychological walls, 16–17
Psychotherapy, and individual break-
  through, 52
Push-back scripts, 230–231

Q

Quindlan, A., 51
Quinn, Arlie (case history), 251–252

R

Ramachandra, Chitra (case history), 316–317

Reagan, Donna (case history), 318–319

Real Boys (Pollack), 253

Reardon, K. K., 86, 130

Rechtschaffen, S., 292

Reentry, new meaning of, 131, 143

Reflection, 165; in breakaways, 45

Reinvention of Work, The (Fox), 95

Relational abilities. *See* Emotional intelligence

Relationship: *versus* deeds, as basis of success, 33; and relationship scripts, 232–233

Relevance, 79

Repetition, 186

Respect, 187–190

Results, producing, 203

Reviving Ophelia, Saving the Selves of Adolescent Girls (Pipher), 39, 254

Rimm, S., 147

Risks, 50–52, 126–129

Road to Coorain, The (Conway), 207

Roddick, A., 104, 214

Rodriguez, Maria (case history), 37–38, 47

Role models, 54, 145–148, 266

Rommel, E., 192

Rorschach test, 301

Rosen, Amy (case history), 175–204

Rosener, J. B., 63, 74, 75, 80

Rubin, H., 190, 201–202

Rukeyser, L., 80

S

Sacred time, 44–45

Sacrifice, compromise *versus,* 159–162

Sainthood, 47

San Jose State University, 4

Sculley, J., 51

Second shift, 1, 114, 138

Self, reinventing of, 100–101

Self-acceptance: as central task of successful adult development, 58; and living with choices, 8

Self-awareness, *versus* self doubt, 9–12, 239

Self-awareness/self-doubt inner dialogue, 11, 69, 86, 103, 103–104, 108–109, 142, 179, 211–212, 225, 246–247, 256–257, 264, 265–266, 284

Self-confidence, 59, 123

Self-discovery, voyage of, 44

Self doubt, and working mothers, 140, 141. *See also* Self-awareness/self-doubt dialogue

Self-expression, 105, 121

Self-investment, 56–57

Self-reflection, 41–43

Separation, *versus* attachment, 36

Service, to others: indirect, 305–308; opportunities for, 301–305. *See also* Balance challenge

Shandel, Rose, 170–172

Shellenbarger, S., 3

Silicon Valley, 4, 29, 43, 99, 100, 102, 105, 130, 139, 144, 196, 257, 288

Simmons, Dawn (case history), 299

Smiley, J., 243

Soft relational skills, 36–37

Solitude, 52

Sophie's Choice (Styron), 166

Sponsorship, 76–77

Stanford University, 71, 76, 146, 181, 285, 307

Stanton, E. C., 320

Starcarbon (Gilchrest), 169

Start-ups, differences between male and female, 121

Strengths, working from, 193

Stretch assignment, 79

Style: development of, 81–84; standing up for one's, 83

Styron, W., 166

Subjugation, cohabitation *versus,* 85–90

Submissiveness, 87

Subordinate culture, 31

Subordination: and authenticity, 31; and identity challenge, 30–31

Success: lure of conventional, 102; metrics of, 76; need for distinctively feminine standard of, 33

Success syndrome, 79

Support: personal, 109; professional, 54

T

Tannen, D., 230

Tanzania, 190

Task challenge: for corporate women, 176–178; gender related differences most salient to, 239–240; overview of, 169–174; self-awareness *versus* self-doubt in, 179

Task challenge, in domestic setting, 239–240; and burnout, 268–272; conscious parenting, 251–254; and conscious parenting, 251–254; and definition of current relationship to work, 254–259; developing intellectual life for, 251–254; structure of time and energy for, 251–254

Task challenge, in entrepreneurial setting, 203–240; and being own role model, 220–223; customer management for, 224–228; management of time and energy for, 216–218; passion and positive energy in, 215–216; professional identity and leadership skills for, 213; and saying no, 228–233; and worry about right stuff, 233–237

Task challenge, managing: and building respect from men in power, 187–190; and competing as a woman, 181–183; and control of thoughts, 184–187; in corporate workplace, 180–202; and implied power, 190–192; and permission to fail, 200–202; and understanding

supervisor, 192–196; and use of positive political skills, 196–200

Tavris, C., 4

Thatcher, M., 214

Theory Z Management (Ouchi), 300

Third shift, dilemmas of, 5–8

Third Shift, The (Bolton), 7, 11, 17–19, 202, 320

Third-shift inner dialogue, 11, 69, 86, 103, 103–104, 108–109, 142, 179, 211–212, 225, 246–247, 256–257, 264, 265–266, 284

Third-shift voices: sharing of, with others, 293–295; true test of, 44

Thurer, S., 140, 156

Toxic worry, 11

Trade-offs, 71–72, 77, 106, 194, 262

Transitions, 42, 51, 109, 140, 154–155

Tubman, H., 190

Tzu, Sun, 189

U

Uniqueness, personal, 120–123

United States Bureau of Labor Statistics, 289

V

Validation, 96, 105, 301

Venture financing, 115

Virgil, 36

Visibility, 79

Vision, personal, 115–120

Vogue magazine, 67, 222

Voice, development of, 81–84

Volunteerism, 13, 110

W

Walking Out on the Boys (Conley), 71

Wall Street Journal, 3

"Wall Street Week with Louis Rukeyser," 80

Weekly work plan, sample, 217

Wharton, E., 29

Where Women Stand: An International Report on the Status of Women in 140 Countries (Neft and Levine), 290

Whetten, D. A., 308
White, Maxi (case history), 236–237
Whyte, D., 47
Whyte, W., 95, 203
Williams, Suzanne (case history), 89–90, 94
Willpower, 52, 185–186
Woman Warrior, The (Kingston), 99
Woman's identity, 64
Women of the Street (Herera), 81
Women's research, 73
Women's work, 13
Wood, J., 183
Workaholism, 53–54

Working Mother, 39, 40
Working Woman, 104
Workplace behavior, 70
Workplace culture, dominant: mastery *versus* intimacy approach, 35
World War I, 170
Worry, and children, 273
Wu, Tina (case history), 160

Y

Yale University, 76
Yiddish language, 72
Yin and yang, principles of, 169

338

This page constitutes a continuation of the copyright page.

The epigraph on p. iv is from *In A Different Voice* by Carol Gilligan. Cambridge, Mass.: Harvard University Press. Copyright © 1982, 1993 by the President and Fellows of Harvard College. Reprinted by permission of the publisher.

The epigraph on p. 25 is from *Tracks* by Robyn Davidson. Reprinted by permission of Random House, Inc.

The epigraph on p. 62 is from *The House on Mango Street* by Sandra Cisneros. Copyright © 1984 by Sandra Cisneros. Published by Vintage Books, a division of Random House, Inc., New York, and in hardcover by Alfred A. Knopf, Inc. in 1994. Reprinted by permission of Susan Bergholz Literary Services, New York. All right reserved.

The epigraph on p. 99 is from *The Woman Warrior* by Maxine Hong Kingston. Reprinted by permission of Random House, Inc.

The epigraph on p. 169 is from *Starcarbon* by Ellen Gilchrist. Little Brown & Company.

The epigraph on p. 175 is from *Heat Wave* by Penelope Lively. Copyright © 1996 by Penelope Lively. Reprinted by permission of HarperCollins Publishers, Inc.

The epigraph on p. 207 is from *The Road from Coorain* by Jill Ker Conway. Reprinted by permission of Random House, Inc.

The epigraph on p. 243 is from *The All-True Travels and Adventures of Lidie Newton* by Jane Smiley. Reprinted by permission of Alfred A. Knopf, Inc.

The epigraph on p. 279 is from *Composing a Life* by Mary Catherine Bateson. Copyright © 1990 by Grove/Atlantic, Inc. Used by permission.

The epigraph on p. 283 is from *The Golden Notebook* by Doris Lessing. Copyright © 1962 by Doris Lessing. Copyright renewed 1990 by Doris Lessing. Reprinted with permission of Simon & Schuster.